KW-179-717

# Poland and the European Union

This authoritative volume assesses how the recently democratised political system in Poland is adapting to the challenges posed by the country's desire to 'rejoin Europe'. Its excellent panel of highly respected Polish academics considers various issues not generally well known to the English-speaking world, but of great importance in the light of Poland's impending entry into the European Union.

This book is the first English-language study of this subject, and highlights key themes and issues ordinarily unavailable to the non-specialist. Its authors demonstrate that the evolution of political forms and life in Poland is related to, and sometimes governed by, Poland's desire to join the EU. Subjects covered include:

- the changing nature of Poland's foreign policy
- the value system of Polish politics
- the changing nature of party politics
- the reform of public administration and local government
- bilateral relations with Ukraine and Germany

*Poland and the European Union* is essential reading for students of Polish politics, and for all those interested in EU enlargement.

**Karl Cordell** is Principal Lecturer in Politics at the University of Plymouth. His previous publications include *Ethnicity and Democratisation in the New Europe*, and *The Politics of Ethnicity in Central Europe*.

**Europe and the nation state**
Edited by Michael Burgess and Lee Miles
*Centre for European Union Studies, University of Hull*

**Poland and the European Union**
*Edited by Karl Cordell*

# Poland and the European Union

**Edited by Karl Cordell**

London and New York

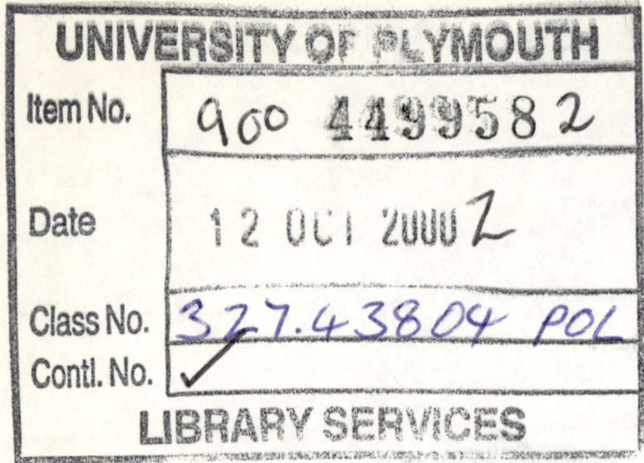
UNIVERSITY OF PLYMOUTH
Item No. 900 4499582
Date 12 OCT 2000
Class No. 327.43804 POL
Contl. No.
LIBRARY SERVICES

First published 2000
by Routledge
11 New Fetter Lane, London EC4P 4EE

Simultaneously published in the USA and Canada
by Routledge
29 West 35th Street, New York, NY 10001

*Routledge is an imprint of the Taylor & Francis Group*

© 2000 Karl Cordell for selection and editorial matter; individual contributors their contributions

Typeset in Baskerville by Exe Valley Dataset Ltd, Exeter
Printed and bound in Great Britain by
T. J. International Ltd, Padstow, Cornwall

All rights reserved. No part of this book may be reprinted or reproduced or utilised in any form or by any electronic, mechanical, or other means, now known or hereafter invented, including photocopying and recording, or in any information storage or retrieval system, without permission in writing from the publishers.

*British Library Cataloguing in Publication Data*
A catalogue record for this book is available
from the British Library

*Library of Congress Cataloguing in Publication Data*
Poland and the European Union/edited by Karl Cordell;
[contributors Antoszewski Andrzej . . . et al.].
p. cm. – (Routledge studies of societies in transition; 15)
Includes bibliographical references (p. ) and index.
1. Poland – Politics and government – 1989. 2. European Union – Poland. 3. Poland – Foreign relations. I. Cordell, Karl, 1956. II. Antoszewski Andrzej. III. Series.

JN6760.P654 2000
327.43804—dc21 00–020055

ISBN 0–415–23885–4

**For my parents**

# Contents

# Illustrations

## Figures



## Tables

# Contributors

**Andrzej Antoszewski** is Professor of Political Science in the Department of Politics at the University of Wroclaw. His research centres on the fields of comparative politics, parties and party systems, and democratisation in post-communist countries. His most recent books include: *Social Demcratic Parties of Western Europe* (1995), *West European Democracies* (1997), and *A Handbook of Political Science* (1997).

**Wieslaw Bokajlo** is Professor of Political Science in the Department of Politics at the University of Wroclaw. In recent years his research interests have focused on the theory and practice of federalism in Europe, and federal thought and practice in the European Union.

**Karl Cordell** is Principal Lecturer in Politics at the University of Plymouth in the United Kingdom. His research interests include the Evangelical Church in east Germany, the German minority in Poland, German–Polish relations, and the politics of ethnicity. He is the editor of *The Politics of Ethnicity in the New Europe* (1999) and *The Politics of Ethnicity in East Central Europe* (2000).

**Andrzej Dybczynski** is a doctoral student in the Department of Politics, University of Wroclaw. His academic interests centre upon the theory of International Relations. He is also conducting research on the G8 and Polish foreign policy.

**Kazimierz Dziubka** teaches political science at the Department of Politics at the University of Wroclaw. He has published English, Dutch and Polish language texts. His main areas of research include contemporary political value systems, the political culture of Poland, and the modern ideal of citizenship.

**Ryszard Herbut** is Professor of Political Science in the Department of Politics at the University of Wroclaw. He is author or co-editor of many books and articles on parties, party systems and public administration. His publications include *An Encyclopaedia of Parties and Party Systems* (1999), *Politics in Poland in the 1990s* (1998), and *Democracies in East-Central European Countries in Comparative Perspective* (1998). In recent years, his research interests have focused on party models and strategies in the process of democratic transformation.

**Andrzej W. Jablonski** is Professor of Political Science in the Department of Political Science, the University of Wroclaw. His teaching and research interests include political theory and methodology; comparative politics, and the democratisation process in East-Central Europe.

**Tadeusz Lebioda** is a lecturer in the Institute of German and European Studies, the University of Wroclaw. He has published numerous works on the German minorities in East-Central Europe, German–Czech relations, the history of international relations, and German expellee and refugee associations.

**Teresa Los-Nowak** is Professor of Politics in and Head of the Department of Politics at the University of Wroclaw. She has published extensively in the fields of international relations theory, international law, and issues of peace and security. Her publications include *Disarmament Problems in Poland's Foreign Policy* (1980), and *Poland's Position in the European Security Structure* (1993).

**Elzbieta Stadtmüller** is Professor of International Relations in and Deputy Director of the Institute of German and European Studies, the University of Wrocclaw. She has authored and co-authored several books including: *The Border of Fear and Hope. The Poles and Germany in the 1990s* (1998), and *Political Problems of the Contemporary World* (1998).

**Robert Wiszniowski** is a researcher and lecturer in the Department of Politics, University of Wroclaw. His doctoral dissertation was a comparative study of political marketing in Finland, France, Poland and the USA. He is the author of numerous articles on parties, elections, and marketing management in public administration in Poland. His main research interests are in the fields of political marketing, party advertisements, public communication, and elections.

# Acknowledgements

There are many people to whom I owe a debt of thanks with regard to this publication. They include, those members of staff at the Institute of German and European Studies, and the Department of Political Science at the University of Wroclaw who contributed to this book, and who managed to cope with my constant requests for amendments and alterations. Special mention is due to Professor Elzbieta Stadtmüller, for taking care of things at the Polish end, and to Andrzej and Barbara Dybczynski for their hospitality and translation services. Thanks are also due to both my former Head of Department, Mr Adrian Lee, and his successor, Professor Michael Thrasher, for supporting me in this endeavour. Finally, my thanks also go out to the Leverhulme Trust for their generous financial support by means of research grant F/568/b.

# Series editor's preface

This is the first volume in the new series published by Routledge on 'Europe and the nation-state'. As Lee Miles and I have briefly emphasized, the series has as its empirical focus the complex relationship between European integration and the nation-state principally, though not solely, in the context of the European Union (EU) and its member states as well as those applicant states that are currently on the threshold of membership.

Edited by Karl Cordell, the present collection of essays comprises a work of twelve chapters on Poland and the European Union (EU). It is tantamount to a 'tour de force' of Poland's complicated and fascinating relations with the EU and with its immediate neighbours both within and without that organization. Karl Cordell has managed to bring together an impressive array of Polish scholars who have brought their considerable intellectual weight and authority to bear upon the many contemporary problems and challenges that confront the Polish nation-state in its drive to join one of the most successful political projects in European history.

The underlying theme of these twelve essays is about adjustment and adaptation. It is about how far the Polish state, society and economy have the capacity to adjust and adapt to the huge changes implicit in membership of the EU. Consequently the emphasis of the essays is differentiated but they include Poland's history, geopolitical position, social and economic structures, political parties, party system and machinery of government, and ultimately how they interact with its basic political values, beliefs and attitudes towards Europe. Tradition collides with modernity. Contemporary public expectations are characterized by a conspicuous ambiguity that veers between the optimism of economic prosperity, political stability and military security and the scepticism of far-reaching structural change that could conceivably render Poland socially, economically and politically enfeebled.

Cordell makes it clear that Poland is a nation-state at yet another crossroads in its long constitutional and political evolution. Its current attempt to remove all traces of its troubled past and replace them with the promise of a much more peaceful, prosperous and secure future serves appropriately to underline the contemporary struggle of the European nation-state to come to terms with its novel role in the EU. In this respect the book has an enduring significance for the study of contemporary European politics and history.

Michael Burgess
University of Hull, March 2000

# 1 Introduction

## Aims and objectives

*Karl Cordell*

There are few countries in Europe whose history has been as turbulent and indeed sometimes tragic as that of Poland. The first Polish kingdom was founded in 966, but after having played an important and sometimes a decisive role in the politics of Europe, Poland disappeared from the political map at the end of the eighteenth century. Despite various uprisings and other more peaceful endeavours aimed at achieving national independence in the nineteenth century, it was not until 1918 that a Polish state was re-created. The new Poland which emerged at the end of World War One was a very different state from its predecessor. The old Poland had been a multi-ethnic monarchical commonwealth, in which the nobility had enjoyed great autonomy from the sovereign. The new Poland was forged in the crucible of modern nationalist doctrine and leaned to the principles of statecraft which had been popularised by the French Revolution.

As a result, the new state veered toward both centralism and chauvinism. In a country in which approximately one-third of the population was not in fact ethnically Polish, such policies were likely to be laden with danger. With so many of its citizens failing on ethno-linguistic and religious grounds to meet the criteria of the 'true Pole', internal tensions were bound to arise. Such tensions were exacerbated by a parlous economic situation and the related inability of either consensus politics or liberal democratic structures to take root. In effect between 1926 and 1939 Poland was run by the military, with parliament being reduced to an institution of marginal importance. Although the *Sanacja* (recovery) regime of the military kept the lid on internal tensions and foreign policy disputes it did not solve them. With the coming to power of Adolf Hitler in 1933, Poland's already frosty relations with Germany took a decisive turn for the worse. The authorities in Warsaw proved to be either unwilling or unable to buy time with either Hitler or Stalin, and instead counted on speedy Anglo-French assistance in the event of an attack from either of its more powerful neighbours. In the event in September 1939, Hitler and Stalin launched their joint invasion. The British and French security guarantees proved to be hollow, Poland was overrun within days, and once again partitioned.

During the Second World War, the Nazis established a reign of terror aimed at destroying the Polish intellectual elite, and enslaving the large remainder of the population. In those areas which initially fell under their control, the policies of the Soviet Union were little better. The main victims in this situation were, of course, Poland's Jews. Their status in the Polish Republic had never been assured, and now they found themselves to be at the mercy of Himmler's death squads. The result was that around three million of them, or 90 per cent of the pre-war population Jewish population, met their deaths in the various extermination centres dotted around the eastern marches of the *Großdeutsches Reich.* When delivery from the Nazis appeared in 1944 and 1945, it came in the shape of the same Red Army which had helped partition Poland in 1939. Stalin was determined to restore the territorial gains made in 1939. He also realised that no section of Polish society including the communists, would tolerate such a situation unless Poland received territorial compensation from elsewhere. Therefore a decision was taken to compensate Poland at the expense of Germany. Poland was in effect shunted westwards. The large majority of the German population in these areas was then subjected to forcible expulsion by the new Polish authorities and their Soviet allies, and the 'Recovered Territories' as they became known, were re-populated by displaced Poles.

Given Cold War rivalries, fear of a vengeful Germany, habitual distrust of Poles, and his highly suspicious nature, Stalin decided that the only way to guarantee Polish allegiance to Soviet foreign policy goals was to ensure that a communist government came to power, by all available means. All internal opposition was crushed, where necessary by military force, and by 1949 the process of Sovietisation was all but complete. Stalin is alleged to have once said that attempting to install socialism in Poland would be like 'trying to put a saddle on cow'. He was not wrong. The peasantry successfully resisted collectivisation, and although bloodied, the Catholic Church remained unbowed and retained the allegiance of the large majority of society. The years 1956, 1968, 1970, 1976 and in particular 1980 bear testimony to the resistance of ordinary people to a regime which most of them regarded as little more than a Soviet stooge. Although the communists, especially in the early years, took advantage of a popular demand for reform, they were never able to obtain the legitimacy they craved.

Another quite possibly apocryphal quote which encapsulates this ongoing struggle is alleged to have been uttered in the Gdansk shipyard in 1980 by an unemployed electrician who said to his former employers: 'Do you remember me? I used to work here'. The electrician was of course Lech Walesa. The movement he helped found and came to dominate was Solidarity. This trades union cum mass movement for reform gripped the imagination of the developed world as it began its titanic struggle with the authorities in Warsaw and Moscow. Despite the imposition of martial law in 1981, and years of harassment, the government was no more able to crush the opposition than it was able to institute effective political, social and economic reform. Eventually, in 1988, in the light of Mikhail Gorbachev's reforms in the Soviet Union, the communist party and their military backers in effect abandoned the notion of one-party rule, and agreed to talk to Solidarity. The result of these 'Round Table' negotiations was an agreement by government and opposition to share power. Semi-free elections were held in 1989 which resulted in the humiliation of the communist party. No longer able to rely on the military might of the Soviet Union, and in fact for the most part now desirous of reform, the communist party agreed to relinquish power. The end of communist rule in Poland presaged the fall of communism throughout the Eastern bloc and eventually in the Soviet Union itself. However, it did not of itself signal instant prosperity.

Although the Warsaw Pact and Comecon were in their death-throes, a majority of both the new political class and the general public were of the opinion that Poland could not and should not stand alone in Europe. Rather, the consensus was that the road to economic recovery and the institutionalisation of liberal democracy lay through membership of the North Atlantic Treaty Organisation (NATO) and the European Community/ Union (EC/EU). In the euphoria which surrounded the defeat of communism and in part due to mutual misperception, it was blithely assumed that integration with the 'West' was a given and could be speedily achieved. However, as this book demonstrates, as the scale and nature of the differences between Poland and even the least wealthy of EU member-states became clearer, such early hopes proved to be misplaced. Neither should we forget that although for years the EC/EU had proclaimed its desire to one day embrace East-Central Europe, it had never had to evolve policies aimed at dealing with that eventuality. Given that neither a policy of exclusion nor the creation of an EU Mark-2 was on the cards, the EU had little alternative but to develop a vision of accession.

Throughout the 1990s, successive Polish governments found themselves in something of a cleft stick with regard to the EU. On the one hand and particularly in the early 1990s, they operated within a climate of rising expectations, to which politicians of all almost all stripes had contributed. On the other, with the EU itself, they faced an organisation which now had to match its rhetoric with concrete fact, and which sometimes gave the impression that it was trying to fight shy of the whole issue. As this volume demonstrates, in recent years common sense has prevailed on both sides. Polish expectations have been dampened and EU member-states have realised that pursuing a policy of exclusion could result in the destabilisation of the continent.

In the past few years both sides have been engaged in substantive talks aimed at securing Polish admission sometime between 2003 and 2006. The terms of membership have been laid down explicitly or otherwise in a variety of documents and fora. They include the Amsterdam Treaty, and the Dublin, Copenhagen and Luxembourg summits. Poland, along with Hungary, the Czech Republic, Estonia, Cyprus and Slovenia, is now locked into a process which, barring last-minute disasters, will lead to full accession. The enormity of this task cannot be understated, especially as it is the current government's avowed aim to prepare Poland not only for EU membership, but also for early accession to the Euro zone. Certain of the problem areas are well known, even to those with only a passing interest in the area. They include the restructuring of Polish heavy industry, and the design of a programme of environmental regeneration, particularly in the former industrial powerhouse of Upper Silesia. Most famously, there is the issue of how to reform Polish agriculture. Indeed from the perspective of a variety of Polish conservatives and traditionalists, the question is one of whether the agricultural sector is actually in need of substantive reform. Poland's communist rulers found to their cost that Polish peasants could be tenacious to the point of bloody-mindedness. The question today is one of whether Poland's farmers, well-served by pursuing such a stance when dealing with the EU, which unlike the Soviet Union in the 1940s and 1950s is not possessed of a 'Polish complex', could *in extremis* simply walk away. It should not be forgotten that some EU governments are wary of Polish membership, precisely because subsidies paid to inefficient Polish industries and farmers would mean less money for them.

These and related topics form part of the backdrop to this volume, and are referred to as and when occasion demands it. However, we are more concerned with changes to Polish political behaviour, culture and political institutions than we are with analysing specific areas of domestic public policy. Thus our analysis commences with an assessment of changes to the basic contours of Polish foreign policy since the late 1980s. As a result, it is to be hoped that the reader will become familiar with elements of both continuity and change in this area, the rationale which lay behind changes to strategies employed, and the goals sought by successive Polish governments. One thing that will become immediately clear is that in the early 1990s, EU membership was thought of as simply constituting one of a number of alternatives which were available to Poland. Yet due to combination of circumstance and necessity, by the mid-1990s, it had become the *sine qua non* of Polish foreign policy. Having so established these facts, the book moves on to an examination of the relationship between changes in public perception, and the process of negotiation itself. Within this context, three key groups have a significant role to play. They are the general public, the political parties, and the Catholic Church. It is noticeable that as the realisation that the EU was neither a piggy bank to be placed at Poland's disposal, any more than it was an entity that looked upon Poland as the prodigal son, so attitudes among ordinary Poles began to change. A majority of the general public still favours Polish entry, but there is a vociferous anti-EU lobby at work, and even those who remain in favour possess an enthusiasm which is tempered by reality. Similarly, the attitude of the major political parties has become clearer over the past few years. In Poland, nationalist and chauvinist elements tend to embrace both the far left and the right. As such they have always been sceptical of the benefits of exchanging Soviet tutelage (in the case of the right), or really existing socialism (in the case of the left) for inclusion in a supranational institution which will submerge Polish traditions within an alien 'Euroculture'. What the reader may actually find surprising is that, as in the United Kingdom, such fears embrace significant sections of the Polish right, and are by no means confined to the fringes of domestic politics. As various contributors show, such attitudes are very often linked to age, education levels, residence and socioeconomic status, and they cannot be ignored. Similarly, the attitudes of the Catholic Church must be taken into account. Despite the fact that the overwhelming majority of Poles are baptised Catholics, we should be wary of assuming that Polish society forms a homogeneous unit with regard to religion. Neither should we assume that the clergy itself moves and thinks as one. Although some of the most reactionary elements in Polish society are to be found in the ranks of the Catholic Church, there is little sign that they are able to turn this notoriety into mass support at election times. The clergy nevertheless remains a significant player, and its opinions are important. The Church, following the lead of the pope is by and large in favour of Polish entry into the EU. Yet, it is also wary of embracing values which it sees as being both negative and alien to the Polish experience. It should be noted that its concerns are not solely or even primarily to do with areas of private morality.

The volume also considers the growth of civil society in Poland, changing notions of citizenship and the extent to which liberal democratic values have permeated Polish society. Such an analysis in turn facilitates those sections of the volume which deal with the nature of political competition in Poland, and the extent to which it differs from that which is to be found in EU states. These points are important. If we wish to understand why Polish politics functions in the way in which it does, and why it differs from Western European patterns, we have to beware of glib explanations which account for disjunctures solely by reference to over forty years of communist rule. By necessity we must examine the nature of Polish society, its cleavages, the nature of its parties, party alliances and the like. We must also be able to account for the roots of these contemporary patterns and structures. In so doing we are better able to understand why certain groups of parties exhibit the attitudes they do toward such issues as the EU, whom these parties seek to represent, and the extent to which they have been influenced by North American and West European campaigning styles.

Moving on, another area of reform which this volume covers is that of changes to the organisation of the machinery of government. In order to render itself compatible to the EU's *acquis communitaire*, Poland along with all other applicant states has been obliged to take a long hard look at the organisation of both its central administrative structures and those of subnational government. As is shown in the volume, this has necessitated defining and re-defining the roles of the cabinet, the prime minister, numerous re-organisations of ministries and attempts to restructure the senior civil service. Bold though these initiatives may be, those undertaken in the field of sub-national government have been even more comprehensive, and to some extent have been designed to render sub-national government in Poland compatible with the idea of a Europe of the regions, should such an entity ever come about. Thus the pattern of centralised, or indeed over-centralised, government which has characterised Poland since the creation of the modern state has at last been overcome. Yet, we should note that the debate over reform stirred quite fundamental emotions concerning whether or not Poland should pursue the path of decentralisation, and in whose interests such plans were.

This leads us into another important theme with which this volume deals. Poland has often suffered from uncertainty, annexation and invasion due to its exposed geopolitical position and it being unable to secure efficient working relationship with at least some of its more powerful neighbours. Throughout the course of history, Germany and Russia have of course been the most powerful of these neighbours. At present, the Kaliningrad enclave to one side, Russia has been removed from the equation.

Germany, however, remains, and moreover the united Germany, no matter how reluctantly, is the major player in European politics. As the volume shows, in the 1990s German–Polish relationships improved immeasurably. That such an improvement was possible, bears no small testament to the endeavours of a courageous group of prominent public figures in Poland, who were prepared to confront the post-war stereotypes, face history honestly, and admit that German–Polish relations had not been characterised by centuries of unremitting aggression by Germany against Poland. In return, Germany agreed to act as Poland's ambassador to Brussels, and has proven to be Poland's main partner in the process of post-communist reconstruction. The progress of recent years has been remarkable. However, the honeymoon period is at end, and as is demonstrated in the text, as the date of accession looms, some uncomfortable shared historical legacies will have to be overcome once and for all.

Turning eastward, we find that with Russia (temporarily) removed from the equation, Poland's relationship with Ukraine is of utmost importance. For the first time ever, Poland shares the bulk of its eastern border with an independent Ukraine. Polish–Ukrainian relations have often been complex, not least since the rise of modern nationalist doctrine in the nineteenth century, and the engendering of consequent ethno-territorial disputes. Today, in some respects, Poland's eastern border is in effect the EU's eastern border. The objective of both Warsaw and Kiev at the moment is to as far as possible to replicate Warsaw's current relationship with Berlin, so that Poland may eventually come to act as Ukraine's unofficial ambassador to Brussels much in the same way that in recent years, Germany has for Poland.

The authors of this book do not pretend to have provided a definitive account of every single issue which confronts Poland as it seeks to join the European venture. However, we do hope that most of the key features have been analysed in an informative and erudite manner. That being the case, we are convinced that the reader of this volume will better appreciate the problems which face this remarkable country as it enters both the new millennium and a new political venture.

# 2 Contemporary government attitudes towards the European Union

*Teresa Los-Nowak*

## Historical contexts and antecedents

Following the collapse of the Soviet Union and the entire Eastern bloc between 1989 and 1991, just about the only certainty with regard to Poland was its geopolitical position. In many respects Poland was in a paradoxical situation. Although the country was now free from Soviet tutelage, its room for manoeuvre was constricted by its lack of capability in various fields such as the economy, finance and technological development. In theory, Poland now had freedom of choice in determining the contours of its foreign policy and alliance strategy. As we shall see, the choices made were in reality consequent upon past experience and (perception of) contemporary realities.

Throughout the 1980s the majority of Poles had called into question both the authenticity and legality of the communist regime. With the downfall of communist hegemony in 1989, prima facie conditions were created for Poland's smooth entry into the political and military organisational structures of Western Europe. However, from the very beginning of this process of transformation, difficulties emerged concerning the ability of the Polish polity to adapt Poland's economic and political structures to the Western European integrational framework. To be blunt, the expectations of both Polish decision-makers and Polish society at large were manifestations of a somewhat pretentious attitude and, on occasion, irrational expectations of what such membership would bring. Unfortunately, space does not permit of any detailed analysis of the circumstances which facilitated the growth of such views. Suffice it to say that this mentality had arisen partly as a consequence of short-term political experiences, and partly through a misperception of how the remainder of the continent viewed Poland.

It is self-evident that the ideological factors prevailing in the foreign and internal policies of Poland during the period of communist rule ended with the fall of the Polish United Workers Party (PZPR). Although it was recognised that many obstacles still existed, the new situation, which provided the opportunity for Poland to take part in West European integrative structures, was perceived as being relatively unproblematic. It was taken as given that membership of a range of organisations would in fact be automatic, and that the only issue was that of the modalities of entry. As it has turned out, especially with regard to the European Community/Union (EC/EU), the construction of a strategy which met the requirements of all interested parties had first of all to be based upon a sober analysis of the facts. Such an analysis includes a reliable analysis of the economy and a prognosis of the consequences upon the domestic environment of joining supranational institutions.

What seems to have been forgotten in the post-communist euphoria is that the east–west division of the continent pre-dated the rise of the communists to power, and that this division was not likely to disappear in the space of a few years. Consequently, there were drawbacks and difficulties for all parties concerned with the admission of countries such as Poland to the then EC. For former communist countries, the danger was that the reform process would simply not deliver the promised gains, and that as and when this became clear to the general public, renewed and deeper crisis would ensue. Although such a crisis has not occurred outside of the former Yugoslavia and Albania, there was and there remains an awareness in the western part of the continent that failure on the part of West European governments to wherever possible reach out to East-Central Europe, could contribute to the growth of instability throughout the region.

For Poland, in the period of immediate post-communism, what was particularly dangerous was the assessment in various West European capitals that the Polish economy was too backward for Poland to be considered a genuine candidate for EC membership. At the time, Foreign Minister Krzysztof Skubiszewski acknowledged the logic of this position by arguing that the capability and range of Polish foreign policy options was to a large extent derivative of Poland's economic condition. For Skubiszewski, the EU could play a significant role in the efforts to reconstruct the Polish economy. He also sought to accentuate the positive, and argued that continued emphasis on Poland's economic backwardness and the difficulties in eliminating it, could lead to Poland remaining isolated from the European mainstream. This perspective was in fact quite realistic. In effect a choice had to be made between genuine aid in the process of transformation, and declarations of goodwill. Unlike in 1945 when geopolitical reality dictated otherwise, the West was confronted with the choice of aiding in the process of political regime change in Poland and other countries in the region, or doing nothing and fostering instability and stagnation. Although the latter option was never exercised, even from the very beginning of the transition period one could observe a decline in interest in the fate of East-Central Europe on the part of West European governments. The reasons for this change in attitudes were quite simple. The initial aims of the reform movements in Poland and other countries in the region had been achieved; domestic communist hegemony had been broken, and the Soviet Union had performed a political U-turn.

The new governments in East-Central Europe declared their determination to create a liberal democratic order based on the rule of law. With regard to Poland, the belief that superficial regime change would of itself lead to a resolution of all of society's ills, proved to be misplaced. Similarly, the belief that the former communist countries had the economic and political capacity necessary to achieve rapid and profound reforms with ease was also ill-founded. In fact, both domestic and West European political elites underestimated the nature and magnitude of the problems inherent in the transition from communist authoritarianism to liberal democracy.

As we shall see, the transformation process was to prove much more difficult and more complex than first envisaged. In the remainder of our analysis we shall focus on the choices faced by Poland in terms of its integration strategy. In so doing, it will be argued that whilst Poland has sought to maintain correct relations with Russia, part of the aim of its integration strategy has been to create a set of conditions which renders the return of Russian influence all but impossible. Finally, we shall highlight the fact that perception of reality, as opposed to reality itself, is often an important factor in the determination of outcomes.

## External and internal implications of the process of change in Poland

The new position of Poland on the geostrategic and geoeconomical map of Europe was one of the most important consequences of the demise of the post-war political order (Los-Nowak 1992: 523). As such, it signalled the destruction of Poland's existing network of alliances and created the possibility for Poland to enter into new arrangements with the states of Western Europe and North America. Each of the participants in this process had to face the new challenges as best they could. Some, such as Poland, were better situated to handle it than others, for example the Soviet Union. The fact that some states actually disappeared from the map bears testimony to just how traumatic these changes were.

The process of transformation was being engineered in two main spheres. In a broad sense they can be subdivided into the sphere of institutional transformation and that of social transformation. Institutional reform concerned wide-ranging changes to the political and socioeconomic systems of the country. Within the social sphere, the process referred to transformation of the individual and collective mentality of society, its attitude towards the state and its understanding of the notion of citizenship. The transformation process also covered the redefinition of notions of internal and external security and economic wellbeing. Concepts such as the sovereignty of the state came under scrutiny, particularly as it was Poland's declared aim to join a raft of explicitly supranational institutions. The hegemonic system in which Poland functioned for over forty years, as well as limiting the autonomy of the individual, had limited that of the state in terms of domestic and foreign policy. Although Poland was technically a sovereign state, all major decisions taken in Warsaw had to be seen to be compatible with both the official policy of 'really existing socialism' and the 'Brezhnev doctrine'.

The year 1989 therefore constituted both a break with the past and a new beginning. The first ingredient of the negotiated transfer of power had been the Round Table Agreement between Solidarity and reformist elements in the PZPR headed by General Wojciech Jaruzelski on 5 April 1989. The second was the elections to the Sejm and the Senate on 4 June 1989, and the consequent appointment of a non-communist government headed by the Solidarity activist Tadeusz Mazowiecki. The Round Table Agreement sought to define the guiding principles of the new political system, and formed the basis of co-operation among the parties for a guided transformation away from the politics of the past. In turn, the elections also signalled the final defeat of the PZPR, and the end of its de facto monopoly of power. As a result, a new set of orientations for both foreign and domestic policy could be created. The selection of Mazowiecki as prime minister symbolised both the transition and the opportunity.

What had begun was a multilevel and multipolar process of transformation, the culmination of which was to be the full democratisation of the state along and its relocation from the political periphery of Europe to its centre. The new political class had therefore quickly to acquaint itself with not only the real domestic situation in Poland, but also with the requirements and expectations of the West European policy community (Kuzniar 1993). The great majority of Polish citizens claimed to identify with 'Western values', as did the political elite. Therefore, at a superficial level, the new government did not have much of a role to play in the process of the 'Europeanisation' of Polish society, the respect of human rights, political pluralism and the like. Rather it saw its primary function to be one of engineering institutional and constitutional reform and the creation of the foundations upon which civil society is created. Having said that, we must acknowledge the problem of perception. It was one thing for Polish society to proclaim itself in favour of an abstract series of 'Western values'. It was quite another to apply such values in a society which had little first-hand knowledge of those values.

## Polish integration strategy: 1989–1990

Despite the above-mentioned elections to the Sejm and Senate in 1989, the relations and interactions between Poland and the international environment were still determined by a basic question. This was one of how to disentangle the country from its existing network of alliances, and then of how to integrate it into the North Atlantic and West European alliance network. There was also the question of how best to proceed without prejudicing either the Polish 'national interest', or indeed that of the still extant Soviet Union.

The foreign policy of a state is the process through which a government attempts to further its national interest. In the case of Poland's integration strategy, the question was one of pursuing a policy which would lead to Poland's 'return to Europe', whilst at the same time maximising Poland's overall room for manoeuvre. Claims that Poland had never left Europe, or alternatively that it had at last taken up its rightful place at the European table, bore witness to an emotional identification with the world of democratic values and political solutions. They were, however, not the deciding factors in the process of economic, political and military integration with the West. The deciding factor was to be the state, based on its own its capacity for radical transformation. This is what Western Europe governments also expected, although we must note that expectations were asymmetrical and the difficulties were understated. Western Europe governments did not appreciate just how difficult the transformation would be. For their part, the new rulers of East-Central Europe blithely seemed to assume that they were walking through an open door.

It is appropriate to note at this juncture that the new Polish political elite did not constitute an exception to this general rule. On the other hand, all parties can be forgiven for failing to realise that rather than use force to maintain the German Democratic Republic (GDR), the Soviet Union would actually allow it to become submerged within an expanded Federal Republic of Germany (FRG). Neither can anyone be criticised for failing to predict that the newly united Germany would adhere to the entire alliance network of the old FRG. Not only had the post-war edifice been destroyed within the space of a few months, but its most powerful symbol, the division of Germany, had been overcome. The governments of Western Europe now had to face three related issues. The first was how to incorporate the newly united Germany within the alliance structure with the minimum of disruption to all interested parties. The second was how to enter into co-operation with the remainder of the former communist bloc. The third was to acknowledge the fact that although the continent was no longer divided in terms of ideology, rhetoric apart, it was by no means united.

## From European Community to European Union: the implications for Poland

In 1986 with the passing of the Single European Act (SEA), the EC embarked upon a massive strategy of internal reform, aimed above all at reviving the process of integration. The Madrid and Strasbourg summits of 1989, and especially that of Dublin in 1990, laid the groundwork for a further deepening of the integration process and to the eventual transformation of the EC to the EU. At this point a strategy for widening the EC/EU to embrace any of the states of East-Central Europe was not on the agenda. Given the apparent immediate unlikelihood of such an eventuality the EU was preoccupied with the dynamics of internal reform.

'Policy' with regard to the potential expansion of the EU eastward, continued to be little more than a series of statements in which the readiness of the EU to embrace new members was reaffirmed.

This is the backdrop which faced the new Polish government in 1989. The question was one of what could and should be attempted in the short term. What alternatives if any, to immediate EC entry were available to Poland and other would-be applicants? Polish policy-makers were also acutely aware that Soviet sensitivities still needed to be taken into account. Therefore they knew they had to explore a range of possibilities, and not necessarily select the most optimal of alternatives. These factors help explain why the new Polish authorities appeared to show an early interest in transforming the Council for Mutual Economic Assistance (CMEA) into a genuinely supranational institution. Certainly, reform-minded former communists, who it must not be forgotten, still wielded influence and power, were of the opinion the CMEA could somehow be rescued and transformed. President Jaruzelski, in a speech to parliament in January 1990 on the occasion of the visit of Czechoslovak President Vaclav Havel, alluded to the hope that the CMEA could transform itself into a genuine supranational organisation. However we should note that even at this early stage, the fully post-communist governments of Czechoslovakia and Hungary held a different position in this matter from that of Poland (*Sprawozdaia Sejmowe*, 1990: 78). In a speech to the Sejm in January 1990, Prime Minister Mazowiecki echoed these sentiments in the Sejm when he stated: 'While gradually building a unified Europe, we do not wish to demolish anything . . . [the] . . . CMEA, since that is what we are concerned with, is an agreement open to the world and fully linked to the global economy' (*Sprawozdaia Sejmowe* 1990). Whether Mazowiecki genuinely believed in what he was saying is open to question. Regardless of whether he did or not, his words indicate that he appreciated the reality of the situation, and the fact that he could not afford needlessly to antagonise either the Soviet Union or its Polish allies.

Rather than simply terminate the CMEA, it was suggested that it be transformed into an international forum aimed at promoting the marketisation and integration of the economies of East-Central Europe. Indeed, this had been the official position of CMEA states from October 1989, by which time the GDR was already in a state of collapse. By the turn of the year, it was clear to all concerned that the CMEA was likely to go the same way as every other part of the Soviet bloc. Evidence for this comes in the shape of a decision by the Polish Parliamentary Commission of Foreign Affairs to commence a formal dialogue with the EC on matters of bilateral concern.

Not only was there uncertainty over Poland's future geopolitical role, Poland was shortly to experience the 'shock therapy' of future Finance Minister Leszek Balcerowicz, who believed that as a result of such policies the Polish economy would become leaner, fitter and more capable of early

EC/EU membership. On the other hand, such measures in the economic sphere were not complemented by progress in the reform of the political system, as years of wrangling over the future shape of the constitution were about to demonstrate.

By April 1990, a change in mood had become apparent toward both the CMEA and the EC. In parliament, the CMEA was referred to as 'a relic of a past epoch' (*Sprawozdaia Sejmowe* 1990, 160). The idea of Polish admission to the European Free Trade Association (EFTA) as a first step to eventual membership of the EC/EU was also floated at this time. By the autumn of 1990, the Polish government had moved yet further, after condemning the Warsaw Pact and CMEA, as structures that served 'foreign domination in our part of Europe' which should vanish 'next year' (*Sprawozdaia Sejmowe* 1990: 4).

The major problem that Poland and other states in the region faced at that time was in fact not one of which Western institutions they should join. Rather, it was the Soviet Union and its attitude toward a state of affairs which had unwittingly been created by its leadership, created through its fatal, albeit well-intended, policies of glasnost and perestroika. The Soviet leadership remained hostile toward the idea of Poland or any other state within its rapidly crumbling sphere of influence entering into alliance structures which it considered to be in some way hostile to the world socialist movement. In March 1990, at a CMEA summit, Moscow made a final attempt to save the situation and failed. Shortly thereafter, Poland, Czechoslovakia and Hungary announced their exit from the organisation. On 14–15 February 1991, during at a meeting in the Czechoslovak city of Visegrad, it was decided that all three states would resign from the Warsaw Pact, and that the CMEA should be dissolved on grounds of obsolescence. These talks signalled the simultaneous creation of the of the Visegrad Group by Poland, Hungary and Czechoslovakia, a joint declaration on the part of the signatories confirming their aspiration to EU membership, and a series of bilateral agreements aimed at enhancing trade and co-operation among the signatories.

In addition, Poland was busy mending its fences with Germany. On 14 November 1990 the two signed a treaty confirming the position of Poland's western border. This treaty was supplemented by a further treaty signed on 17 June 1991 on Good Neighbourly Relations, which, importantly from the German side, provided for official Polish recognition of its German minority, and as such marked real progress in the endeavour to create a genuinely pluralistic society in Poland. In return, Germany offered to act as Poland's unofficial ambassador in Brussels. This latter point was of crucial importance to the Poles. In December 1990, with ideas for transforming the CMEA all but dead, they had submitted an application for associate membership of the EU (*Sprawozdaia Sejmowe* 1991: 20). In turn this application sparked off a wide-ranging domestic debate on how and whether the state, economy, the social security system and just about every other aspect of public life should be reconstructed. Again the issue of perceptions raised its head. Negotiations on entry had not even begun. Yet having made an application for associate membership, and having secured German support for it, talk of accession by the year 2000 became commonplace among both the general public and policy-makers.

As mentioned earlier, the reforms pioneered at this time by Minister of Finance Balcerowicz, were designed to effect a transition away from the centrally planned economic model as quickly as possible, in order to facilitate Poland's speedy entry into the EC. These moves in the economic sphere were complemented by the initiation of a programme of institutional reform in other areas aimed at creating civil society and a liberal democratic political culture.

Inevitably, the sheer scale of these reforms coupled with their final goal raised fears that Poland's hard-won sovereignty was once again about to be surrendered. The right of centre Confederation for an Independent Poland (KPN), and the Union for Real Politics (UPR), both claimed that if Poland opened itself too readily to foreign capital it would simply be exchanging one form of neo-colonial domination for another (*Sprawozdaia Sejmowe* 1992: 161). These fears notwithstanding, the majority of parliamentarians accepted the inevitability of the reform process, even if they did not necessarily agree with either its form or content. Above all they were convinced that only radical surgery could provide long-term guarantees of Polish independence (Wiberg and Kostecki 1996: 59–60).

With respect to relations with Moscow, the picture was still rather cloudy. Although the Soviet Union finally imploded in December 1991, the fact that no treaty was signed with the Russian Federation until May 1992 indicated two things. The first was that Poland did not feel secure as long as Russian troops were still stationed in the country. The second was that whereas correct relations with Russia were desired, Moscow was no longer an ally. Indeed, initially at least, the new regime of Boris Yeltsin in Moscow proved itself to be no more enthusiastic at the prospect of an eastward expansion of the (newly created) EU than had its communist predecessors. On the other hand, the situation was complicated by the fact that a majority of Western politicians were seemingly unable to break with past patterns of thinking. Hence, despite the political vacuum that now existed in East-Central Europe there was a climate of indecision which inevitably had repercussions in Poland.

Indecision on the part of the EU states was in many ways perfectly understandable. It was the consequence of decades of ideological glacis on the continent. Furthermore, EU member-states were quite simply preoccupied with other more pressing matters. First of all there was the Gulf War, which affected EC member-states both individually and collectively. The EU was also preoccupied with 'Agenda 2000', the creation of a single internal market, and the preparations for the Maastricht summit of 1991, which paved the way for the creation of the EU. As it was to turn out, the meeting at Maastricht in December 1991 represented the triumph of those who wished to deepen the process of integration. It also inadvertently contributed to the transformation and extension debates becoming more complex.

## Poland and the European Union: 1991–94

By the end of November 1991, the first phase of Poland's rapprochement with the EC had been completed. A Treaty of Association between Poland and the EC created a legal framework for multilateral co-operation in the economic, political, social and cultural sectors, and promised to add impetus to Poland's programme of internal reform. The overall objective of this programme was now to uproot the remaining elements of 'really existing socialism' from all walks of life in Poland, and simultaneously to adapt the Polish political, socioeconomic and legal frameworks to EC/EU norms.

However, the EC/EU was still wary of committing itself to a firm date for Polish accession. Instead, detailed solutions were sought on questions concerning the operation of the internal markets of the Visegrad Group of states, the introduction of free trade in agricultural commodities, protection of intellectual assets, and liberalisation of the labour market. It is an open question as to whether or not, as some have claimed, the East-Central European states were in some way being discriminated against. It may be argued with a degree of certainty, that previous 'late applicants' such as Greece and Portugal did not have to face as many obstacles. On the other hand, such late applicants had been admitted under wholly different circumstances from those which pertained in the 1990s. Neither had they laboured under Marxist–Leninist regimes for over forty years.

In fact, sceptics have argued that the Treaty of Association was an ambiguous document, which could, depending on interpretation, mean different things to different people. On the one hand the treaty laid down the general principles to which Poland is supposed to adhere if it wishes to accede to the EU. On the other, nowhere was it made clear whether Poland was being offered full political membership of the EU or some kind of associate status based on economic association. According to Daniel Lasok, Poland was placed in 'a legal never never land' (Lasok 1995: 204). Alternatively, and indeed more realistically, it could be argued that all the EC/EU was trying to do was to proceed sensibly and cautiously, so that in the event of the negotiations running into serious difficulties it would not find itself beholden to a set of unrealistic target dates. The Association Treaty in fact replaced an earlier agreement of 19 November 1989 signed between Poland and EC regarding trade and economic co-operation. The Polish negotiating team had been led by Jan Saryusz-Wolski, Plenipotentiary of the Government of Poland for Integration into the EU, who declared himself satisfied that Poland now had set of operational guidelines within which to work, and that without fulfilling them, integration into EU would be impossible and that the price of such a state of affairs would be the isolation of Poland.

Given that for most isolation was not a realistic alternative, the question was one of how quickly could the transition process be safely implemented, and by what date Poland could actually enter the EU. Although Poland was expected to meet EU standards on a whole range of issues, there was also the expectation on the Polish side that the EU would make concessions to Poland, particularly in the spheres of heavy industry and agriculture (Wiberg and Kostecki 1996: 57). Why this should be the case becomes clear only if we once again take into account the question of perceptions. For the EU, Poland's crumbling heavy industry represented little more than a drain on funds and a threat to the environment. For the Poles, such industries were still symbols of national virility, staffed by those who had been at the forefront of the struggle against communism. That their fate on entry to the EU should be redundancy was to many Poles simply an incomprehensible betrayal of trust.

Matters became somewhat clearer after the Copenhagen summit of June 1993. First, the EU stated explicitly that what was on offer to Poland and other applicant states was full membership, thus easing the fears of those who were worried about the terms of the Treaty of Association. Second, the general criteria of membership for aspirant countries were agreed. They were requested to amend their legal codes in order to embed notions of individual civil liberties and rights for national minorities. Whereas the former had been an explicit goal of the reform movements, the question of minority rights, especially for Roma, Germans and, to a lesser extent, Jews, had barely featured on the agenda. The fact that Poland in common with the other applicants, broke with post-war traditions in this area and worked for the creation of such rights shows the extent to which perceptions were beginning to change. In more general terms they were asked to ensure that domestic legislation was rendered compatible with EU norms. The importance of completing the process of transition from a centrally-planned to a market economy capable of functioning effectively within the EU was also reiterated. Moves were also begun aimed at ending tariffs on the export of Polish industrial goods to the EU, and more importantly on dismantling Polish tariffs on imports of finished goods from EU countries.

All such objectives were viewed as being indispensable if Poland was to meet the requirements of EU membership (Lasok 1995: 204). The results and ramifications of the Copenhagen summit also effected a change in another area, this time that of public opinion. Opinion polls on the attitude of the Polish population towards the various aspects of economic integration indicated an attitude in which paradoxes dominated. This was most apparent in the fields of sovereignty and territorial integrity. For example, in 1994, results revealed that 76 per cent of respondents held a positive view of the EU, with only 6 per cent being opposed. The remaining respondents were either undecided or held no firm opinion. By 1996 the results were, superficially at any rate, even more positive, with 80 per cent of respondents in favour of EU membership, and only 7 per cent being firmly against. However, when asked specific questions regarding costs and benefits that EU membership might bring, the presence of a sense of doubt became clear. In 1994, 50 per cent of respondents were convinced that EU membership would be beneficial for Poland, whereas by 1995, the number had dropped to 35 per cent (BSE Informacja No. 408 1996: 12). Although the trend was downward, the message was clear. What is also clear today is that a sizeable section of Polish society is still sceptical towards EU membership, precisely because they see it bringing more costs than benefits, especially to the way of life in small towns and villages.

In order to ensure that both the Treaty of Association would and could be implemented in a satisfactory manner, in 1992 parliament established an Extraordinary Commission to oversee implementation of the treaty (*Sprawozdaia Sejmowe* 1992: 149 ff.). At the time it was the opinion of then President Lech Walesa, that the process of economic transformation had been so slow that all talk of early accession was illusory. The pace of privatisation was slower than had been anticipated, public budgetary and financial procedures had still not been overhauled, and agriculture was still in its semi-crippled archaic state. For Walesa, this all meant that Poland did not constitute an attractive proposition for potential foreign investment (*Sprawozdaia Sejmowe* 1992: 149–151). The Commission was Walesa's solution to the problem. Whether it worked or not is an entirely different matter. The important point is that it added to the dynamic of integration.

From March 1992 the so-called Transition Agreements came into force. Their purpose was further to facilitate the transformation of the economic and legal codes of the applicant states. Importantly, Poland's ratification of the Treaty of Association in July 1992 enabled the government finally to prepare its application for full EU membership. On 7 April 1994 the government formally presented its application for approval by the Sejm. The Minister for Foreign Affairs, Andrzej Olechowski, commented: 'Lying at the base of this decision was the conviction of the necessity of a rapid advance in political and economical co-operation with Western Europe . . . we acknowledge that the efficiency of reform will depend to a significant extent on its correlation with the integration process in EU' (*Sprawozdaia Sejmowe* 1994: 7). Following the securing of parliamentary approval on 13 April, Prime Minister Waldemar Pawlak officially lodged the letter of intent with the embassies of the EU's member-states.

The application may be viewed as two-dimensional. On the one hand it symbolised the ending of one stage of Poland's endeavours to join the EU, and the commencement of the final phase of negotiations. On the other, it represented the final confirmation that Poland saw its future as lying with what had previously been viewed as a West European institution. Poland together with other former communist states in the region had firmly turned its back on Russia.

## Poland and the European Union 1994–98

Poland's application was formally accepted at the Luxembourg summit of 29–30 October 1994. At the same time it was agreed that negotiations on the Polish application, together with those from Hungary, the Czech Republic, Estonia, Slovenia, and Cyprus, would formally commence in the spring of 1998. The entry into force of the Treaty of Association in April 1994 and the decisions of the Luxembourg summit, opened the next stage of Poland's integration policy. The dominating issues were as ever, compliance with the programme of adaptation, the timetable for membership, the question of the Polish economy, and the transformation of the Polish legal code. Forming a kind of road map for the negotiating process was the 'Strategy for Poland' devised in June 1994, which contained the blueprint for domestic economic, social and institutional reform. The specific issues to be discussed included the continuation of economic reform, balancing the budget, reducing state subsidies to heavy industry, the reform of working practices and employment laws, the capacity of Polish domestic producers to cope with foreign competition, and of course agriculture.

Once again the question of perception is important here, particularly with regard to the implications for national sovereignty entailed by membership of the EU. This issue dovetailed into concerns expressed following the accession to power in December 1994 of a post-communist coalition of the SLD (Democratic Left Alliance) and the PSL (Polish Peasants Party). Doubts were raised over whether or not these parties, and luminaries such as Waldemar Pawlak, Jozef Oleksy and Wlodzimierz Cimoszewicz, were actually committed to Polish entry into the EU and especially to Polish membership of the North Atlantic Treaty Organisation (NATO). These fears were compounded after the victory of Aleksander Kwasniewski in the presidential elections in December 1995. Whereas fears concerning the PSL and its attitude toward the EU were proven to have some substance in fact, the SLD has proven itself in and out of government to be a whole hearted supporter of both endeavours. If anything, the current dominant coalition partner, Solidarity Electoral Action (AWS), has proven to be less solid on the EU question, and more concerned with the potential surrender of sovereignty that membership might entail.

During the period 1994–8, a series of issues which previously existed only as an undercurrent to the entire debate finally came to the fore. Poland was now locked into a co-ordinated negotiating mechanism. It gradually became clear both to society at large, as well as to members of the policy-making community, that 'the EU à-la-carte' was not on offer. Although there was a small-scale revival of talk about seeking alternative solutions outside or within the framework of the EU, nothing has so far materialised which could be viewed as a serious and effective alternative. What increasing numbers of Poles also found irritating was the fact that Poland was not going to be invited to become a full member by the year 2000. In turn this realisation called into question the need for having pursued such a vigorous adaptation programme in the early 1990s.

These facts provoked a public admission on the part of the government that the EU was not simply a source of revenue for Poland, and that the negotiations had to be viewed in a wholly new light. The Minister for Foreign Affairs in the government of Wlodzimierz Cimoszewicz, Wladyslaw Bartoszewski, stated: 'This meant a clear shift in discussions of membership of Poland in EU from the level of "benefits that Poland was to gain" to the level of common benefits for all the members of this organisation' (*Sprawozdaia Sejmowe* 1995: 11–14). In terms of events, the next important juncture was reached with the submission on 1 March 1996 of the second report on the progress of the programme of adaptation of the economy and legal system to EU norms (*Sprawozdaia Sejmowe* 1996, 226 ff.). Its content and also the main premise showed beyond all doubt that in essence the fate of Poland's application to join the EU was dependent above all on Poland's desire and ability to adapt:

> 'It is a rare case of realising the aims of foreign policy on home ground . . . It embraces arduous and not always effective *prima vista* work on the adaptation of the national economy, our legal system, public institutions and mentality to the standards of EU . . . it is concluded that for membership of the European Union to be achieved, work must first be done in the country and only then can we negotiate with the European Union'.
>
> (*Sprawozdaia Sejmowe* 1996, 22)

What is significant about the above statement is that it was made in reference to the negotiations that had taken place in 1994. The next two years witnessed a continuation and deepening of the adaptation process in the areas of the economy and finance. The fact that in November 1996 Poland actually applied to join the Euro zone, demonstrates the extent to which official perceptions of the relationship between Poland and the EU have changed. However, they also demonstrate that there is still an air of unreality concerning what can and cannot be achieved. Such an application can be viewed as evidence that Poland appreciates the true dimensions of the European project. A date of 2002 for Polish accession to the Euro zone has also been suggested. Admirable though the intention is, it is also completely unrealistic. The problems which have surrounded the Euro since its launch aside, the Polish domestic policy arena is simply not geared to it. Apart from anything else, Poland will not be a member of the EU by this date. Having said that, we should not forget that this whole issue could complicate the entry negotiations. The unwritten condition of entry into the Euro zone is the legal capacity of a state to undertake and execute the obligations resulting from the Maastricht and Amsterdam treaties, and the *aquis communautaire,* and that in theory includes meeting the criteria for economic and monetary union. Whether or not Poland or any of the other applicants from East-Central Europe will be in a position to fulfil these criteria in the early years of the twenty-first century is open to question.

In addition, this issue is entwined with that of constitutional reform. The previous 'Small Constitution' of 1992 contained no clauses allowing for the incorporation of internationally agreed statutes into domestic law. With the coming into force of the constitution of 2 April 1997 the problem was solved by the insertion of clauses which allow in general terms for the incorporation of international law into domestic law (The Constitution of the Republic of Poland 1997, Article 90), and specifically for the incorporation of EU law (The Constitution of the Republic of Poland 1997, Article 91). Once again the question of national sovereignty played a major role in the ratification debates. It was difficult for elements of the Polish public to accept such a fundamental change to constitutional and legal practice, especially after so many years of having effectively been under the thumb of the Soviet Union.

Under the terms of the 1997 constitution, a new body, the European Integration Committee, has the task of preparing the government's negotiating stance with respect to Brussels, whilst the Ministry of Foreign Affairs has responsibility for the actual conduct of the negotiations. In reality this division of labour is unclear and demarcation disputes have arisen. This was particularly the case between the Minister for Foreign Affairs, Bronislaw Geremek, and the former leader of the European Integration Committee, Ryszard Czarnecki.

The next stage of the accession procedure was for Poland to obtain the so-called avis acknowledging that the Polish side was well prepared to commence negotiations. It was distributed to the Polish government and to the governments of the other applicants in April 1996. The inquiry sheet included a series of questions totalling 170 pages and covering twenty-three different subject areas needed to be co-ordinated by Poland. The answers given were of crucial importance to the process of negotiations, given that the European Commission would in part base its judgement on Poland's suitability for eventual membership from these answers. Three months later, the Polish government submitted its response.

The submission in turn enabled the British Foreign Secretary, Robin Cook, to issue an official invitation to the Polish side to begin the formal accession negotiations. For its part, Poland continued with the process of adaptation. Ahead of the Luxembourg summit of 11–12 December 1997, during a session of the (Polish) European Integration Committee, discussions were held on the progress made toward compliance with the Treaty of Association, as were controversial questions such as support for the steel industry, the automobile industry, agriculture, and import duties on spirits.

The Commission also considered a series of documents which had been prepared by both sides. Of particular importance were matters referring to implementation timetables, binding decisions, and opinions and comments of the European Commission (*Gazeta Wyborcza*, 29 January 1998). The end result was the production of a 'National Strategy of Integration' and the 'EURO 2006' programme, with as the title of the latter suggests, the year 2006 set as the provisional target date for entry.

From the Polish perspective another step of the pre-accession phase of negotiations had been completed. The decisions of the Luxembourg summit confirmed this, and paved the way for the formal process of negotiation to begin. This process commenced on 30 March 1998 in Brussels with a meeting of the Ministers of Foreign Affairs of the EU and their counterparts from among the candidate members. The key to success in this presumed final phase will be further deregulation of the economy, wide-ranging reforms to the agricultural sector, and the continuing process of reform in areas such as health and education. The choice of Jan Kulakowski to lead the negotiations from the Polish side was one which was accepted with pleasure by both parties. Kulakowski had been post-communist Poland's first ambassador to Brussels in 1990. Thus he will hopefully complete the process which he started at the turn of the decade.

As our survey shows, throughout the 1990s, support for the European project among the Polish population has ebbed and flowed, with a majority being consistently in favour of entry. In the early years of post-communist rule many were naively enthusiastic for all things 'European' without perhaps appreciating the full costs of what was involved. By the mid-1990s a more sober assessment had become apparent, although enthusiasm for the project was still evident. In more recent years there has been a realisation that in order to make gains in some areas, Poland has to be prepared to make losses in others (Wiberg and Kostecki, 1996). A certain degree of naiveté still prevails, as the plans for Poland's entry into the Euro zone indicate. Poland has also made a decisive choice in terms of foreign policy and defining the national interest. Its entry into NATO and its desire to join the EU have sent a signal to all states in Europe that it does not consider itself either to be a natural ally of Russia, any more than it considers itself to be a part of the Russian sphere of influence. For its part, Russia has little choice at the moment but to accept the situation. The attitude in Brussels is, however, not as clear-cut as some in Warsaw would like to believe.

## Bibliography

Biuro Studiow I Ekspertyz (BSE), Kancelaria Sejmu, Informacja No. 48, Wydawnictwo Sejmowe, Warszawa, 1996.

Bucher, A. 'Security cooperation in Europe: domestic challenges and limitations', in A. Classe and L. Ruhl (eds), *Beyond East–West Confrontation. Searching for a New Security Structure in Europe*, Baden Baden: Nomos Verlag, 1991.

*The Constitution of the Republic of Poland*, Sejm Publishing Office, Warsaw, 1999.

*Gazeta Wyborca*, 29 January 1998.

Glenny, M. *The Rebirth of History. Eastern Europe in the Age of Democracy*, Harmondsworth: Penguin, 1990.

Holsti, K. 'National role conceptions in the study of foreign policy', *International Studies Quartely* 14, 3, 233–309, 1970.

Karkoszka, A, 'Poland's security policy', *The Polish Quarterly of International Affairs* 2, 1, 89–112, 1993.

Kostecki, W. and Wiberg, H. 'Adaptation during European Integration 1989–1994, Poland', in H. Mouritzen, O. Weaver and H. Wiberg (eds), *European Integration and National Adaptations. A Theoretical Inquiry*, New York: Nova Science Publishers Inc., 1996.

Kuzniar, I. 1993. 'The geostrategic factors conditioning Poland's security,' *The Polish Quartely of International Affairs*, 2, 1, 9–28.

Lasok, D. Zarys prawa Unii Europejskiej, Torun, Corp. TNOiK, 1995.

Los-Nowak, T. 'Processes of European Integration', in Z. Pietras and M. Pietras (eds), *The Transnational Future of Europe*, Lublin: Marie Curie-Sklodowska University Press, 1992.

—— 'Problemy konceptualizacji modelu bezpieczeflstwa zewnetrznego RP', *Przeglad Zachodni* 4, 273, 1–10, 1994.

Rymarezyk, J. *Polska gospodarka a proces dostosowawczy do Unii Europejskiej*, Wroclaw: Atla 2, 1998.

*Rzeczpospolita*, 29 December 1997.

Sejm Rzeczypospolitej Polskiej I i II Kadencji, *Sprawozdania Sejmowe*, Warszawa, 1999.

*Sprawozdania Sejmowe*, 1989–1997.

Stadtmüller E, *Debaty Polityczne wokol integracji Polski z Unia Europejska – ewolucja pogladow*, Jaka Europa, Wroclaw: Atla 2, 1998.

Wiberg, H. and Kostecki, W. 'Adaptation during European Integration 1989–1994, Poland', in H. Mouritzen, O. Weaver and H. Wiberg (eds), *European Integration and National Adaptations. A Theoretical Inquiry*, New York: Nova Science Publishers Inc., 1996.

*Wprost*, 11 January 1998.

# 3 Polish perceptions of the European Union in the 1990s

*Elzbieta Stadtmüller*

The aim of this chapter is to analyse the objectives of Polish policy-makers since 1990 with regard to the European Union (EU). These endeavours are contextualised within the overall framework of regional and wider European co-operation. The study attempts to identify elements of continuity and change in attitudes among Polish political parties, the still influential Roman Catholic Church and among the general public. Problems of adaptation in such key areas of the socio-economic system such as industry and agriculture are also given due attention. The chapter concludes with an overall assessment of the impact of the ongoing integration process on Polish politics and society.

## Polish integration policy: difficulties and consequences

It is self-evident that the fundamental political changes of 1989 altered the goals of Polish foreign policy. Since the early 1990s such objectives have included: the construction of a state based on the rule of law; the development of multidimensional co-operation with neighbouring countries, active participation in regional initiatives, and involvement in activities that might lead to the re-configuration of the European security system. Rapid and full integration within all the political, military and economic structures of Western Europe, namely the Council of Europe, the North Atlantic Treaty Organisation (NATO), the Western European Union (WEU) and the European Community/European Union (EC/EU), has been a priority for all Polish governments since 1990.

Polish membership of the Council of Europe was obtained relatively quickly, and in June 1989 Poland achieved 'special guest' status. In January 1990 Poland tabled an application for membership which was accepted in October of that year, subject to the holding of a fully free liberal democratic election, which duly occurred in October 1991. As a result, on 26 November 1991 Poland obtained membership of the Council of Europe, thereby confirming Poland's successful progress towards the establishment of a fully functioning liberal democracy.

Since then successive Polish governments have pursued a twin-track strategy aimed at securing accession to both NATO and the EU. Membership of these organisations is seen as being complementary and mutually re-enforcing. Entry into NATO, although initially more controversial for Polish politicians because some of them preferred a broader conception of collective security based on the Conference on Security and Co-operation in Europe/Organisation for Security and Co-operation in Europe (CSCE/OSCE), became much easier with time. Rather than involving long-term adaptation processes or evident economic success, Polish accession to NATO essentially required short-term political decisions and goodwill on the part of all interested parties.

The prospect of full membership of NATO finally appeared after the decisions of the Alliance at the Madrid summit in July 1997. At Madrid the way was paved for Polish, Czech and Hungarian entry into the North Atlantic Alliance (Kupiecki 1998). The process of ratification was then formally initiated and completed in December 1998. On 12 March 1999 Poland became a member of NATO. In so doing, Polish policy-makers achieved one of the two major objectives they had been pursuing since 1990.

In the case of integration with the EU the waiting time has proven to be much longer. The main reason for the delay lies with concerns over the Polish economy and the difficulties associated with the transition from a centrally-planned economy, which accorded primacy to heavy industry, to a consumer-oriented market economy. There is a fear that without rapid and effective structural reforms of the whole Polish economic system it will not be possible to exploit opportunities inherent in the accession process, but instead economic collapse will occur, especially in the most backward sectors.

In the light of such concerns, the development of regional co-operation became one of the paths leading to political stabilisation and more dynamic economic growth in Poland as well as in East-Central Europe as a whole. Poland was involved in these initiatives from the outset. In February 1991 the Visegrad Triangle, later re-named the Visegrad Group was established. Also in 1991 Poland became a member of the Central European Initiative. In 1992 co-operation within the framework of Central European Free Trade Area (CEFTA) began, and that year also saw the establishment of the Council of Baltic Sea States (Szczepaniak 1996). The early 1990s also saw the development of local initiatives, and many Euroregions emerged on the borders of Poland (Malendowski 1998). Among the above-mentioned forms of co-operation, CEFTA proved to be the most productive. Its members abolished all restrictions on trade in industrial goods, and despite a conservative attitude towards agricultural goods, the overall volume of trade among its members increased. CEFTA's future will be a problem as and when its most developed countries leave it to become members of the EU (Kisiel-Lowczyc 1998). In 1999 a revival of the Visegrad Group became apparent. All partners are interested in supporting the Slovakian reform process, in the hope that it will soon cease to be the only country in the region omitted from NATO and the negotiation process with the EU. Prospects for co-operation within the Council of Baltic Sea States seem to be even more promising because of common business interests and the absence of potential conflicts among the member-states.

We have already noted that full membership of the EU has been a priority of Polish foreign policy since the early 1990s. That is why Polish involvement in this process was perceived by the majority of the political elite and society as a whole to be a pre-condition for Polish economic development. If we take into account that the process of transformation began only ten years ago we see just how dynamic the formal process of linking Poland to the EU has been. An initial agreement on trade and economic co-operation between Poland and the EC was signed in September 1989. In the first half of 1990, the Polish authorities began to make efforts to associate more fully with the Community. On 16 December 1991 the European Agreement was signed. The Polish parliament ratified the European Agreement on 4 July 1992 and it came into force with effect from 1 February 1994 (Podraza 1996: 296). In 1993 the government's programme setting out the steps necessary in order to adapt the Polish economy to EU standards was accepted. Poland tabled a formal motion calling for membership of the EU on 8 April 1994.

Little of any substance occurred in this arena until 1997. Then in January of that year, Vice Prime Minister and Minister for Finance, Grzegorz Kolodko, presented to the Committee of European Integration his programme 'Euro 2006' which declared as an undisputed goal of Polish policy that an integration with the EU should be followed by accession to the Euro zone as quickly as possible (*Rzeczpospolita*, 6 January 1997). In the same month the government presented its 'National Strategy of Integration' which although couched in general terms constituted a key mandate for negotiations. It repeated the opinion that Polish membership of the EU was a strategic goal, which despite initial costs would positively influence the development of the country, the adaptation of the legal system and the economy to modern standards, and the requirements of competitiveness (Narodowa 1997).

Finally, in April 1998, real negotiations on Polish accession began. The first phase, which lasted until mid-1999, constituted a review of Polish law. Simultaneously, talks commenced on eight relatively straightforward spheres; namely science, education, telecommunications, culture and media policy, industrial policy, policy towards small and medium firms and the Common Foreign and Security Policy (CFSP). By 10 November, after the first round of talks, agreement on policy toward science, education, and policy toward small and medium firms had been reached. With regard to the remaining areas, Poland declared its willingness to accede to the CFSP, but given the overall difficulties surrounding this policy area, the practical ramifications of this step have been difficult to gauge. Turning to industrial policy, declarations of Polish readiness to adapt to EU norms and practices were deemed to be inadequate by Brussels, which wanted more detail on the extent of government help for industry, and the correlation of such help with the development of a genuine environmental policy. However, Brussels has accepted that in the short term the steel, mining and arms sectors will remain (heavily) subsidised by the state. Doubts were also raised about declaring Polish readiness to accept all agreements regarding culture and media policy. On the one hand, Poland was willing in principle to accept the key proposal, that foreign media companies had the right to enter the Polish market. On the other hand, the Polish government demanded safeguards concerning the levels of foreign investment in this area, with the aim of preserving the production of domestic programming (*Gazeta Wyborcza* 10–11 November 1998).

Negotiating positions in the fields of company law, statistics, consumer protection consumers and health care were presented in December 1998. By 19 April 1999 they had reached agreement only in the field of statistics, although one month later agreement was reached in the fields of industrial policy, telecommunications, health care and consumer rights. By 22 June, agreement had been reached in most of the aforementioned areas, with Poland formally due to present its position on remaining fields by the end of 1999. The most difficult stage in this process will occur in 2000 when negotiations begin on such bugbears as agriculture, environmental protection, the free movement of people, regional and structural policy, financial and budgetary practices, and the purchase of land by foreigners (*Gazeta Wyborcza*, 22 May 1999).

The issue of land ownership ties in with the question of agriculture, which is the field of greatest concern to all those involved in this entire process. Polish agricultural practices are overwhelmingly incompatible with EU norms. We must also remember that almost 40 per cent of EU law concerns this particular field and the Common Agricultural Policy (CAP) absorbs over half of the EU budget. The EU's report on Polish agriculture of September 1998 showed that only 19 per cent of the population lived in urbanised areas, that average farm income was one seventh of the EU average, that 26.7 per cent of the Polish workforce was engaged in the agricultural industry and, most tellingly, that farmers produced a mere 6 per cent of GDP. The report also noted that Polish villages are very small, and that farms are unconsolidated. The approximately two million farms consist of twenty-four million separate fields, and that at current rates of progress consolidating them would take a minimum of twenty years (*Raport o stanie polskiego rolnictwa* 1998). Estimates of the length of time it would take Polish agriculture to reach EU average standards tend toward the thirty-year mark, and then on the premise that Polish and EU growth rates remain at their late 1990s levels. The fact that only 20–25 per cent of Polish farms have a future, and the liquidation and consolidation of the remainder will provoke resistance, is an additional problem. The same is true of Polish industry. Low educational levels and the lack of investment in this field constitute additional problems. Only one-third of the population over 15 years old has completed full basic education. Within the same group only 7 per cent of the population has undertaken a course of higher education (Zielinska-Glebocka and Stepniak 1998: 259, 313).

Such a situation arouses fears in Polish society as well as controversy among existing EU member-states. Such low levels of development create negative rather than positive impressions of what Polish membership of the EU would actually entail. In turn, these facts create resistance from among the poorer EU states who balk at the prospect of having to share development funds with Poland. In turn, richer EU states foresee mass immigration from Poland as being a likely consequence of the freedom of movement for Polish labour.

This last hypothesis is disputed by the Polish side, which predicts a maximum emigration rate from Poland of forty thousand per year. The Poles claim that in any case most migrants would simply seek temporary work, and that they would act as a supplement to existing labour forces. The fact that EU countries may be exaggerating this problem is supported by the fairly low levels of emigration from Spain, Portugal and Greece to more developed EU states. It is also argued that the impact of continuing Polish economic growth, combined with the claimed reluctance of most Poles to emigrate, will act as brake upon any desire on sections of the population to head west (*Gazeta Wyborcza*, 20 May 1999).

However, in Austria and Germany this fear of uncontrolled emigration dampens public enthusiasm for further EU enlargement. The inevitable consequence will be that these states will push for transition periods in order to protect their labour markets. On the other hand, Denmark, The Netherlands, Sweden and Great Britain, which are also potential targets for Polish migrants, do not perceive the need for such protective measures, and the level of public acceptance of Polish membership of the EU is generally higher in these countries (see Table 3.1). Indeed, as the following table reveals, in general, attitudes toward Poland amongst potential members of the EU are positive (see Table 3.2).

## Political debates and public opinion

In the 1990s, the issues and themes in the sphere of the integration policy outlined in the first part of this work were accompanied by a vigorous internal debate. In turn, this debate was interlaced with a broader discussion of ideas of integration and European unity, regional and pan-European structures of economic and security co-operation, and bilateral relations with Poland's neighbours, especially with Germany. Government officials, politicians from governing parties, opposition politicians, activists from all types of professional and social organisations, church dignitaries, journalists and academics were all involved in this discussion.

*Table 3.1* Support for Polish membership in the EU among existing EU members (%)

| *Country* | *B* | *DK* | *G* | *GR* | *E* | *FR* | *IRL* | *IT* | *L* | *NL* | *AU* | *PO* | *FIN* | *SW* | *UK* | *EU 15* |
|---|---|---|---|---|---|---|---|---|---|---|---|---|---|---|---|---|
| For | 31 | 76 | 35 | 59 | 53 | 45 | 48 | 53 | 40 | 62 | 24 | 46 | 55 | 70 | 50 | 47 |
| Against | 50 | 16 | 47 | 30 | 15 | 38 | 20 | 26 | 38 | 26 | 58 | 19 | 31 | 13 | 23 | 32 |

*Source*: Eurobarometer, Autumn 1998: B.62

*Table 3.2* Support for enlargement of the EU among applicant states

| *Country* | *For* | *Against* |
|---|---|---|
| Malta | 52 | 25 |
| Hungary | 50 | 28 |
| Poland | 47 | 32 |
| Cyprus | 45 | 31 |
| Czech Republic | 45 | 31 |
| Slovakia | 40 | 36 |
| Estonia | 39 | 36 |
| Bulgaria | 39 | 36 |
| Latvia | 39 | 36 |
| Lithuania | 38 | 36 |
| Romania | 37 | 40 |
| Slovenia | 36 | 38 |

*Source*: Eurobarometer, Autumn 1998: 88.

Although individuals may and have changed their minds since 1989, the general lines of division on these issues have remained. The first camp consists of those who advocate the speediest possible integration within the EU. The second has many serious doubts but generally is not completely against the process. The third camp consists of firm opponents of the EU and, one might add, most things 'foreign'. At the same time, the commencement of substantive negotiations in 1998 put the question of Polish membership in a completely different perspective and seems to have marked the beginning of a new stage in shaping opinions on integration on the part of politicians and society as a whole. That there has been a rapid transformation of perspectives is beyond all doubt. During the initial phase of the post-communist transition, the debate was characterised by the ripening of delaratory opinions. The commencement of substantive negotiations changed this perspective, forcing quick decisions concerning specific issues and engendering a greater realism. Let us now examine a range of opinions expressed by politicians and others in the debates on integration since 1990, and highlight elements of continuity and change with them.

The first post-communist Minister for Foreign Affairs, Krzysztof Skubiszewski, defined Poland's task vis-à-vis the EU very clearly, saying: 'This tenacity of purpose is directly related to our state interest and . . . it will determine our place in Europe. We must be clear in our minds that it is a goal of highest importance' (*Sprawozdanie Sejmowe*, 27 June 1991: 14). He also emphasised that Poland supported the goals of the Maastricht Treaty, and added that it was in just that kind of structure that Poland saw its place in the future (*Sprawozdanie Sejmowe*, 8 May 1992: 153). The post-communist coalition of social democrats and the Polish Peasant Party (PSL), which came to power after the elections of 1993, re-affirmed Poland's commitment to European integration, whilst simultaneously re-affirming commitment to the regional fora mentioned earlier in the chapter, and the need to develop a coherent strategy toward the former Soviet Union (*Sprawozdanie Sejmowe*, 12 May 1994: 24).

The previous government had contained avowed pro-marketeers such as Andrzej Olechowski and Wladyslaw Bartoszewski who during their period in office had attempted to quicken the pace of Western integration. Indeed, the common adherence of all leading parties to the goal of European integration received sanction in a Sejm resolution in the spring of 1994 which was unanimously supported by all parliamentary groups (*Sprawozdanie Sejmowe*, 7 April 1994). During this period, Bartoszewski expressed hopes that Polish accession could be achieved in the year 2000, but was careful to stress that this could be achieved only if the whole of society was prepared to support the efforts of Polish diplomacy. Although the date of 2000 later proved to be unrealistic, the efforts of Bartoszewski were beneficial because they served to consolidate the market economy and democratic values in Poland (*Sprawozdanie Sejmowe*, 24 May 1995: 13–15). The continuation of policy in this sphere was later emphasised by the social democratic prime minister, Wlodzimierz Cimoszewicz, who during a speech to parliament in 1996, said that:

> the European orientation is dictated by the most basic interests of our country and it is built on values that are common for Poland and the European Union. That is why the integration process . . . is for our country a strategic goal. . . . In this case, there are no differences of opinion between the government and the opposition.
>
> (*Sprawozdanie Sejmowe*, 1 March 1996: 269)

The same sentiments have been expressed in the speeches of both post-communist presidents. Lech Walesa declared his support for the multi-dimensional integration of Poland with the structures of the West, and with institutions which had proved their effectiveness in resolving common problems (*Rzeczpospolita*, 4 October 1995). His successor, Aleksander Kwasniewski has stated that part of his political project is to demonstrate to Western governments that the inclusion of Poland and Central Europe into Western European integration structures would result in fewer, not more problems for all parties (*Polityka*, 28 September 1996).

Despite the gulf that exists between left and right, there was and is agreement among the main Polish parties that EU membership is the most important issue in Polish foreign policy and that such membership is desirable even if it leads to serious short-term problems in the social and economic spheres. This view is best represented by the liberal politicians from the Freedom Union (UW): 'The European orientation is the only one which serves Poland well and we should not concentrate simply on possible losses because in reality the prospects are entirely open,' said present Minister of Foreign Affairs Bronislaw Geremek in 1992 (*Sprawozdanie Sejmowe*, 8 May 1992: 159). A few years later, the former prime minister and fellow UW member, Hanna Suchocka, emphasised that:

> If Poland does not become a member of the EU, it will mean isolation, marginalisation and in consequence the collapse of Polish civilisation. We would like to see a Europe without borders and we can not at this moment let our fears cause the process of building borders to begin anew.
>
> (*Sprawozdanie Sejmowe*, 25 May 1995: 117)

Similarly, the Democratic Left Alliance (SLD) believes that the pro-European option best serves Polish national interests. The SLD claims to have seen in the EU not only a guarantee of further economic development but also a chance for 'a social-market , open, and solidarist Europe' (Nasz 1994: 17). Left of centre parties originating from Solidarity, such as the Labour Union (UP), have made much the same points (*Sprawozdanie Sejmowe*, 1 March 1996: 238).

Inevitably, there were and are parties afraid of the consequences of integration. Moreover, the reasons for such worries are quite diverse. For instance, the PSL which claims to defend the interests of Polish farmers, has been concerned about the fate of domestic agriculture should Poland join the EU. Some PSL politicians have gone further claiming that the EU constitutes a danger to Polish national values such as Catholicism and patriotism. However, they do not reject integration outright, and instead stress the need for a parallel policy of formally strengthening links between Poland and other Central European countries (*Program* PSL: 13; *Sprawozdanie Sejmowe*, 12 May 1994: 54). The attitude of the PSL towards integration was one of the key elements which distinguished it in the SLD in the former governing coalition (*Sprawozdanie Sejmowe*, 25 May 1996: 115). Similarly, the right of centre Confederation for an Independent Poland (KPN) pronounced itself to be in favour of European integration but only after the *Miedzymorze,* that is the countries lying between the Black and Baltic Seas, first integrated with one another. According to the KPN, only later, when Central Europe is richer, can co-operation and integration be extended to Western Europe (Moczulski 1991: 47–54).

Free marketeers of the right such as the Union for Real Politics (UPR), stressed another danger, namely that in an EU dominated by the left and the ubiquitous Eurocrats, economic freedom was a fiction (*Sprawozdanie*

*Sejmowe*, 8 May 1992). The Christian-National Union (ZChN) represented even more sceptical attitudes based in part on a combination of prejudice and historical memory. They were afraid of both the EU and Germany. Apart from being a front for German expansionism, the EU was seen as a danger to Polish sovereignty and independence, Catholicism, traditional moral values, as well as toward the Polish economy (*Sprawozdanie Sejmowe*, 26 April 1990: 70; 8 May 1992: 167–8; 12 May 1994: 22–3, 40–41).

As for opponents of the EU even more radical than the ZChN, they could and can still be found on the wings of both ideological extremes. In general, such groups are relatively small, but they are united in their belief that any kind of integration is bad and dangerous for sovereignty, national identity and Polish national values. Inevitably the most dangerous aspect of all for these parties is that Germany plays a decisive role in the EU. In their opinion, the decisions which have already been made by the Polish authorities in the field of integration are an example of: 'the degeneration of the Polish political class . . . whose price is loss of our national sovereignty' (*Prawica Narodowa*, January 1995).

For those interested in the fate of Polish Marxism–Leninism, it will be of interest to learn that the Union of Polish Communist (ZKP) is not opposed to European integration, just as long as it occurs after a European social revolution. As currently constituted, for them the EU is merely another manifestation of capitalist domination. Recent declarations and programmes of this party state:

> By promoting Poland's membership of the EU we are dooming Poland to play a role of secondary importance as an economic base for the rich Western countries, primarily Germany, a base that will provide cheap raw materials, cheap workers and good markets for Western products . . . Growing unemployment, the liquidation of factories, decreasing industrial and agricultural production, ruin and bankruptcy of 70% of farms – those are the effects of such moves.
>
> (*Deklaracja* ZKP 1996: 2,6)

It was within such a domestic environment that Poland entered a second phase of integration policy that began in July 1997. The election of September of that year was won by Solidarity Electoral Action (AWS), an amorphous mass of approximately thirty groups which were by no more united on the question of EU membership than they were on most other matters. The coming to power of this coalition in conjunction with the UW, aroused renewed interest in the matter of Poland's desire to 'return to Europe'. On the other hand, the creation of a coalition government with the consistently pro-European UW blew away all doubts regarding the current direction of policy. This fact found its confirmation in the first visit of new Prime Minister Jerzy Buzek to Brussels in November 1997, as well as his initial policy statements in which a strong emphasis on NATO membership was supplemented by similarly strong support for EU membership (*Polityka*, 15 November 1997). He put forward the idea that Poland must join: 'As fast as possible. The European Union is undergoing restructuring. It must become the strongest [European] institution. We want to enter such a strong union' (*Gazeta Wyborcza*, 14 November 1997). These declarations were even more important because the programme of the AWS, although generally pro-European, also called for a slowing down of the process of integration, and strongly emphasised that the power of the EU should not supersede that of the nation-state.

In the first period of the new coalition's rule, everyone awaited with interest to see who would be appointed to those positions of prominence with regard to the persual of Poland's envisaged integration. Pro-Europeans were therefore relieved when Bronislaw Geremek was appointed as Minister of Foreign Affairs. The attitude toward integration of the new head of the Committee for Integration (KIE), Ryszard Czarnecki, who represented the ZChN, was unknown. This caused consternation in some quarters because, as we have already noted, his party was decidedly unenthusiastic about the whole affair. However, his initial statements showed his readiness to stress the advantages over the costs of membership. This signalled a fundamental evolution of his views and those of his party. Czarnecki pointed out that the benefits of Poland's membership in the European structures were self-evident; but that care should be taken to ensure that those interests were catered for in the negotiating process. He saw his role as one of mediating between the extremes of both Euro-enthusiasts and avowed enemies of the EU within the coalition. He also tried to soften previous remarks made regarding Germany's role in the EU, the threat to Poland constituted by foreign capital, and the loss of sovereignty EU membership would entail. In essence, he portrayed both himself and his party to be 'Polish Gaullists'. He also emphasised that he was a dedicated follower of the AWS programme and was ready to argue with Europhobes and other extremists in his own party (*Gazeta Wyborcza*, 3 November 1997). After his resignation from the KIE following Poland's failure to secure 34 million ecus in PHARE funding, he described his goals as a minister without portfolio as being unchanged. Neither of his successors as head of the KIE, Maria Karasinska-Fedler and Pawel Samecki, has aroused controversy.

In line with this general spirit of co-operation, a majority of politicians saw the decisions of the Luxembourg summit of 1997 as an opportunity for Poland. In his declaration, the President of Poland stressed that this event had been a success of historic importance: '. . . created by the effort of all political forces and by the effort of all Poles, who, feeling themselves Europeans, saw the future and the development of our country in a united Europe.' As a result of the outcomes at Luxembourg, several essential questions were addressed. They included the requirement that all candidate members would be supportive of one another's applications, and that the result of the negotiations depended on Poland's own efforts, on the continued implementation of reforms, and on being properly prepared for the negotiations (*Trybuna*, 15 December 1997). Taking care over both reforms and negotiations was also a concern of Polish parliamentarians. Tadeusz Mazowiecki thought that the negotiators had two main tasks. The first was the achievement of full membership. The second was the securing of adaptation periods that were advantageous to Poland (*Gazeta Wyborcza*, 13–14 December 1997).

By and large, those parties and politicians who had earlier declared their support for the processes of integration maintained their opinions. The resolution of the third congress of the Social Democracy of the Republic of Poland (SdRP), which is dominant within the SLD, proclaimed that 'the most important assignment for us is to support the process of Poland's entry to the European Union'. It stressed the contributions of social democrats in accelerating this process in the past, declaring at the same time its support 'for difficult reforms which would adapt our economy and state to the requirements and mechanisms of the EU (*Trybuna*, 9 December 1997). In the words of SdRP member Tadeusz Iwinski, the 'SdRP and SLD create today the most pro-European political formation in Poland' (*Trybuna*, 16 July 1998). Although Iwinski may have somewhat exaggerated these sentiments, neither the SdRP nor the SLD as a whole are as prone to division on this issue as are the various components of the AWS.

However, worries and doubts do persist. In the opinion of some, the real danger of movement towards the EU lies not with the Eurosceptic arguments of some political groups, but in anxieties which exists in some parts of society, especially among rural dwellers. That is why it has been argued that the preparation for EU membership requires first of all the creation and realisation of three programmes: the reconstruction of agriculture, education and social security (*Gazeta Wyborcza*, 25 November 1998). Within this context, former SLD Foreign Minister Dariusz Rosati has directed his attention toward the AWS/UW, arguing that the coalition should overcome its differences in the treatment of Polish integration with the EU and be constant in adhering to a single strategy which takes into account the qualifications of staff and not their political roots (*Gazeta Wyborcza*, 24 August 1998).

Another former Minister for Foreign Affairs, Andrzej Olechowski, warned against Polish negotiators adopting a prejudicial approach in the negotiations. He characterised the governing parties as containing three factions on the issue of Poland's entry. First, there were those who stubbornly sought options other than membership of the EU. The second group he identified were those who agreed with the principle of integration, whilst hedging their support with numerous doubts and qualifications. The third group he identified as being genuinely and unreservedly in favour of EU entry. He tried to show that the arguments of the first group were built on unrealistic prerequisites, and that the second included many errors in their analysis, because there is no place in Europe for competitors to the EU, and that delaying accession because of the low competitiveness of the Polish economy did not in reality serve Polish interests. Unsurprisingly, he advocated the quickest possible entry of Poland to the European structures (*Gazeta Wyborcza*, 31 December 1997).

Following their return to power in 1997, politicians and journalists from the centre-right sought to change Western opinions of the new government. In Western Europe, Polish rightists tended to be associated with strongly Catholic, traditional, anti-European views. They were especially eager to calm German fears concerning the coming of the right to power in parliament, and tried to show that the AWS was open to dialogue and amenable to reason (*Zycie*, 7 March 1997). Henryk Goryszewski, Marian Pilka, Ryszard Czarnecki and Michal Kaminski from the ZChN stressed the evolution in their thinking by coming out in favour of the speedy accession of Poland. According to them, their national democratic roots allowed them to take this new position because the process of integration served the cause of the Polish nation, and would allow for a final resolution of the apparently still-open 'German Question'. From this perspective, the EU was above all an open market, which helped rather than hindered the pursuit of national interest. They saw integration as an inevitable process in which Poland had to take part once Polish politicians had obtained terms favourable to the national interest (*Gazeta Wyborcza*, 23 July 1998).

On the other hand, Jan Lopuszanski was representative of those who had not changed their opinion. He argued that, as currently constituted, the EU was injurious for Poland and Europe as a whole. He held this was true especially in the fields of sovereignty, identity and the economy. According to him, 'the method of Brussels' socialists is based on levelling all that does not fit a common pattern', and that 'they build unity on money and by killing identities'. He saw an opportunity for Poland by virtue of 'the fact that we are still not there' (*Gazeta Robotnicza*, 19 December 1997). One year later, debates in the Sejm concerning ratification of the NATO agreement showed that he was isolated in these views even within the ZChN. Of the entire ZChN leadership, only Lopuszanski himself voted against Polish membership of NATO. As much as anything else, this change of view signifies that the ZChN is in fact beginning genuinely to embrace Christian democratic ideology and abandon entrenched nationalist positions (*Sprawozdanie Sejmowe*, 20–21 November 1998).

Many of the groups which identify with the 'Polish national interest' against the 'cosmopolitan powers' of the UW, SLD and AWS, as the process of EU negotiations gathers pace, have consolidated forces within the Homeland Patriotic Movement (*Ruch Patriotyczny 'Ojczyzna'*), a group which contested the local and regional elections of 1998 with some success. The KPN, the Movement for the Restoration of Poland (ROP), a pensioners' party, the National-Democratic Party (SND) and a dozen or so smaller rightist formations, count on attracting support from sitting members of parliament in the Our Circle (*Nasze Kolo*) faction of Lopuszanski and the Polish Family (*Rodzina Polska*) movement connected with the Catholic chauvinist Radio Maryja (*Gazeta Wyborcza*, 16 November 1998). In April 1999, the Polish Agreement (*Porozumienie Polskie*) came into being. However, the level of support it enjoys is difficult to measure, given that the KPN, ROP and pensioners' party have been excluded from it because they give (highly) conditional support to the EU. The Polish Agreement claims to unite in the name of :'Resistance towards accession of Poland to the EU' and is convinced that it must 'support Polish agriculture and Polish production in the face of the threat posed by accession to the EU, and protect Polish property against foreign hands.' (*Gazeta Wyborcza*, 26 May 1999). Their aim is to organise resistance towards Polish membership in the planned referendum on accession, and should they lose the vote, create a Polish version of Jean-Marie Le Pen's National Front.

## European integration and the Catholic Church

Of central importance to Polish society, and especially to traditionalists, is the attitude of the Catholic Church. The evolution of official Polish Catholic views was expressed by the superiors in 1997 when they accepted the idea of a united Europe, declaring their full engagement in the realisation of this goal 'despite fears about what it might awaken'. This evolution away from a Euro-sceptical stance is a favourable factor for greater acceptance of integration among practising Catholics (*Gazeta Wyborcza*, 10 November 1997). According to Bishop Pieronek, at that time a spokesman of the episcopate: 'Europe should be accepted as a wonderful opportunity, a difficult challenge and a great apostolic assignment for the Church.' For his part, the Primate of Poland, Jozef Glemp has stated:'The Church is not afraid of a united Europe, quite the reverse, it looks on this process with hope' (*Gazeta Wyborcza*, 6–7 December 1997). A visit by a delegation of Polish bishops to Brussels in 1996 served to change the picture of the Polish Church in Western Europe, but it was also a symbolic expression of the Church's own interest in integration. Church dignitaries also responded to the fear most often repeated by Polish Catholic traditionalists, namely the loss of national identity. During the press conference, Bishop Pieronek declared that the Church did not see that any of the EU's member-states had lost their identity, and because identity can be viewed as being analogous to the soul, ' we do not share any anxieties about souls of the Poles' (*Polityka*, 15 November 1997). The support of the Episcopate for Polish membership of the EU is connected with goals which the Church sees for itself in a united Europe: 'The Church will endeavour to restore Europe for Christianity which determined and can still determine the spirit of Europe for which today's leaders search' (*Polityka*, 6–7 December 1997). This new tendency has since been re-affirmed. The General Secretary of the Episcopate Conference of Poland, Bishop Piotr Libera, not only declared his support for speedy EU membership but also saw it as a great opportunity for the Polish Church to return to its European roots and incidentally for agriculture to restructure itself (*Gazeta Wyborcza*, 21 April 1999).

However, this new attitude, so different from that previously held, has not been accepted by all members of the clergy. Nationalist, traditionalist and integralist interpretations, close to the views presented in Radio Maryja (whose guiding light is father Tadeusz Rydzyk), are also shared by some bishops, such as Stanislaw Stefanek, who view the EU as an amoral set of institutions controlled by strong countries which wish to reduce their weaker European counterparts to a state of vassalage (*Gazeta Wyborcza*, 21 April 1999). As for the papacy itself, it is difficult to estimate the level of influence of the pope's teaching upon Polish society because, on the one hand, admiration for John Paul II is enormous, but on the other, Catholic values do not determine all Polish behaviour. However, the opinions expressed during his last pilgrimage to Poland (June 1999) concerning the idea of a united Europe will strengthen the arguments of supporters of Polish membership of the EU. In his speech to parliament he affirmed that Poland's policy of EU membership was fully supported by the Holy See. He elaborated upon this theme, indicating that the Poles can bring to the unifying of Europe values which have served them well in the past, together with contemporary ideas of freedom, security and co-operation among nations that stem strongly from Christianity. This latter factor was particularly stressed as a necessary element for the future European structure. The pope gave a similar message to the Conference of Polish Episcopate (*Gazeta Wyborcza*, 12–13 June 1999).

The evolution of the Church's opinions opens a new opportunity for debate among Catholics about Europe, European unity, and Polish membership of the Union. That the bulk of the clergy supports Polish entry is not in doubt. In an opinion poll of the clergy conducted in February 1998 by the Institute of Public Affairs, 84 per cent respondents accepted Polish accession to the EU. The corresponding figure for the adult population at large was only 64 per cent (*Polityka*, 28 March 1998).

## Contemporary trends

Returning to the secular powers, we find that a majority of politicians favour a 'fast track' approach, as was indicated by the resolution accepted by the Sejm during the March debate on the preparations for EU membership. A total of 335 MPs, including all UW and SLD deputies, together with a large majority of AWS members, voted in favour of the resolution. Only thirty-three MPs, all from either the AWS or the PSL, voted against the resolution. A total of thirty-nine MPs from the PSL and the ROP abstained (*Gazeta Wyborcza*, 21–22 March 1998). The resolution emphasised that one of the principal conditions of integration with the EU, apart from legal and economic reforms, is that it must have the support of society. Such support will be essential as negotiations begin to touch upon such thorny issues as agriculture and freedom of movement.

As for the attitude of the general public, we have to note that the results of polls conducted by the numerous opinion research organisations show that there is decreasing support for entry into the EU (see Table 3.3). We will comment upon this phenomenon shortly.

When we analyse the fine detail of these results we find that there is a clear correlation between residence, age and education and attitudes toward the EU. Rural dwellers, people resident in the east of the country, and people on low incomes are inclined to express a negative opinion. Integration is most strongly favoured by respondents under 24 years of age, the well educated, managers, professionals and students. Although all of these groups tend largely to right of centre in terms of their thinking, both the SLD and the AWS have a solid pro-European base of support (see Table 3.4).

In the initial declaration of the Polish government at the start of negotiations, the current Minister for Foreign Affairs, Bronislaw Geremek, repeated that:

> Poland accedes to the negotiations with the conviction that our membership in the European Union is the most profitable choice for reasons of national security, stability of the democratic order, quick and stable economic development and the building of a modern civil society.

He also stressed that EU membership was the choice of a sovereign state based on unanimity among political forces and the wide acceptance of the principle among Polish society (*Gazeta Wyborcza*, 31 March 1998). Undoubtedly he had a good reason for making such a statement because, in spite of the indicated hesitations of public opinion, most respondents agreed that membership of the EU should remain a major goal of Polish policy.

As we can see clearly from the above analysis, the number of politicians declaring pro-integration attitudes has increased. However, the core element of the second stage in Poland's integration endeavours will be the fact that debate will shift from the general to the specific. In fact, as the negotiations are beginning to shift in this direction, so greater sections of Polish society are becoming less sanguine over the costs of EU membership. Political discussion is beginning to focus upon support not only for ideas but, first and foremost, for concrete reforms, which in the short term will be painful for influential social groups which form the electorate of many parties. Hence the next phase of the debate will determine the tempo of reform whilst taking into account its social consequences. Moreover, it will also have to take into account the fact that any delay in the reform process will retard Poland's development and its chances of meeting the requirements of global, political and economic processes. Interestingly, research indicates that there are widespread doubts regarding the speed of integration with the EU (see Table 3.5).

*Table 3.3* Support for membership of the EU: evolution of views in the 1990s (in percentages)

| *If a referendum concerning Polish membership of the EU were held now, would you vote:* | *VI' 94* | *V' 95* | *V' 96* | *III' 97* | *IV' 97* | *VIII' 97* | *V' 98* | *VIII' 98* | *XII' 98* |
|---|---|---|---|---|---|---|---|---|---|
| for Polish membership | 77 | 72 | 80 | 72 | 72 | 72 | 66 | 63 | 64 |
| against Polish membership | 6 | 9 | 7 | 12 | 11 | 12 | 19 | 19 | 19 |
| I do not know | 17 | 19 | 13 | 16 | 18 | 15 | 15 | 18 | 17 |

*Source*: Na drodze, January 1999: 1.

*Table 3.4* Support of the parties' electorates for Polish membership in the EU (in percentages)

| *Potential electorates of Polish parties* | *If a referendum concerning Polish membership of the EU would be held now, would you vote:* | | |
|---|---|---|---|
| | *For* | *Against* | *I do not know* |
| UW | 82 | 12 | 6 |
| AWS | 74 | 14 | 12 |
| SLD | 73 | 19 | 8 |
| PSL | 51 | 36 | 13 |

*Source*: Na drodze, January 1999: 3.

*Table 3.5* The relationship between Polish membership of the EU and Polish economic strength (in percentages)

| *In your opinion:* | *Evolution of opinion* | | |
|---|---|---|---|
| | *IV'97* | *VIII'97* | *XII'98* |
| Poland should first improve and modernise its economy, and then try to become a member of the EU | 48 | 43 | 50 |
| Poland should become a member of the EU as quickly as possible because membership will speed up the improvement and modernisation of Polish economy | 40e | 39 | 34 |
| I do not know | 12 | 19 | 16 |

*Source*: Na drodze, January 1999: 5.

In the late 1990s, a new dimension of debate has concerned the question of the role Poland eventually wants to play in the EU, and whether and how can it contribute to stabilisation of its own geopolitical region which has again become involuntarily involved with the decisions on NATO and EU enlargement. The debate therefore increasingly impinges upon issues which until recently have been sidestepped, such as the future shape of the EU, the direction of its development, and the reform of its institutions. This last point was only expressly mentioned for the first time by foreign minister Geremek in his policy statement of May 1999 to the Sejm. He asserted that, at the very least, Poland must prepare an outline of its own position on these matters and must participate in this most important of current debates, even if only indirectly as a candidate-member (*Gazeta Wyborcza*, 9 April 1999)

As is well known among the political class, if not society as a whole, the date of Polish accession to the EU is still open. At the beginning of the process there was a convergence of opinions as expressed by the Polish chief negotiator Jan Kulakowski and his counterpart from the European Commission, Nikolaus van der Pas. At the beginning of 1998 they jointly declared that Polish accession could take place towards the end of 2003 (*Polityka*, 28 February 1998). Then in the middle of 1999 they acknowledged that in order to keep to this target date, the aim should be to complete the negotiations by the end of 2001 (*Gazeta Wyborcza*, 10 May 1999). However, the member-states themselves refuse to be pinned down to an exact timetable. The year 2005 is now given as the most likely for accession, on the condition that not only will candidate countries achieve significant results in their reforms, but that the EU will solve its own internal problems (*Gazeta Wyborcza*, 5 May 1999).

## Conclusions

At the beginning of the 1990s Poland formulated new foreign policy goals. They included endeavours to join the integrative structures of Western Europe, above all the EU and NATO. This aim stemmed from the conviction of the political elite that only membership in these structures can provide Poland with the multi-level security guarantees it requires. This goal was supplemented by the pursual of other objectives, such as establishing and maintaining the best possible relations with all other states in the region, and participation in regional initiatives.

Polish–German relations were of crucial importance here. Germany strongly supported Polish membership of NATO and the EU and played a prominent role in Polish integration policy. The speedy settlement by treaty in 1990 of all residual questions arising from World War Two facilitated German–Polish rapprochement and enabled Germany to act as Poland's strategic partner in Brussels. This unparalleled evolution in Polish tradition and policy was carried out with widespread social support. In surveys, Germany has been perceived by as many as 59 per cent of respondents as the state which has been most helpful for Poland on the road to EU membership (*Czy zmiana* 1999: 4). The Poles have accepted Germany as the

most apt and logical partner for economic and political co-operation, although levels of 'affection' towards Germans still remain low. Within this context we should also stress that the nationalist right still seeks the play the 'German card' by portraying Germans as incorrigibly malevolent, and Germany as a country which will dominate Poland from the moment EU membership is achieved.

In our survey we have demonstrated that the major parties are in broad agreement that entry into the EU will be of benefit to Poland. We have seen how the goals formulated by Krzysztof Skubiszewski, the first post-communist Minister for Foreign Affairs after 1989, were pursued with the support of the then largest opposition grouping, the SLD, who when they obtained power in 1993 did not substantially change them in any way. The policy of integration with the EU has been supported consistently by a wide range of parties throughout the 1990s.

In theory, if not in practice, there are three options now available to Poland, and they centre around the attitudes towards the EU outlined earlier in the text. The first is to join at the earliest possible opportunity. This is the goal of the UW, and is one which is shared by elite groups within the SLD, the UP and part of the AWS. The second option is favoured by groups which accept the principle of EU membership, but for different reasons, such as anxieties concerning agriculture, the economy, land and property ownership rights, national identity and Catholic values, would prefer that the integration process expressly takes these concerns into account. In the 1990s those who held such views could be found in the ranks of the PSL, the KPN and elements of the AWS, ROP and ZChN. The third group contains the firm enemies of Polish membership of the EU. Their justifications for this attitude are varied. Nationalist and fundamentalist Catholic groups views the idea of a united Europe as a threat to national sovereignty, national interests and the economy. For some at least, the EU is a symbol of moral deterioration, loss of Christian faith, and the capture of Europe by an unlikely coalition of international freemasonry, Jews and Germans. On the extreme left, parties such as the ZKP accept the principle of a united Europe but not in the framework of a capitalistic order. Finally, in order to put these views into perspective, we must note that those who hold them have only localised and occasional regional influence, and barely influence policy-making at the national level.

As for wider public perceptions of the EU, there has been a general decline in support during the 1990s. Given that at the beginning of the decade over 80 per cent of the population supported the endeavour, this fact should come as no great surprise. Such massive support was motivated more by the wish to 'rejoin Europe', and by the deeply rooted idea of a Europe without frontiers, than by any real knowledge of the EU's mechanisms and rules. A good example of such ignorance concerns opinions on controversial issues such as the right of abode of foreigners in Poland, and the right of foreigners to purchase land, where only about one quarter of the population approves of what in fact is a EU prerequisite of entry (Ocena 1996 11).

The above analysis of Polish integration policy and attitudes towards the EU suggests the following tendencies in Polish foreign policy. First, political groups and politicians who are convinced of the indispensability of including Poland in the European integration process will continue to dominate the Polish political scene. The goal of achieving EU membership as quickly as possible will be adhered to, but it is difficult to see whether the present domestic schedule of membership in 2003 and joining the Eurozone between 2005 and 2008 is actually feasible (*Rzeczpospolita*, 19 April 1999).

Second, the political scene will become increasingly polarised as the human and financial costs of the adaptation process become ever more clear. Inevitably, extremes of both right and left will seek to make political capital from this eventuality. Yet societal support for integration should stay at a sufficiently high level to ensure a 'Yes' vote in the referendum planned for 2002–3 (*Gazeta Wyborcza*, 5 May 1999). This is despite the fact that the government is still failing to implement its promised information policy on the EU, and the fact that many voters are still ill-informed on the whole issue.

On the whole, Polish foreign policy during the 1990s is rated as having been a success. However, we can observe that in the new century Poland will need to pursue somewhat different ideas. A Poland with a strengthened democratic system, considerable economic progress, friendly relations with its neighbours, and as a member of NATO and candidate to the EU may wish to, and perhaps should, play a greater role in the region. For this reason, the Polish government continues clearly to articulate support for the development of regional integrative structured co-operation in the Baltic area and with Ukraine, and indeed with Belarus in the event of liberalisation in Minsk. This trend is connected with the conviction, deeply rooted in Polish policy, that it is impossible to create a stable Europe whilst at the same time drawing new lines of partition.

In conclusion we need to note that other factors scarcely considered need to be taken into account. Hitherto, the problem of institutional reform within the EU was not a subject of debate in Poland, unlike the future of European security arrangements. Not only that, questions concerning the ultimate destination of the EU divides Poles very deeply. There is no consensus as to whether the EU should deepen federal co-operation, or whether it should simply be a collection of sovereign nation-states. As negotiations with the EU progress and as they begin to touch on questions of real substance, so the collision of state interests that is likely to occur could reconfigure both public attitudes and current alliances, for example that which currently exists with Germany. Whatever the case, playing an active part in the processes of European integration will still be an ambition of Polish foreign policy, and a majority of Poles will continue to support its general thrust.

## Bibliography

AVIS, Euro-Biuletyn, Warszawa, Centrum Informacji Europejskiej przy Urzedzie KIE, 1997.

Böhne, T. 'The eastward enlargement of the European Union – can the financial implications be estimated?', Working Paper, Strasbourg: The European Parliament, February 1997.

Czy zmiana rzadu w Niemczech wplynie na stosunki polsko-niemieckie? Komunikat z badan, Warszawa: CBOS, January 1999.

Deklaracja ZKP Proletariat, Dabrowa Gornicza, Zwiazek Komunistow Polskich, 1996.

*Eurobarometer* 50, 'Public Opinion in the European Union', Autumn 1998.

*Gazeta Robotnicza*, various issues December 1997–June 1999.

Integracja Polski z Unia Europejska. Komunikat z badan, Warszawa: CBOS, August 1996.

Kaczmarek, J. and Skowronski, A. *NATO, Europa, Polska*, Wroclaw: Atla 2, 1997.

Kisiel-Lowczyc, A.B. 'CEFTA in PanEuropean Integration', in A. Zielinska-Glebocka and A. Stepniak (eds), *EU Adjustment to Eastern Enlargement Polish And European Perspective*, Gdansk: Fundacja Rozwoju Uniwersytetu Gdanskiego, 1998.

Kupiecki, R. *Od Londynu do Waszyngtonu, NATO w latach dziewiecdziesiatych*, Warszawa: ASKON ,1998.

Malendowski, W. and Ratajczak, M. *Euroregiony. Pierwszy krok do integracji europejskiej*, Wroclaw: Atla 2, 1998.

Moczulski. L. *U progu niepodleglosci*, Warszawa: Konfederacja Polski Niepodleglej, 1991.

Na drodze do Unii Europejskiej. Komunikat z badan, Warszawa: CBOS, January 1999

Narodowa Strategia Integracji, Warszawa: Komitet Integracji Europejskiej, 1997.

*Nasz Dziennik*, 27–28 March 1999.

Nasz program dla Polski, Warszawa: Sojusz Lewicy Demokratycznej, 1994.

Ocena niektorych konsekwencji przystapienia Polski do Unii Europejskiej. Komunikat z badan: Warszawa: CBOS, August 1996.

Odezwa ZKP "Proletariat", *Brzask*, January 1995

Opoka, October 1995.

Podraza, A. *Stosunki polityczne i gospodarcze Wspolnoty Europejskiej z panstwami Europy Srodkowej i Wschodniej*, Lublin: Wydawnictwo Katolickiego Uniwersytetu Lubelskiego, 1996.

—— *Unia Europejska a Europa Srodkowa i Wschodnia*, Lublin: Wydawnictwo Katolickiego Uniwersytetu Lubelskiego, 1997.

*Polityka*, various issues September 1996–March 1998.

*Prawica Narodowa*, January–February 1995.

*Program* PSL, Warszawa: Polskie Stronnictwo Ludowe, 1990.

Raport o stanie polskiego rolnictwa, VI Dyrekcja Generalna Komisji Europejskiej, Bruksela, 1998.

*Rzeczpospolita*, various issues October 1995–April 1999.

*Sprawozdania Sejmowe*, 1989–1999.

Stadtmüller, E. 'Panstwa Europy Srodkowo-Wschodniej w procesie integracji europejskiej', in A. Antoszewski and R. Herbut (eds), *Demokracje Europy Srodkowo-Wschodniej w perspektywie porownawczej*, Wroclaw: Wydawnictwo Uniwersytetu Wroclawskiego, 1997.

Szczepaniak, M. (ed.) *Panstwa Wyszehradzkie. Systemy polityczne, gospodarka, wspolpraca*, Poznan: Akademia Ekonomiczna, 1996.

Tezy programowe IV Kongresu KPN, Warszawa: Konfederacja Polski Niepodleglej, 1993.

Uklad Europejski ustanawiajacy stowarzyszenie miedzy Rzeczypospolita Polska, z jednej strony, a Wspolnotami Europejskimi i ich panstwami czlonkowskimi, z drugiej strony z 16 grudnia 1991, Bruksela, *Dziennik Ustaw RP*, zalacznik do nr 11, pozycja 38, 27 stycznia 1994.

*Trybuna*, various issues December 1997–July 1998.

Wojtyna, A., Wilkin, J., Hausner, J., Marody, M. and Zirk-Sadowski, M. *Przystapienie czy integracja? Polska droga do Unii Europejskiej*, Warszawa: Fundacja E. Brosta przy Fundacji im. Friedricha Eberta, 1998.

Zielinska-Glebocka, A. and Stepniak, A. (eds) *EU Adjustment to Eastern Enlargement Polish And European Perspective*, Gdansk: Fundacja Rozwoju Uniwersytetu Gdanskiego, 1998.

*Zycie*, 7 March 1997.

# 4 Emergent democratic citizenship in Poland

## A study of changing value patterns

*Kazimierz Dziubka*

Arriving at a new definition of citizenship is one of the most fundamental issues that faces Poland as it moves closer to full membership of the European Union (EU). This chapter does not seek to explore initiatives undertaken by the Polish government independently of, or in conjunction with, the EU, which seek directly or indirectly to promote the growth of a civic culture in Poland. Rather, it examines the concept of citizenship, its historical and contemporary presence in Polish society and offers some observations on the political values found in Poland today. In essence it seeks to inform the reader of the extent to which Poland is a society which possesses the psycho-political attributes of the states of Western Europe, and offers an explanation as to why Poland differs from the West European norm.

The first part of the chapter comprises of a rigorous analysis of the concept of citizenship, and examines both the attributes and the forces which have shaped its operationalisation. The roots of the term are examined by means of its origin in Greek antiquity and its subsequent development. An explanation is offered as to why the condition of Poland during the phase of nation- and state-building was not conducive to Western models of civil society, and why, as a result, an organic view of society developed in Poland. This is important in the analysis of the contemporary endeavours of the Polish government vis-à-vis the EU, because it helps us understand the politico-cultural determinants of the situation in Poland today and the roots of Polish concerns over such matters as the right of foreigners to live, work and own land in Poland.

We also show how that once Poland regained its independence, organic notions of society were re-enforced by governmental practice and expectations. Of crucial importance here is the communist experience, which if nothing else re-enforced certain negative attributes in Polish society, atomised society and created further distortions to the notion of citizenship as applied to Poland. As we shall see, the cumulative result has been the entrenchment among certain sectors of society of negative attitudes towards capital accumulation and certain forms of individualism. Naturally, such attitudes run counter to certain fundamentals held to be of value by EU governments. However, the analysis is by no means bleak, and positive signs and characteristics which point toward a change in attitudes are also highlighted. Indeed, one of the objectives of this chapter is to demonstrate that the construction of a democratic citizenship in Poland, and elsewhere in Europe, is important in terms of cultural integration. All in all, the chapter represents an important contribution to the debate on Poland's desire to 'return to Europe'.

## The basic attributes of citizenship

Like most categories, such as those of civic culture, civil society, community, political inclusion, and social balance, which have been described in contemporary empirical and normative sociopolitical research, the notion of citizenship is ambiguous and multidimensional in both its ontological and heuristic sense. One may find in the very etymological origins of the notion of citizenship, the definitional attributes which can be regarded as derivatives of the term 'citizen'. It is often assumed that one of the most significant and imminent elements of the latter term is that a set of certain rights and duties belongs to each individual due to their membership of a given state–national community (Ehrlich 1979: 205–18). In accordance with this view, the legal status of a citizen is perceived as grounds for establishing his/her subjectivity, and thus the bilateral relations between the individual and other subjects of legal and sociopolitical order, including the state and the other members of the political community. Although there exist numerous and specific kinds of such bilateral relations, it may be presumed that they generate four types of rights and responsibilities. These are: those of the state/community toward the individual; the duties of the individual toward the state/community; that the individual has the right to determine the extent to which other individuals contribute to her/his rights; and that the individual has to fulfil certain duties towards other individuals (Dekker 1994a: 1)

With regard to the juridical system, analysis of rights and duties is strictly related to the very structure and functions of legal norms binding all members of a political community. Their characteristic is that the legal norms – by way of reference to the notion of 'the good' – play an instrumental role in establishing and/or protecting given moral standards, values and behavioural patterns. This normative aspect of legal norms can be analysed at the level of the decision-making process as an expression of the selective (evaluative) approach of the legislative body (individual or collective) towards reality. In other words, any legal decision made by the law-makers depends on whether a certain kind of individual or group activities, behaviours, or attitudes will be accepted or not. Such outcomes result from the very structures of legal norms, which are bound up with varied types of patterns referring to the preferable (or prohibited) civic behaviours and attitudes. The entirety of these attitudes and behaviours, taking the form of conceptualised and abstract normative rules and norms, creates a more or less coherent juridical ideal of citizenship. As constitutionally defined moral and legal obligations, some of these norms and behavioural patterns are incumbent on society as a whole and are performed by public institutions. The others, often defined as civic virtues, rest with individuals and refer to their attitudes and behaviours, for instance: loyalty, obedience of the law, tolerance, and one's contribution to the realisation of public goods and values.

One also has to admit that the patterns and norms mentioned above are simultaneously of great importance as a device in the field of legal and in sociopolitical estimation of individual/group behaviours. This aspect of the juridical (normative) ideal of citizenship is strongly related to the fundamental function of legal norms under a democratic regime, which is deemed to be the establishment of such societal feelings as safety, self-development, freedom and justice. Like legal norms, idealised elements of citizenship are aimed at introducing the 'rules of fair-play' in the public and private spheres. For political science, the most important functional and teleological aspect of this issue is the set of methods and means brought into play by a regime in order to strengthen cognitive and behavioural components of social consciousness. In this sense, citizenship involves social facts, among which the most significant are: obedience and esteem of legal norms, constitutionally admissible forms of civil disobedience, and rules and mechanisms of social and political co-operation (Borucka-Arctowa 1981: 78–84).

All the above mentioned categories shape an ideal image of citizenship when they become a part of the political culture of a given sociopolitical community. In this sense, the core is behaviour, while other components seem to be as more or less supportive of behaviour. There is no doubt that a narrowly interpreted idea of citizenship may practically, either by state institutions or by individuals, lead to many deformations and pathological events in public life. The stability and effectiveness of a democratic order necessitates continuous attempts to find *modus vivendi* between the needs and demands of political organisations, on the one hand, and individual aspirations for more freedom, autonomy and self-development, on the other.

The impact of such phenomena is crucial if one takes into consideration that legal systems and political cultures are defined by boundaries reflected in the minds and by habits of people living between these boundaries. They form the framework through which each sovereign influences people's behaviour through the law, institutions, organisations and associations of civil society, and the education system. Living together inside the same boundaries has a strong impact on what people believe, think, and find good or bad (Kalberg 1993: 91–114).

When discussing the relevance of legal and cultural value systems in shaping the ideal of citizenship one also has to pay attention to the theoretical and practical consequences stemming from the exaggeration of the causative role of this issue. Herman van Gunsteren posed this question in the following way:

> The quality of civil democracy depends upon such matters as civic-mindedness, religion, education in democratic rules or the development of a public ethic. A total absence of these things means that democracy cannot exist. To embrace them too intensely, however, would mean the same.
>
> (van Gunsteren 1994: 40)

Appeals for responsibility and civic-mindedness serve little purpose. Civic-mindedness will not arise nor develop simply by being summoned. Civic-mindedness, legitimacy and public support arise as a by-product generated by other activities and events. They do not come into existence by directing our will, intention or manipulation towards them. As the evolution of many political regimes has shown, the desired outcome is often contrary to the the desired result.

It is important to stress that legal and institutional aspects of citizenship situate this notion systematically in terms of the psycho-political grounds of the everyday actions exercised by individuals and the state agencies. The ways, forms and methods of these activities, however, go beyond the narrow meaning of citizenship embraced by constitutional or juridical definitions of the term. The operationalisation of the notion of citizenship, whose key expression is the subjective feelings of 'being a citizen', is conditioned by a complex of varied factors determining such feelings directly and indirectly. Among these factors, and of equal importance as one's perception of rights and duties, is an individual's social and economic position, cultural and mental determinants, hierarchy of needs, and moral capabilities. All these determinants influence the individual's structure of thinking and behaviour. Personal self-estimation of 'being a citizen' has a substantial effect on the individual degree of identification with membership patterns, loyalty, types of activity and, eventually, the character of one's perception of the whole *universum* of political and social events. Due to these contextual settings and contrary to juridical ideals, the notion of citizenship is characterised on the operational level by a heterogeneous mental–cultural structure containing variable and often self-contradictory cognitions, affectations and behaviours.

Following the above conceptions and characteristics of citizenship and also taking into account the analytical purpose of this chapter, one may assume that citizenship is a form of individual cognitive and normative attitudes, and associated with them, patterns of activities, which among other things are expressed by the feelings of interrelations between an individual and the community, spontaneous self-acceptance of obligations to act for the benefit of this community, and the sense of self-limitation in exercising individual rights and duties. As an element of collective consciousness, citizenship manifests itself in legal, societal, moral and cultural acknowledgement of the equal status of all persons, their equality under the law, and the endowment of each person with a set of rights and liberties. In this sense, democratic citizenship is a synthesis of many elements implying institutional and legal infrastructure of a given democratic order as well as being related to its mental and cultural characteristics, which are usually described in such terms as 'legal citizen', 'democratic character', 'civic culture', 'civic education' and 'public activities'.

## The evolution of the notion

Anticipations of the concept of citizenship as presented are deeply rooted in the political practice of the Greek *polis* and in philosophical and moral schools which legitimised this practise (cf. Pythagoreans, Sophists, Aristotle). In both academic literature and common consciousness, *polis* is perceived as an archetype of democratic order, under which all those who belonged to the category of citizens enjoyed many opportunities for genuine spiritual and physical self-development. Yet *polis* also meant a relatively coherent political and moral community – *koinonia* – whose members (*polites*) were united by a common ethos comprising a system of shared rules, norms and values. Besides its religious and cultural functions related to maintaining the internal integrity of the city-state, the ethos played a crucial role in promoting value patterns and behaviours necessary for the 'just conduct' of each citizen in the public and private spheres. For the ancient Greeks the term 'citizen' was strictly connected not only with an arrangement of democratic institutions or legal norms but also, as in the Aristotelian ideal of *zoon politikon* for instance, with an active participation in making political decisions, and further, with a certain way of civic thinking and behaviour.

The basic elements of this deontological conception of citizenship, in its legal, political and moral senses, were adopted by the main architects of republican Rome and later, during the empire, by politician-philosophers, such as Marcus Aurelius and Marcus Tulius Cicero. One of the most important elements of the Roman legal system, which lasted longer than the empire and became a solid component of European juridical culture, was the conception of citizen as a subject whose status implied not only civil rights and obligations but the moral–mental capacity (*virtus Romana*) to understand and exercise them. Bryan Turner's examination of this issue led him to the conclusion that:

> The term for citizen was derived in classical times from *civitas*, giving rise in Roman times to the notion of a *civitatus*. This etymological origin provided eventually the French term *citoyen* from *cité,* namely an ensemble of citizens enjoying limited rights within a city context. Thus in French we find in the twelfth century the notion of *citeaine* and

> eventually in the thirteen century the notion of *comcitien*. . . . In English, the notion of a citizen can be detected in the medieval concept of *citizen*, but until the sixteenth century at least this term was interchangeable with the notion of denizen (*deisein*). This limited notion of the citizen as simply the inhabitant of a city was both extensive and continuous.
>
> (Turner 1990: 203)

During the following centuries various attempts were made at defining the legal, political and moral connotations of the term citizen and the words correlatively related to it. These efforts were intensified in the nineteenth century, and were accompanied by the popularisation of liberal-positivist conceptions of the state of 'law and order' (*Rechtsstaat*, *L'Etat de droit)* in the literature and the governmental practice of many Western states. At its initial stage, that is until the middle of the nineteenth century, the essence of these concepts was compatible with the Anglo-Saxon model of the 'rule of law'. These models were based upon the assumption that activities undertaken by both the state and citizens were to be submitted to the general rules of law. The fundamental thesis put by the Scottish moralists, John Locke, David Hume, Adam Ferguson and Adam Smith, and also examined by German liberal-positivists such as Adam Müller, Robert von Mohl and Lorenz von Stein, consisted in tracing a set of necessary self-limitations that were to be imposed on both state institutions and individuals. Despite the substantial theoretical and cultural differences between the German school of positive law and the Anglo-Saxon model of common law, these two schools focused on providing each citizen with solid grounds for their feeling of subjectivity (*Freiheit des Bürgers*, freedom under law).

From the latter part of the nineteenth century, such limitations turned out to be of primary importance. In this period one may notice that the development of most European political regimes was combined with a significant growth of state power regarding its regulative and control functions over the basic domains of public life. The permanent extension of state activities, which had been accompanied by the extensive state regultions and subordination of citizens, brought to light several new questions and controversies. The search for equitable answers to such concerns was motivated by the very fact that whereas some such policies enhanced the idea of democratic citizenship, for example the New Deal, others paved the way for authoritarian and totalitarian regimes.

The strategy directed toward the development of democratic citizenship became an integral objective of political and economic strategy initiated by West European countries after the Second World War. In analysing implications of this strategy, Desmond S. King and Jeremy Waldron observed that: 'Citizens in these countries have grown used to a consistent expansion in the state's provision of goods and services, in particular goods and services associated with the welfare state like education, health, social security and employment' (King and Waldron 1988: 415). Under the conditions created in such welfare states as well as their modified German version, the *sozialer Rechtsstaat,* a citizen is both governor and governed. In order to be able to practise this double role it is assumed that a citizen must display a minimum of autonomy, sound judgement, loyalty and have broad access to social services and goods.

The theoretical grounds for contemporary debates on citizenship were developed by Thomas H. Marshall. His conceptualisation of citizenship was based upon the analysis of the history of social welfare in Britain during the eighteenth and twentieth centuries, at which time three dimensions of citizenship, civil, political and social, were shaped. According to Marshall, the value of each of these dimensions consisted of:

> [in] . . . providing civil rights, society mitigates the impact of force and violence in relations between people. By providing political rights, it [the state] ensures that power is not confined to an elite. And by providing minimum standards in these areas the state offsets the vagaries of market processes and corrects the gross inequalities of distribution arising from the market.
>
> (King and Waldron 1988: 419)

Following these propositions, Marshall concluded that citizenship is:

> a status bestowed on those who are full members of a community. . . . Citizenship requires a . . . direct sense of community membership based on loyalty to a civilisation, which is a common possession. It is a loyalty of free men endowed with rights and protected by a common law. Its growth is stimulated by the struggle to win those rights and by their enjoyment when won.
>
> (Marshall 1964: 84,92)

Marshall's theory of citizenship particularly influenced the works of Reinhard Bendix, Ralf Dahrendorf, Ronald Dore, Seymour M. Lipset and Peter Townsend among others. The basic assumptions of his model remain prominent today and are adopted by a number of theorists who, despite some elements of criticism, attempt to use Marshall's concept of citizenship. Unfortunately, space precludes us from entering into further discussion of these issues. Suffice it to say they propose a broader and more innovative analysis of citizenship (Mann 1987: 339–54; Roche 1987: 363: 99).

## Some historic aspects of Polish notions of citizenship

Retrospective analysis of Poland's political development indicates that due to real dangers to national sovereignty and because of partition and occupation by foreign powers, on a societal level Polish political culture was dominated by the norms and values related to an organic concept of political community. Therefore, community was characterised by strong links with an idealised nation-state. For many years, the issue of how to regain national sovereignty constituted the core of various political programmes, formulated by the main Polish political and social movements. Under these conditions there was no room for the Anglo-Saxon concept of civil society, based on the principle of autonomous local public bodies and on a clear distinction between political and civil society, i.e. between the public and the private interest.

The need to preserve national identity, exemplified mainly by the Roman Catholic Church with its traditional values, petrified a civic community of the organic type. It is essential to note the fact that despite the nascent capitalism of the nineteenth and twentieth centuries, the idea of the national interest remained the supreme criterion for all political and social activities. Moreover, the weakness of the middle class coupled with the very slow process of urbanisation hampered the reception of the liberal ideas, which constituted the cultural background of the modern politics in the West. The influence of the Catholic Church on Polish political culture and a mythologisation of the state contributed to the peculiar political consciousness of Poles, which Marcin Krol has called a corporatist way of thinking about politics. As Krol says, in Poland:

> the idea of citizenship was intertwined with belonging to the nation. . . . In an individual's life it was more important to guard the fulfilment of the national duties of fellow citizens and oneself, than individualistic actions. It was this attitude which hampered capitalist developments in Polish lands.
>
> (Krol 1993: 2)

It must be admitted, however, that the permanent reliance on the national value system played a substantial (positive) role in maintaining a high degree of national mobilisation against 'invaders'. On the other hand, it often led to the promotion of nationalism as a basis of individual/group identity patterns and loyalty. This subsequently led to the establishment of a closed ethno-political and cultural form of community. The political and social implications of this process are summed up by George Schöpflin who noted that:

> nationalism as a political doctrine provided answers to very few questions of political organisation and the distribution of power. It created strong identities and a sense of belonging to the state – for members of the dominant group – but said nothing about political structures, the resolution of conflicts of interest, the allocation of resources and values, participation and representation, i.e. the day-to-day problems of political, economic and social life.
>
> (Schöpflin 1990: 75)

The disjuncture between the slow but gradual development of capitalist relationships in Poland's economy and value system, generated by political and sociocultural sub-systems, seems to be an important factor holding up demands for individual rights and thus the establishment of a certain level of autonomy of particular segments within Polish society. Under these circumstances the process of structuralisation of political consciousness featured many self-contradictions and tensions: values and motivation related to the functioning of the market economy, contrasted with societal homogenisation in both ideological and political terms. Even when Poland had been re-established as a nation-state after World War I, there appeared many symptoms of the dominance of the national value orientation. They forced a process of societal homogenisation that shaped most of the democratic forms of civic identity. As Henk Dekker observed, the status and political consciousness of citizens were 'marked by subordination rather than possession of a set of democratic political, economic and cultural rights' (Dekker 1994b: 20).

The very political language of the inter-war *Sanacja* (recovery) regime of Jozef Pilsudski, was permeated with a corporatist spirit. The political discourse of this camp was composed of moralistic ideals calling for national unity, the improvement of citizens' understanding of their civic obligations, the implementation of a state of commonwealth and the motivation of citizens to undertake collective efforts for the sake of a moral revival of the nation. In that discourse the public duties of the citizens prevailed over the rights of the individual and legal protection of citizens against state power. The state was perceived in a mythologised way and was defined in terms of conservative moralistic philosophy of the superior goodness and organic commonwealth. The idea of the 'fatherland' overshadowed the concept of state of law as well as the liberties of citizens and other values so important in modern British or French liberalism (Jablonski 1996: 41). A similar attitude can be also found in the language of other influential political formations in inter-war Poland, including even those acting as the opposition to the *Sanacja*.

## The deformed idea of 'citizenship' under 'state socialism'

There is no doubt that the practice of state socialism in Poland not only enforced these negative tendencies, but, more importantly, destroyed the seeds of democratic citizenship, which had developed in the previous period. It can be assumed that the most critical institutional principle of state socialism was that society as a whole had to be run as a single organisation via relationships of command and subordination. Thereby, the autonomy of the party/state vis-à-vis society was secured either by the exclusion from the social and political scene of all other forms of power or by negative inclusion. The latter practice resulted from an ideological principle according to which only those associations and political groupings whose activities were not directed against the ruling regime, thus confirming loyalty to the communists, were permitted to exist in public life (Misztal 1993: 455). So there were limits not only for institutionalised representation and the defence of political interests of various groups, but also to the very emergence and survival of groups which did not fit the image of the political interests of the regime. Legitimacy was based on the communist bureaucracies' claim of possessing 'a superior truth', and a monopoly with relation to political discourse. Thus 'their truth could not be falsified by reality, their commands were always correct, their tasks could never fail by their shortcomings' (di Palma 1991: 57). Independent intellectuals were replaced by party bureaucrats who viewed themselves as a form of 'collective mind' (Kennedy 1992: 30–58).

Ideologically defined systems of mechanism and rules of public life promoted a peculiar form of citizenship, of which the essence was a set of aggregated values: including 'class identity', 'collective co-operation', and 'loyalty to the party-state party' (Volgyes 1975: 29–30). Simultaneously, the communist regime launched a widespread assault on traditional 'capitalist' value orientations and virtues. The regime stigmatised and persecuted the values and relations of the capitalist economic and sociopolitical system, as a result driving them underground. This included norms and values relating to private property, market activities, and personal autonomy, freedom and self-responsibility. In the view of the regime it was also necessary and justified to dismantle or at least to curb the autonomy and the influences of the traditional value-generating institutions, such as local communities, social movements and churches. They were to be replaced by a network of quasi-representative organisations closely associated with the communist party.

A closed circle of decision-makers affected, directly or indirectly, the formulation of esoteric forms of political communication. Deprived of an authentic public life and opportunities for free activity, citizens were forced to behave according to the rules and norms imposed on them by the paternalistic state. The institutional structure of the system induced a peculiar form of sociopolitical relations, which were characteristic of an atomised mass society. Its distinctive feature was the dualistic structure of societal self-identification 'us and them', which in turn involved 'ethical dualism'. Standards and rules observed in 'our' group were invalid with respect to 'them'. In addition, because of the lack of crystallised political interests, the goals of collective activities were set by the reference to an idealised vision of 'normal life', the shape of which was defined by fundamental social values such as freedom, justice, equality and general affluence. All these attitudes and expectations were associated with phenomena, frequently reported in sociological studies, such as social mimicry and a strong tendency towards the levelling of socioeconomic differences.

On the whole, the impact of the communist order on structures of societal systems had a levelling effect. Yet, a serious limitation of freedom was the a price to be paid for this outcome. As Ellen Parkin pointed out:

> Egalitarianism seems to require a political system in which the state is able continually to hold in check those social and occupational groups which, by virtue of their skills or education or personal attributes, might otherwise attempt to stake claims to a disproportionate share of society's rewards. The most effective way of holding such groups in check is by denying them the right to organise politically, or in other words, to undermine social equality.
>
> (Wnuk-Lipinski 1990: 324)

The social policy of the communist regime was aimed at achieving equality of conditions rather than equality of opportunity. Due to economic constraints it was generally a process of equalising downward: cheap food, housing and transport, free education and health care, accompanied by low salaries. Nearly all resources were concentrated under state control, and the redistribution of resources followed the political priorities of the ruling elite: stabilisation of the system, forced industrialisation, reproduction of manpower, social peace, full employment and social security. During this period, social policy was an integral part of more general domestic policy orientated towards a total reconstruction of society. The socialist state possessed a range of political instruments to ensure that all 'deserving citizens' enjoyed a minimum standard of living. To be sure, in the communist system, the political and economic elite, the nomenklatura, enjoyed a wide spectrum of privileges. In general, these privileges involved access to goods or services not available to the population at large (Ferge 1991). Yet at the same time, many other social and occupational groups also enjoyed some of these privileges. This produced the illusion that the regime was not the exclusive incumbent participating in 'extraordinary distribution' of goods. However, it would be naive to maintain that state-socialism contributed to the growth of 'citizenship' in Marshall's sense of the term. It must be stressed here that although social rights under socialism may have reduced risk and insecurity, they did little to enrich civilised life. Thus, the collective as well as individual aspects of social rights, and the provision for society as a whole and for individual instances, were rejected.

The destruction of political society, the negation of the public sphere and, finally, the accommodation between the party state and the society, produced a huge clientele system. Grzegorz Ekiert argues that 'clientele networks' consisted, in a selective and arbitrary way, of the distribution of privileges and resources in exchange for political compliance or withdrawal from politics:

> The party-state targeted intellectuals, professionals and selected groups of highly concentrated and educated workers (miners, steelworkers and shipyard workers) with higher salaries and special privileges. Such practices caused the corrosion of law, demoralisation and a widespread sense of moral crisis in all segments of society.
>
> (Ekiert 1991: 303–04)

In the 1980s, research findings focusing on this issue showed the existence of two fundamentally varied opinions in the Polish population (see Tables 4.1 and 4.2). The first and at the same time the most common one (nearly 50 per cent of the national sample) singled out the structure of power as a source of illegitimate privileges. The second opinion (which was much less common, 12 per cent of the national sample) was the perception of the socialist market as a source of undeserved privileges. There was also a third option, which located the source of illegitimate privileges in various pathological micro structures, 'cliques', but this option was rather peripheral (4 per cent).

After having analysed these findings, Edmund Wnuk-Lipinski (1990: 326) came to the general conclusion that:

> People have learned from common experience that money is not the most important regulator in the distribution mechanism. This function, at least partially, was taken over by position in the power structure, while distribution itself was regulated by the enigmatic sultanic principle: *to each according to his functional usefulness to the system*.
>
> (Wnuk-Lipinski 1990: 326).

The data suggests that this principle and the redistribution mechanisms were not only commonly visible, in spite of the hidden process of distribution, but also generally questioned. The instrumentalisation of the value system turned out to be one of the most significant elements in the process of decision-making. This in turn made it possible for the communist regime to keep full control over each form of public activity and to shape political discourse. By combining repression with negotiation, the regime neither established constitutional and legal opportunities for exercising civil rights nor provided real political citizenship, though it provided some elements of the institutional arrangement of social citizenship. Civil liberties under the communist social order were preserved as long as they were used in support of the existing regime; otherwise they were limited or entirely suspended. Thus, an individual who supported the ruling state-party leadership could enjoy his or her civil rights, but an individual who did not support the order usually was deprived of their civil rights. A study undertaken in Poland in 1983/84 showed that this kind of inequity gave a source of strong sense of deprivation for over 80 per cent of skilled workers and engineers employed in big enterprises (Wnuk-Lipinski 1989).

This type of a generalised sense of relative deprivation was especially widespread among professionals, skilled workers, owners, members of Solidarity, the middle aged and city dwellers. The results of empirical studies are absolutely explicit with regard to social groups' assessment of opportunities to influence policies through participation in the existing sociopolitical organisations or use official channels and procedures. The existence of such opportunities was acknowledged by about 6 per cent of respondents in

*Table 4.1* The answers to the question 'Who could you rely on in settling important matters?' presented by respondents in 1980, 1984 and 1988. (in %)

| *Who could you rely on?* | *1980* *N=2340** | *1984* *N=1798** | *1988* *N=2247** |
|---|---|---|---|
| On myself | 47.6 | 63.4 | 43.4 |
| On family, folks, friends | 20.4 | 36.1 | 43.2 |
| On public institutions or organisations | 9.6 | 8.1 | 4.2 |
| On government, central/local authorities, party | 9.3 | 5.8 | 2.4 |
| On enterprise I work at | 5.8 | 3.3 | 2.4 |
| Other possibilities | 7.3 | 12.8 | 4.5 |

*Source*: Wnuk-Lipinski 1989 : 57.
*Respondents could select more than one of possible answers.

*Table 4.2* Persons pointing to different segments of authority perceived as a source of undeserved privileges (the survey was carried out in December 1981).

| *Categories of respondents* | *Groups perceived as the main socio-political forces exercising undeserved privileges* | | | |
|---|---|---|---|---|
| | *Total* | *Including :* | | |
| | | *Authority* | *Members of the Polish United Workers' Party* | *Army and militia* |
| Inhabitants of town | 49.8 | 32.8 | 5.4 | 12.4 |
| Inhabitants of village | 32.8 | 22.0 | 61,0 | 4.7 |
| *Membership of trade unions (in XII 1981)*: | | | | |
| Solidarity | 69.4 | 39.0 | 14.8 | 15.6 |
| So-called pro-establishment trade-unions (OPZZ) | 44.0 | 27.8 | 7.8 | 8.4 |
| Not belonging to trade-unions | 40.7 | 25.0 | 7.7 | 7.7 |
| *Occupational groups*: | | | | |
| Intelligentsia | 60.8 | 32.3 | 15.5 | 13.0 |
| Civil servants | 55.4 | 34.9 | 7.5 | 13.0 |
| Skilled workers | 61.1 | 37.7 | 12.8 | 10.6 |
| Unskilled workers | 33.5 | 24.4 | 1.7 | 7.4 |
| Farmers | 25.0 | 15.3 | 7.4 | 2.3 |
| Owners | 72.4 | 37.7 | 18.8 | 15.9 |
| Unemployed | 40.2 | 24.0 | 8.1 | 8.1 |
| *Level of education*: | | | | |
| Elementary | 33.4 | 21.5 | 5.6 | 6.3 |
| Secondary | 60.2 | 33.1 | 12.1 | 15.0 |
| University | 65.6 | 35.6 | 18.3 | 11.7 |

1985. Characteristically, among the relatively few respondents, who in general admitted the existence of the possibility of ordinary people to influence government policies, the largest number (13.2 per cent) pointed at more productive and thorough work as the form of this influence. In other surveys held in 1984, as many as 72.8 per cent of respondents when asked: 'What do you think about the elections to people's councils? Do you think that people should go to the polls?', answered in a way which indicated that they attached no importance to that form of participation and deprecated it as a political fact and social event. What was interesting was the fact that at the same time over 80 per cent of respondents said they believed people should turn out at the polls. Therefore, one may say that for more than 50 per cent of respondents, the only reason for taking part in the elections was the fact the latter were being held.

Of course, the motives which led people to participate in the officially established forms of political life were characterised by much complexity, including both the sense of civil duty as well as fear of presumed political sanctions. However, irrespective of the different motives for such participation, what was common for statements spoken by respondents was the denial of its *political* significance. The area of officially established forms of political life under state socialism was perceived as a domain governed by customary norms, an area for rituals in which participants played roles designed for them in some other dimensions of reality. The perception of politics as the exclusive domain of authorities was accompanied by a low level of interest in official political life, scant knowledge concerning official political events as well as by the absence of political beliefs on the part of a majority (61.5 per cent) of respondents (Marody 1991: 134–47).

Due to the lack of credible and profound sociopolitical studies there is not sufficient data to estimate precisely the extent to which the rules and norms of state socialism were internalised by particular sections of Polish society. It can be said, however, that a series of worker's protests in 1956, 1970, 1976 and 1980, and the 1968 social unrest, led by students and intellectuals, clearly showed that the communist regime was not successful in establishing the anticipated degree of loyalty and obedience. The accumulation of societal discontent undermined the normative foundations of the structure of state socialism; thus it became the main source of an open legitimacy crisis in Polish society.

Analysis carried out in 1984 revealed a remarkably high level of social acceptance of the view that the system did not function in accordance to universal moral norms, such as justice, legal equality, and respect for human dignity. There was a widespread opinion that the aforementioned values and norms had been frequently violated by the communist regime. Many respondents indicated also that even in the domain of systemic rules there existed a huge discrepancy between declarations and political practice (Jasinska-Kania 1990: 267–92).

## Citizens between political inclusion and social exclusion

In contrast to the development of capitalism in most West European countries, political elites in Poland had to implement a market economy 'from the top', i.e. they were forced to adopt methods and measures inherent in the realm of *politics*. This in turn jeopardised 'classical' liberal-democratic rules and procedures by crossing the dividing line between the political and the non-political spheres of social life. This specific feature of systemic transformation in Poland was noticed by Grzegorz Kolankiewicz, who rightly pointed out that whereas in Marshall's sequence civil rights predated political rights, in the case of Poland, the establishment of industrial and social rights, such as those existing under real socialism, was (the platform of trade unionism that was) used to press for civil rights (Kolankiewicz 1992: 141–158).

One year after Solidarity came to power, the incoherence concerning the way in which the elites and the rest of society judged and interpreted the objectives of transformation generated what one may call *the rationality gap*. It originated from the dissimilarity of experiences and cognitive attitudes of these groups. Considering the process of transformation, elites were supposed to think in terms of institutional order and laws serving as the basis for their evaluation of the reforms, whereas individuals perceived and underwent the change of systems through their subjective feelings reflecting their achievements in terms of values and satisfaction of needs (Wnuk-Lipinski 1991: 22). The ever-greater tension between the visions of the politicians and the 'revolution of unsatisfied expectations' on the part of the citizens resulted in the loss of social capital.

In the light of data offered by successive public opinion polls, one could easily see that a substantial part of Polish society perceived the 'politics of real interests' with growing discontent. In the period between 1990 and 1997 public opinion polls reported a continuous scepticism and uncertainty as to whether the neo-democratic normative and institutional order was a systemic value or not (cf. Figures 4.1 and 4.2).

Taking the evidence into consideration, it seems to be true that a breakdown of ethical–moral values in the early phase of the establishment of the neo-democratic order and a shift toward 'politics as a marketplace', has created division lines in the formerly integrated anti-totalitarian political culture. One line of division is drawn between the weakening culture of the 'Solidarity ethos' and the strengthening culture of real adversarial politics, consisting of numerous political conflicts, particular political ambitions of the leaders and egoistic motivations of interest groups and parties.

There also appeared another type of political behaviour that occurs in everyday life, which one can name as 'defensive adjustment'. Many individual citizens and groups try to gain benefits for their place of residence or work by forming informal relationships with, and within, state institutions and

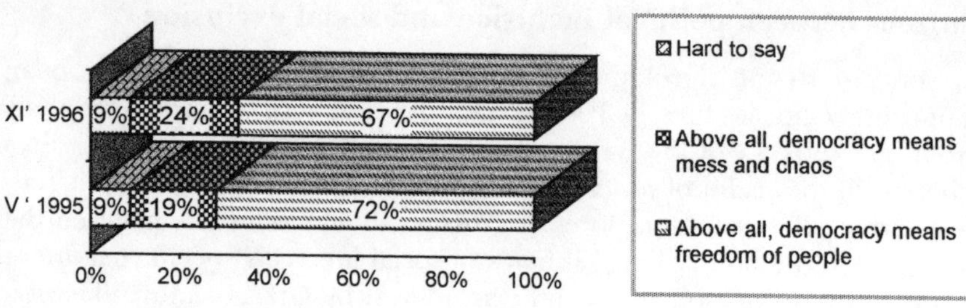


*Figure 4.1* Answers to the question: 'With which of the following opinions do you agree?' (The survey was carried out in November 1996; N=1,134).

*Source*: Serwis Informacyjny CBOS (Centre for Public Opinion Research) , January 1997: 7.

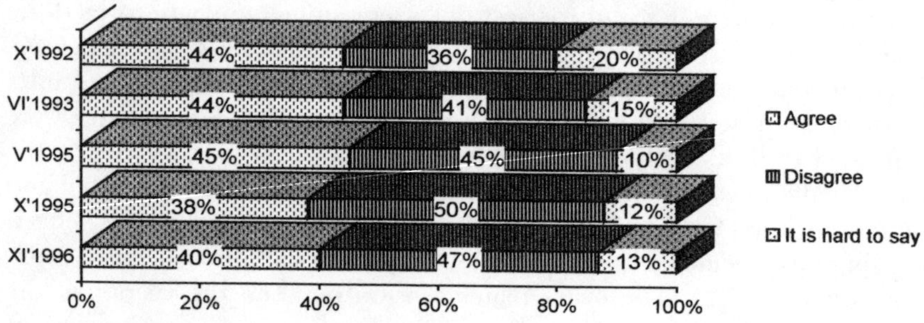


*Figure 4.2* Answers to the question: 'Do you agree with the proposition that for people like you it does not really matter whether the power is exercised by democratic or undemocratic government?' (The survey was carried out in November 1996; N=1,134).

*Source*: Serwis Informacyjny CBOS, January 1997: 13.

public organisations in order to speed up the bureaucratic procedures and be treated better than others. Although access to institutions and organisations is much easier nowadays than it used to be under 'really existing' socialism, many individuals and social groups still habitually look for 'access' and connections, and seem to forget that their business could be formally arranged with no bother at all.

Retrospectively, it may be said that the gap between the value systems created by 'the world of politics' and 'the world of individuals', having being petrified during the period of communism, has remained or, as some argue, increased in size. Three years after the successful abolition of the totalitarian institutions, as few as 7 per cent of Poles were of the opinion that they would like to participate in public life, while 86 per cent expressed the view that they would like to be well-governed (Glinski 1993: 3). The delegitimisation of political elites and the withdrawal from political par-

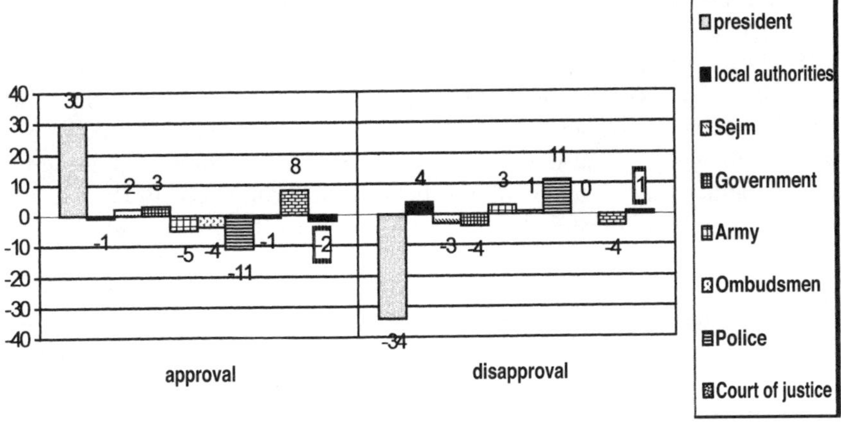


*Figure 4.3* Changes in public opinion between July 1995 and January 1997.
*Source*: *Serwis Informacyjny* CBOS, 1997.

ticipation, show that a serious conflict between the preferred macro-level order and its perception by different sections of society has been maintained. This estimation seems not to be exaggerated: since 1995, public opinion surveys have shown a definite decline of trust in basic public institutions in Poland, such as parliament, the army, local authorities and the public administration.

A more detailed analysis of the character of the political consciousness of Poles reveals also many other inconsistencies concerning cognitive and behavioural attitudes. Such an ambiguous conclusion springs, for example, from a survey conducted by Jan Garlicki in 1992, of a sample group of 578 people including 303 students from Warsaw colleges and universities, and 275 students from Warsaw secondary schools and universities. According to the results of the survey:

> many of the declared pluralists are, at the same time, ardent defenders of tradition, ready to sacrifice some aspects of freedom of speech. The group of *pluralist-traditionalists* accounts for a total of 59,3 per cent of the population. For comparison, the consistent pluralists who are really tolerant, and who would not like to sacrifice the freedom of speech for the sake of tradition constitute a group of less than 20 per cent (the exact number is 19,4 per cent). On the other hand, there is 5,5 per cent of clear separatist-traditionalists. The figures presented may prove a certain social personality split among young people. The majority of them display declarative support for pluralism, under which they hide traditionalism and resistance to foreign ideas. The latter being stronger than their devotion to the freedom of speech.
>
> (Garlicki 1994: 170)

Searching for an explanation of the sources of these phenomena, one has to keep in mind that despite the new opportunities originated by democratic order, many forms of civic passivity have survived as living examples of the enduring nature of socialist experiences, habits and patterns. They discourage association and action on behalf of others and provide citizens with a justification for civic non-participation. Such attitudes are frequently accompanied by the belief that public activity is merely a 'springboard' to political privileges or a career in the civil service (Swida-Ziemba 1994: 35–50).

Whilst not deprecating the significance of post-communist influence on current behaviour and social attitudes, in the analysis of the reasons of both the feeling of distrust and the lack of positive constant images of public institutions, one has to stress the links between political opportunities and increasing disapproval of the socioeconomic changes which have been introduced since 1989 (Reykowski 1993: 41–2). However, as Aleksander Smolar noted, the population has started to believe that 'their lives depend less and less on the political scene, [and] politics no longer fills the people with great dread or great hope' (Smolar 1994: 81). Surveys have also revealed a strong correlation between negative attitudes towards democratic values and those persons who feel the pain of transition. In the first place such remarks concern: pensioners, the less educated, women and inhabitants of underdeveloped regions of the country, primarily the eastern and south-eastern regions of Poland. On the other hand, surveys have shown that 'pro-democratic' attitudes occur mostly among representatives of such groups as the young, the well-educated, managers, skilled workers and inhabitants of large towns.

From the very beginning of the introduction of market rules, there appeared a typical syndrome of hopelessness, especially amongst those groups who were afraid of changes and did not support the principle of reduction of state protection. A study carried out in 1990/91 showed that none of the social and occupational groups among the urban population was free from the threat of poverty, even those working on their own account (Beskid 1992). The process of impoverishment has mostly affected the middle-income strata. This is best shown in the ratio of average income to the minimum subsistence level, accepted in Poland as the most adequate criterion of poverty. Compared with 1989, in the first three quarters of 1991 the ratio fell from 1.78 per cent to 1.32 per cent in employees' households, from 1.90 per cent to 1.25 per cent in workers-farmers' households, from 2.06 per cent to 1.11 per cent in farmers' households, and from 1.39 per cent to 1.30 per cent in old age and invalid pensioners' households (Danecki 1993: 48–9).

During the first two years of shock therapy, levels of poverty increased. In comparison with 1989, the data from 1991 indicates that the percentage of persons living in poverty in employees' households rose from 14.9 to 37.4 per cent and in the households of pensioners from 27.4 to 33.9 per cent. During these two years the percentage of people living in families of income less than 70 per cent of the social minimum rose in employees' households from 4.9 to 14 per cent and for pensioners from 10.7 per cent to 13.3 per cent.

The considerable fall in Polish living standards in the years 1990–3, brought about the revival of an old normative dilemma, usually an integral part of the policy-making process, namely that between freedom and equality or political citizenship and social citizenship. The social perception of the relations between these two values is presented by OBOP (Centre for Public Opinion Research) findings, which were carried out from 1988 to 1993. The data indicate that the growth of public support for equality is closely related to such negative side effects of economic change as frustration, deprivation and pauperisation of many social groups.

Subsequent research conducted in 1993 revealed that social acceptance of 'freedom' was strongly associated with an expectation of equal rights and equal opportunities for each person. The investigation also showed that the principle of justice became one of the most important criteria of the individual's evaluation of social and political reality. It must be stressed here that these empirical results do not indicate that there existed a popular support for a radical levelling of inequalities among various groups. A study carried out among urban dwellers in 1991 showed that only one-fifth of respondents favoured radical egalitarianism. The opinion that 'all people deserve the same and, thus, they should have the same living standards' was expressed by only 20 per cent of respondents. On the other hand, the opinion that 'not all people deserve the same and they should have different living standards' was supported by 74 per cent of respondents.

A greater level of support for radical egalitarianism has been observed among those with the lowest level of education, while the highest percentage of the supporters of social differentiation is to be found among those with the highest levels of education. The greatest supporters of social differentiation included private proprietors (95 per cent), and non-technical specialists (91 per cent). The supporters of radical egalitarianism formed the biggest group among the unemployed not in receipt of benefit; unskilled and skilled workers formed 46 and 39 per cent respectively (Beskid 1992).

Recently published research reports have indicated a significant shift in the social perception of structural determinants and the sources of poverty and wellbeing. In comparison with the survey carried out in December 1994, the percentage of respondents accepting wellbeing as a natural circumstance grew from 69 per cent to 74 per cent in January 1997, while 53 per cent (as opposed to 45 per cent previously) expressed the view that wellbeing should be regarded as an 'advantageous' to the structure of Polish society.

The idea of economic freedom has now begun to be perceived as a virtue in a selective way only. If the market is not treated as the ideal mechanism

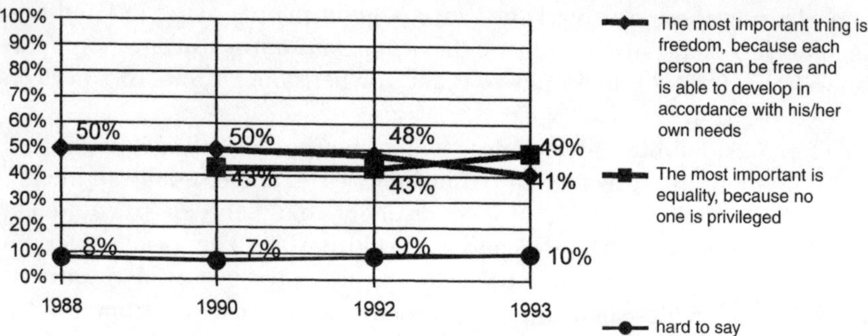


*Figure 4.4* Although both freedom and equality are very important, if you have to make a choice between one or another, which one would you choose?

*Source*: OBOP, 1993 (N=1,111).

of providing goods, then people expect the state to correct market forces in favour of citizens who assume they do not have the possibility of securing jobs, housing, education for their children through their own endeavours. However, demands for more egalitarian policies, supported by syndicalist or Catholic ideas, may limit the emergence of new political and civil rights. Such pressures of public opinion on the state may lead to serious disturbances connected with socioeconomic infrastructures, and particularly with the reconstruction of private ownership relations and related types of social attitudes.

The last topic reveals its special significance when considering the issue of the nature and the range of main structural barriers which Polish society has to overcome in order to rebuild a civil community. From the perspective of the structure of modern Western societies, the class-strata structure of Polish society, inherited from the communists, seems to be one of the main barriers to its transformation toward democratic citizenship and a self-governing society. As strictly defined within a market economy, the systems of 'open' upper, middle and lower strata, are important factors shaping the order of civil society. Acting as self-control systems – while distributing nobility, respect and prestige, based on the extent of consumption, property, power, or education – this stratification may also, to some degree, eliminate the repressive functions of the state.

It can be assumed, therefore, that such attitudes and beliefs will have a great impact on how people will interpret their constitutional social rights as well as the particular forms of social citizenship, i.e. forms of social co-operation, social stability and interpersonal relations. This issue, however, depends on clearing up many other detailed theoretical and practical dilemmas, including: how to reconstruct Poland's economy without jeopardising equality and social security provision; how to invigorate the functioning of democratic institutions under conditions of social apathy and excessive demands and expectations; and, finally, how to protect and improve the 'the bargaining position' of the nascent bourgeoisie whilst maintaining social peace.

## In search of the paradigms of the development of democratic citizenship

One of the characteristics of the debate concerning citizenship in Poland lays great emphasis on its active dimension whilst simultaneously deprecating every behaviour that expresses civic passiveness. The followers of such thinking can be observed both on the left and right of the political scene. These groups both refer to the example of Western societies, which are treated as the personification of civic activity and competence. Such opinions are held especially by those who advocate a participatory model of citizenship as a necessary structural component of democratic reforms in Poland. The central thesis of this social project springs from the assumption that active engagement in public activities brings about a better understanding of the public good, civic competence and, eventually, interpersonal relations. To begin with, this type of democratic citizenship order has much to do with a social democratic ideal of the active state, in which the principal objective is to provide each citizen with an equal access to basic welfare service, and thus to counteract socioeconomic inequalities. Based on empirical data, the proponents of this direction of democratic transformation emphasise the inseparability of three dimensions of citizenship: civil, political and social. As such, they are supposed to be a condition *sine qua non* for an establishment of a genuine democratic citizenship in Poland. Moreover, it is assumed that, as a result, the prerequisites for a deeper interest in current affairs may appear, and citizens' interest in political issues and their willingness to participate actively in public life, accompanied by a sense of political efficacy and a knowledge of actual democratic rights and duties, may grow.

Following these principles, Kazimierz Przeworski expressed the view that: 'Citizens in new democracies expect to enjoy social as well as political rights' (Przeworski 1995: 76). In opposition to such views, some theoreticians and politicians claim that the re-emergence of citizenship and civic virtues in Poland must be supported principally by the strengthening of the legal and political components of individual liberty and a sense of autonomy rather than a further stimulation of social expectations. Such opinions are inspired mostly either by neo-Hegelian or neo-liberal thinking. Both sets of theories and programmes are focused on the mental, cultural and social implications of individual rights, in particular those associated with property relations. According to this view, 'in all Eastern European societies the base for the patterns of socialisation typical of civil society would emerge only after the dissolution of state ownership' (Staniszkis 1992: 222). Criticising the supporters of the government's commitment to social provision, the representatives of this approach emphasise the positive consequences of privatisation and deregulation policies in the domain of public services. Such policies are felt to be necessary in order to speed up the process of consciousness transformation in Polish society, and to achieve a higher level of individual responsibility, socioeconomic mobility and self-sufficiency.

In consideration of the origins of Polish society's inaptitude for citizenship standards fulfilment being shaped within the framework of liberal democracy, there is no lack of opinions on the extent to which the current situation is the result of the persistence of the romantic model in Polish political culture. Such a view is formulated by Joanna Kurczewska and Hanna Bojar who state that the model has contributed to the creation of value system and attitudes,

> according to which good intentions are what counts, not the practical effects of behaviour. While quixotic behaviour is admired, it is much more difficult to win plaudits for day-to-day individual or group co-operation towards the common good. The negative social effects of the romantic model are also manifest in the respect accorded pathetic failures in the face of reality. In public opinion, individual and group activities which have aborted for some reason or another are still highly esteemed. On the other hand, well-organised and successful co-operation is neither copied nor even accepted since it does not fit the pattern of noble defeat inherited from the nineteenth century.
>
> (Kurczewska and Bojar 1995: 188–9)

The traditional belief in *gloria victis* does not encourage people to undertake practical endeavours, especially if they are to be successful. This is why so many circles respond so negatively to clubs and associations formed by those who have been successful, because many Poles are still convinced that to be successful in the new Poland is something shifty and deplorable. The problem of which of these diagnoses is more adequate remains open. What seems to be necessary in this context, however, is knowledge about the current changes taking place in Poland, and potential and real implications with regard to both normative and systemic dimensions of citizenship. This knowledge, based on further empirical as well as theoretical studies, is essential for an adequate understanding of the nature, forms and specific characteristics of democratic citizenship in Poland. When searching for positive solutions to conflicts and contradictions connected with the restoration of democratic rule, it is necessary to consider the danger that may be implied by the replacement of the old picture describing collective society's passive nature with the myth of the mature citizen (Wolff-Poweska 1998: 146).

There are still many symptoms which suggest political elites perceive democratic citizenship in terms of wishful thinking or simplified images of social life. A possible modification of these attitudes must be united with a mental metamorphosis of the whole society or at least its majority, which regards the development of citizenship as a process from above rather than one of 'self-education'. Although such attitudes may be considered as a side effect of systemic transformation in Poland, one has to keep in mind that they lay the foundations for the establishment of the liberal-democratic citizenship model, as well as of authoritarian or paternalistic forms of policy. Taking into account the problem connected with the restitution of democratic institutions and laws, it is necessary to consider the fact that democracy enables *ex definitione* different forms of political expression to exist, including both those forms that solidify civil society and those that are negations of this sort of society. A general assessment concerning democratic citizenship development in Poland is also influenced by a historically verified rule which sates that different institutional solutions can function successfully within one and the same political culture, yet one and the same institution functioning in the environment of different cultures may have entirely different effects.

## Bibliography


Beskid, L. 'Poziom zycia – potoczna percepcja i oczekiwania', in L. Beskid (ed.) *Warunki zycia i kondycja Polakow na poczatku zmian systemowych,* Warszawa: PAN Instytut Filozofii i Socjologii, 1992.

Borucka-Arctowa, M. *Swiadomosc prawna a planowe zmiany spoleczne*, Wroclaw: Zaklad Narodowy imienia Ossolinskich, 1981.

Danecki, J. 'Social costs of system transformation in Poland', in S. Ringen and C. Wallac (eds) *Societies in East-Central Europe Today*, Prague Papers on Social Responses to Transformation, vol. I. Prague: Central European University Press, 1993.

Dekker, H. 'Democratic citizenship competence', paper presented at the workshop: Nationalism, Ethnic Conflict and the Conception of Citizenship in Western and Eastern Europe, European Research Centre on Migration and Ethnic Relations, University of Utrecht, November 24–25, 1994a.

—— 'Socialization and education of young people for democratic citizenship. Theory and research', in R. Holly (ed.) *Political Consciousness and Civic Education During the Transformation of the System*, Warsaw: Institute of Political Studies; Polish Academy of Sciences, 11–43, 1994b.

di Palma, G. 'Legitimation from the top to civil society. Politico-cultural change in Eastern Europe', *World Politics* 44, 1, 49–80, 1991.

Ehrlich, S. *Wstep do nauki o panstwie i prawie*, Warszawa: Panstwowe Wydawnictwo Naukowe, 1979 .

Ekiert, G. 'Democratisation process in East Central Europe: a theoretical reconsideration', *British Journal of Political Science* 21, 285–313, 1991.

Ferge, Z. 'Social security systems in the new democracies of Central and Eastern Europe: a postlegacies and possible futures', in G. Cornia and S. Sipos (eds) *Children and the Transition to the Market Economy*, Aldershot: Avebury, 69–90, 1991.

Garlicki, J. 'Attitudes towards pluralism', in R. Holly (ed.) *Political Consciousness and Civic Education During the Transformation of the System*, Warsaw: Institute of Political Studies; Polish Academy of Sciences, 162–74, 1994.

Glinski, P. 'Polak obywatelem', *Spoleczenstwo Otwarte* 1, 3–10, 1993.

Gunsteren, H. van. 'Four conceptions of citizenship', in B. van Steenbergen (ed.) *The Condition of Citizenship*, London: Sage, 36–48, 1994.

Jablonski, A. W. 'The politics of virtue versus the politics of interests: the political culture of Poland in the era of systemic transition', in A. Jablonski and G. Meyer (eds) *The Political Culture of Poland in Transition*, Wroclaw: Wydawnictwo Uniwersytetu Wroclawskiego, 39–52, 1996.

Jasinska-Kania, A. 'Wartosci moralne i postawy polityczne', in J. Reykowski *et al.* (eds), *Indywidualne i spoleczne wyznaczniki wartosciowania*, Wroclaw: Ossolineum, 1990.

Kalberg, S. 'Cultural foundations of modern citizenship', in B. Turner (ed.) *Citizenship and Social Theory*, London: Sage, 91–114.

Kennedy, M. D. 'The intelligentsia in the reconstruction of civil society and post-communist regimes in Hungary and Poland', *Theory and Society* 21, 1, 29–76, 1992.

King, D. and Waldron, J. 'Citizenship, Social Citizenship and the Defence of Welfare Provision'. *British Journal of Political Science* 18, 415–43, 1988.

Kolankiewicz, G. 'The reconstruction of citizenship: reverse incorporation in Eastern Europe', in K. Poznanski (ed.) *Constructing Capitalism. The Re-emergence of Civil Society and Liberal Economy in the Post-Communist World*, Oxford: Westview Press, 141–58, 1992.

Kolarska-Bobinska, L. 'Ustroj ekonomiczny a interesy grupowe', w: *Polacy '90. Konflikty i zmiana*, Warszawa: Instytut Filozofii i Socjologii PAN, Instytut Studiow Politycznych PAN, 61–80, 1991.

Krol, M. 'Obywatel miedzy spoleczenstwem, panstwem a narodem' (unpublished manuscript), Warszawa, 1993

Kurczewska, J. and Bojar, H. 'A new society? Reflections on democracy and pluralism in Poland', in G. Bryant and E. Mokrzycki (eds) *Democracy, Civil Society and Pluralism,* Warszawa: IFiS Publishers, 143–204, 1995.

Mann, M. 'Ruling class strategies and citizenship', *Sociology* 21, 3, 339–54, 1987.

Marody, M. 'Perception of politics in Polish society and its consequences for political participation', in G. Meyer and F. Ryszka (eds), *Political Participation and Democracy in Poland and West Germany*, Warsaw: Osrodek Badan Spolecznych, 134–147, 1991.

Marshall, T. H. *Class, Citizenship and Social Development*, New York : Doubleday, 1964.

Misztal, B. 'Understanding political change in Eastern Europe: a sociological perspective' *Sociology* 27, 3, 451–70, 1993.

Przeworski, A. *Sustainable Democracy* (*A Joint Report*), Cambridge: Cambridge University Press, 1995.

Reykowski, J. 'Zmiany systemowe a mentalnosc polskiego spoleczenstwa', in J. Reykowski (ed.) *Wartosci i postawy Polakow a zmiany systemowe*, Warszawa: Instytut Psychologii PAN, 1993.

Roche, M. 'Citizenship, social theory, and social change', *Theory and Society* 16, 2, 363–99, 1987.

Schöpflin G, 'The political traditions of Eastern Europe', *Daedalus* 119, 1, 55–90, 1990.

Serwis Informacyjny, CBOS 1990–1997.

Smolar, A. 'The dissolution of Solidarity', *Journal of Democracy* 5, 1, 70–84, 1994.

Staniszkis, J. 'Main paradoxes of the democratic change in Eastern Europe', in K. Poznanski (ed.) *Constructing Capitalism. The Re-emergence of Civil Society and Liberal Economy in the Post-Communist World*, Oxford: Westview Press, 1992.

Swida-Ziemba, H. 'Mentalnosc postkomunistyczna', *Kultura i Spoleczenstwo* 1, 35–50, 1994.

Turner, B. *Citizenship and Capitalism: the Debate over Reformism*, London: Allen & Unwin, 1986.

Turner, B. S. 'Outline of a theory of citizenship,' *Sociology*, 24, 2, 189–217, 1990.

Volgyes, I. 'Political socialization in Eastern Europe: a conceptual framework', in I. Volgyes (ed.) *Political Socialization in Eastern Europe. A Comparative Framework*, London: Praeger Publishers, 1–37, 1975.

Wnuk-Lipinski, E. 'Nierownosci, deprywacje i przywileje jako podloze konfliktu spolecznego', in W. Adamski *et al.* (eds) *Polacy '88. Dynamika konfliktu a szanse reform*, Warszawa: Uniwersytet Warszawski, 1989.

—— 'Freedom or Equality: An Old Dilemma in a New Context,' in P. Ploszajsk (ed.), *Philosophy of Social Choice*, Warsaw: IFiS Publishers, 317–331, 1990.

—— 'Deprywacje spoleczue a konflikty interesow i wartosci' in *Polacy* '90 Konflikty i zmiana, Warszawa: PAN Instytut Filozofii i Socjologii, 1991.

Wolff-Poweska, A. *Oswojona rewolucja. Europa srodkowo-Wschodnia w procesie demokratyzacji*, Poznan: Instytut Zachodni, 1998.

# 5 Political competition in Poland

## Traditionalisation or westernisation?

*Andrzej Antoszewski*

All member-states of the European Union (EU) are classified as fully functioning liberal democracies. The length of time each of the member-states has enjoyed liberal democratic rule is by no means uniform. Some countries such as the United Kingdom and Sweden have liberal democratic traditions that stretch back well over one hundred years. Others such as Denmark and Belgium have similarly proud records which have been interrupted only as a result of foreign invasion and not through internal pressures. Some, such as France and Germany have been prone to massive internal dislocation and bouts of revolutionary violence. Yet others, such as Spain and Portugal, have only emerged from long periods of authoritarian rule in recent years.

Poland perhaps possesses similarities with current EU members which fall into the final category. Although liberalism has long been a key element of Polish political culture, prior to 1989/90, liberal democracy had been experienced only between 1919 and 1926. This chapter focuses upon one ingredient of liberal democratic life in Poland since 1989, namely the party system. In particular, it seeks to establish the extent to which the new Poland has developed a party system and modes of political competition which correspond to the norms of more established liberal democracies. The chapter also highlights both commonalties and disjunctures between Poland and similar liberal democratic systems, and assesses the extent to which the question of Poland's participation within the EU informs the conduct of party politics and political competition in today's Poland.

### Political competition in post-communist Europe: general trends

Many scholars who deal with the question of democratisation in East-Central Europe have emphasised that this process is beginning to result in the emulation of the West European model. There is little doubt that countries such as Poland, Hungary and the Czech Republic share the occidental cultural heritage. Hopes for the consolidation of democracy in Poland and other countries in East-Central Europe are placed upon the imitation of patterns of political competition characteristic of advanced liberal democracies. The question is one of whether political mechanisms and devices currently being developed should be or will come to be identical with those of Western Europe. For many reasons the answer has to be no. The main reason for giving such an answer lies in the obvious fact that despite the existence of a common cultural heritage, the political development of East-Central Europe has been different from that of the western part of the continent. It may be argued that the lack of solid democratic traditions, the immaturity of civil society and the weakness of political parties may turn out to be the obstacles in the process of democratisation. On the other hand, pressure from the international political environment may act as a factor in favour of the 'westernisation' of political life, on those countries that aim to join the EU.

It is beyond all doubt that the collapse of the communist regime in 1989 triggered a process of the re-democratisation in Poland. The Round Table Agreement of 1989 paved the way for the historic semi-free, 'contractual' election of that year and all subsequent fully free elections that have been held in post-communist Poland. The Round Table Agreement also opened the way to the institutionalisation of political competition in place of the informal rules that governed this process during the communist period.

It is commonly recognised that democracy revolves around the competition 'among individuals and organised groups (especially political parties) for all effective positions of government power, at regular intervals and excluding the use of force' (Diamond, Linz and Lipset 1990: 6). In essence, the notion of competition refers to the process of political co-operation of political parties within the rules of the democratic game. Inter-party relations may be less or more stable and durable according to case and circumstance. They may differ from country to country and within each country according to the balance of domestic political forces. Patterns of political competition may be defined as the established standards of co-operative behaviour among political parties, upon either a national or cross-national perspective. Such standards become most visible during electoral campaigns and during the process of cabinet formation and maintenance.

As was mentioned earlier, party political competition in post-communist Europe, although sharing certain characteristics with Western Europe, is somewhat different. Above all, it has been and continues to be highly centrifugal and adversarial in character. In part this situation has arisen due to the presence of reformed and renamed former communist parties, which have attempted to monopolise the left of the political spectrum. Some of them have succeeded, as in Bulgaria and to some extent Hungary, some have failed, as in the Czech Republic. In Poland, reform-oriented former communists formed the largest parliamentary group between 1993 and 1997, but until the latter date they were forced to share the left side of the political spectrum together with the post-Solidarity Labour Union (UP).

A second observable trait of political competition in post-communist Europe was the initial fragmentation of party systems. In all countries of the region, numerous parties emerged after the collapse of the old regime, but the majority of them turned out to be typical 'flash parties'. Moreover, we have witnessed a multitude of splits and mergers that have served to confuse the electorate. Poland serves as a typical example of this phenomenon, particularly in the first phase of transition, leading to the party system having been characterised as one of overdeveloped pluralism (Grzybowski 1994). Thus, in Poland, both the effective number of parties and the level of electoral volatility have been relatively high. In addition, as with some other countries in the region, there has been a relatively frequent alternation of power.

It is also worth emphasising that the new party systems in post-communist countries do not reflect the classical structures of Western Europe. Rather, area-specific political conflicts have yielded peculiar axes of competition. Such an example in Poland is illustrated by the competition between post-communists and the sometimes fragmented, sometimes united, anti-communist bloc. As long as the anti-communist forces are dispersed, the post-communists, whether reformed or not, will remain in power. It took Solidarity until the mid-1990s to reach this rather obvious conclusion.

There are also features of political competition which are distinctive to Poland. Four, in particular, are worthy of mention. First, Poland was the only country in the region in which a competitive election was preceded by a semi-competitive one. In July 1989, Polish voters were not asked which political force should govern them. Their choice was limited to the question as to which candidates of two political camps – the communists and their allies, and Solidarity – should enter parliament. Although the election was not fully competitive, it gave people the opportunity to vote for or against the communist regime. As is well known, the communists and their allies lost, despite the fact that the rules of competition had been designed in order to prevent such an eventuality from occurring.

Second, the inaugural competitive election of 1991 followed hard on the heels of the presidential campaign. Lech Walesa, the symbol of the anti-communist opposition, won that election, and his personal victory acted as a spur for Solidarity in the subsequent parliamentary campaign. One has to remember that at that time a plethora of political parties, and interest groups masquerading as parties, occupied the political space. Within this context, it is also important to note that the Solidarity camp disintegrated into a bewildering number of competing factions.

Third, political competition in the first phase of transition in Poland was accentuated by the differing electoral laws which were employed. Each of the parliamentary elections in the period 1989–93 took place under different electoral systems. The competitive element of the election of 1989 was majoritarian. That of 1991 employed a list system with no effective threshold, only to be replaced in 1993 by a list system with a basic 5 per cent threshold. This last model, which has achieved its aim of consolidating the party system, is still in use. The final shape of electoral law was the subject of controversy and fierce dispute in parliament. In effect, during the initial phase of transition, the patterns of political competition were unstable.

Finally, we have to acknowledge that according to standard Western European definitions of the term, Solidarity was and is not a political party. Since 1989, Solidarity has taken a part in every parliamentary and presidential election, whilst maintaining its function as a trades union. It gained parliamentary representation in the Sejm of 1989 and that of 1991, but in 1993 failed to gain representation owing to excessive internal factionalisation. Having learned a rather painful lesson in 1993, a degree of cohesion was achieved through the formation of Solidarity Electoral Action (AWS), which succeeded in gaining the largest share of the votes in 1997. When represented in the Sejm (its representation in the less powerful Senate has been continuous), AWS/Solidarity has acted in a sometimes cavalier fashion. Having entered the cabinet of Jan Olszewski (1991–2), it later brought about the downfall of the government of the former Solidarity luminary Hanna Suchocka. Its support for the government of Jerzy Buzek, appointed in 1997, has been decisive for and conducive to political stability. The role of Solidarity, as both a trades union and political party, distinguishes Poland from other post-communist countries in Europe.

The instability of the party system in Poland has hindered the growth of party identification among voters. Given that pre-war parties did not re-emerge in Poland, pre-war patterns of party identification did not re-appear. The newly formed parties are not entrenched in society and they have yet to form strong links with the bulk of the electorate. 'It has been argued that between 1990 and 1993 neither small parties, nor the larger . . . crystallised their ideologies or clearly formulated long-term programmes . . . several parties also avoided taking any definite standpoint on particular controversial issues' (Wesolowski 1996: 237). Small wonder then, that voter-party identification has proven to be so elusive. In light of these findings it is useful to research political competition on three levels. The first is at the level of elections. Parties compete for votes, but the central question is one of how the parties formulate their appeals; to which kinds of values they seek to appeal and to whom are they addressed.

The question of political competition can and should also be examined at the parliamentary level. As a consequence of deformations brought about by the various electoral laws, the distribution of the seats after elections has not and does not fully reflect the distribution of votes. The degree of parliamentary representation of a given party has not only been an indicator of its relevance, but has also helped determine party parliamentary and governmental strategies. Thus, we have to take into account such variables as the effective number of parliamentary parties, the strength of the first and the second parties, the aggregation of the parliamentary party system and the size of the opposition.

The third level of political competition is connected with the process of formation and maintenance of coalition governments. In Poland such administrations are the norm. The patterns of political competition on this level are predictors not only of possible alliances but also of their durability. It is obvious that the main aim of the parties is to form or to enter the cabinet in order to translate their programmes into governmental policies. The actual political relevance of the parties is determined mainly by that what Sartori terms their coalition potential (Sartori 1976: 122). Thus, in this field, the first question is to determine the relevance of particular parties, and the second is to reconstruct the criteria of coalition formation.

When analysing party competition in Poland, it is worth bearing in mind that approaches used in the analysis of West European societies may be appropriate. In his often-cited conception of consociational democracy, Arend Lijphart has argued that in segmented societies there is more than one area of inter-party conflict. He cites ethnicity, religion, class, language and attitudes toward the political regime as forming the basis for political cleavage and party competition (Lijphart 1984: 127–140). In turn, Hans Kitschelt distinguishes three types of political competition in Western Europe. The first is based on a unidimensional left–right division. The second is termed one and a half dimensional, and involves the combination of class and religious cleavages. The third is two-dimensional competition which appears when the class and religious cleavage are 'supplemented by a cross-cutting ethno-linguistic division that generated its own parties' (Kitschelt 1997: 134). In the opinion of this author, Poland constitutes an example of this second type of political competition. Alternatively, following Wesolowski, we could consider political competition in Poland occurring around a number of axes: (1) nationalism versus universalism, (2) confessionalism versus secularism, (3) authoritarianism versus democracy (or presidentalism versus parliamentarism), (4) laissez-faireism versus interventionism, (5) elitism versus populism and (6) communism-purging versus communism-forgiving (Wesolowski 1996: 239–41).

Finally, when considering the phenomenon of political competition at the electoral and parliamentary levels we must take into account the fact that contemporary democracies may differ as to the degree of competitiveness. Morlino has suggested the use of such indicators as the effective number of parties, the level of net and inter-bloc volatility, the absence or presence of new parties and the difference between the strongest party and its nearest competitor (Morlino 1995; Bartolini and d'Alimonte 1996). Having established the theoretical basis of our study, let us now move directly to the case itself.

## Political competition in Poland in the electoral and parliamentary arenas

The most striking features of political competition in the first democratic election in Poland were the absence of strong parties, the slight difference in votes gained by those parties which came first and second, the extremely high level of fractionalisation of the party system, and the effective number of parties represented in parliament. If we compare these indicators with the results of the first, transitional elections in other countries in Western and Eastern Europe, during the 'third wave of democratisation', Poland appears as a deviant case (see Table 5.1). The effective number of parties is more than two times higher than in the in the next example, namely Slovakia (9.8 and 4.0 respectively). Support for the strongest party was almost three times lower than in Slovakia and Hungary, and more than four times lower than in Greece and the Czech Republic. In only three countries is the difference between the first and the second parties lower than 10 per cent (Spain, Hungary and Poland) but only in Poland it did it not exceed 1 per cent.

After the dissolution of the Sejm in 1993 by President Lech Walesa, the electorate passed judgement on the government's performance. This was a difficult moment for the incumbents because of the deterioration of the standard of living, and the growth of unemployment and inflation over which they had presided. The presence of these factors helps explain their subsequent defeat. For some the dissatisfaction of the voters with the economic and social policies of Tadeusz Mazowiecki's and Jan Bielecki's cabinets was the decisive factor for the defeat of the 'post-August 1989' forces. Voter dissatisfaction was manifested in relatively strong support for those parties that rejected such policies (Raciborski 1997: 43). Such parties were perceived as supporters of the austerity programme introduced by Minister of Finance Leszek Balcerowicz in the first non-communist government and gained only 20 per cent of the vote. In the opinion of Polish sociologists, the defeat of the governing camp, particularly the liberal forces, indicated the growth in significance of a socioeconomic cleavage (Morawski 1998: 214; see also Antoszewski 1993: 10). In interpreting these electoral results, many observers of the Polish political scene have emphasised the shift to the left that took place in 1992/3 (Dudek 1997, 272–5). Parties that the voters perceived to be on the left gained over 27 per cent of the vote, or almost two times more than in 1991 (see Table 5.2). The 'post-August' camp suffered from internal fragmentation and the introduction of the 5 per cent threshold, rather than from a considerable decline of electoral support.

The victory of the post-communists in the parliamentary and presidential elections led to an intensification of efforts on the part of the anti-communist right to unite. In June 1997 unity was finally achieved with the formation of the AWS by the leaders of Solidarity and several small parties,

*Table 5.1* Political consequences of transitional elections in selected European countries during the 'third wave of democratisation'.

| *Country* | *IF* | *ENP* | *S1* | *S2* | *D* |
|---|---|---|---|---|---|
| Greece | 0.64 | 1.7 | 54.4 | 74.8 | 34.0 |
| Portugal | 0.73 | 2.9 | 40.7 | 69.0 | 22.4 |
| Spain | 0.77 | 2.9 | 34.8 | 65.1 | 4.5 |
| Hungary | 0.85 | 3.7 | 32.8 | 58.3 | 7.3 |
| Czech Republic* | 0.68 | 2.0 | 55.3 | 66.6 | 44.2 |
| Slovakia* | 0.82 | 4.0 | 32.5 | 51.5 | 12.5 |
| Poland | 0.92 | 9.8 | 12.3 | 24.3 | 0.3 |

*Sources*: Morlino 1995: 324; Wiszniowski 1997: 97; Herbut 1997: 151–2; Toka 1997: 17.

*Note*: *The values of indicators for Czech Republic and Slovakia are calculated on the base of voting for the candidates to both the Czech and Slovak Chambers of the People.

*Abbreviations*: *IF* – Rae's fractionalisation index, *ENP* – effective number of parties (Laakso-Taagepera index) – on parliamentary level, *S1* – support for the strongest party, *S2* – support for two strongest parties altogether, *D* – difference between the first and the second parties.

including, among others, the Non-party bloc for Reform (BBWR), the Christian National Union (ZChN), the Centre Alliance (PC), and elements of the Confederation for an Independent Poland (KPN). The main aim of the founders of the AWS was to form an electoral coalition capable of winning the next parliamentary election (Gebethner 1997: 61). The AWS presented itself as the successor of Solidarity in its struggle with communism. Despite these efforts to attract all anti-communist parties, some of them have remained outside the AWS, the main one being the Movement for Restoration of Poland (ROP) headed by Jan Olszewski, which itself is a successor to the Movement for Poland (KdR).

A glance at Table 5.2 reveals that in the 1997 parliamentary election the AWS gained victory with 33.83 per cent of the votes and 43.69 per cent of the seats. Although voter support for the post-communist Democratic Left Alliance (SLD), increased from 20.41 per cent in 1993 to 27.13 per cent in 1997, they came second to the AWS. The main losers of the election were the Polish Peasants Party (PSL), whose support dropped from 15.4 to 7.31 per cent, and the UP, which experienced a drop in support from 7.28 to 4.74 per cent. The newcomers, but only in a formal sense, were the Freedom Union (UW), which had been formed in 1994 from a merger of the Democratic Union (UD) and the Liberal Democratic Congress (KLD); together with the aforementioned ROP. From among ten parties that stood on the national lists, five failed to enter parliament. They were the UP, two Pensioners Parties, the nationalist Bloc for Poland (NBP) and the conservative Union of Polish Right (UPR).

Comparison of the results of these three parliamentary elections allows us to answer the question of whether or not Poland has developed a stable party system. Prior to 1997, the overall consensus was that no such thing had

*Table 5.2* The 1993 and 1997 electoral results

| *Party* | *Votes 1993* | *Seats 1993* | *Votes 1997* | *Seats 1997* |
|---|---|---|---|---|
| AWS | – | – | 33.83 | 43.69 |
| SLD | 20.41 | 37.17 | 27.13 | 35.65 |
| UW | 14.58* | 16.07 | 13.37 | 13.0 |
| PSL | 15,40 | 28.69 | 7.31 | 5.87 |
| ROP | – | – | 5.56 | 1.30 |
| UP | 7.28 | 8.91 | 4.74 | – |
| KPN** | 5.77 | 4.78 | – | – |
| BBWR** | 5.41 | 3.48 | – | – |
| Others | 31.15 | 0.87*** | 8.06 | 0.43*** |

*Source*: Gebethner 1995: 1; Monitor Polski 1997, No 64.

*Notes*: *This figure includes votes gained by the UD and KLD, which merged in 1994, forming the Freedom Union (UW).

**Now part of the AWS.

***German minority.

occurred. Five factors were cited as evidence in support of this view. The first was the high number of parties. Second, support for parties was fragmented. Third, the main parties, including governing parties were unable to gain significant support. Four, the level of voter volatility was still high, and five there were frequent mergers and splits which brought about deep changes in the composition of parliament. In the light of the 1997 election results there are grounds for arguing that only the third factor still applies. Taking into account the indicators of stability within party systems one is able to discern symptoms of stabilisation within the Polish party system. This is expressed above all in the concentration of electoral support for a smaller number of parties and in a decrease in the fragmentation of parliament (see Table 5.3).

With regard to the effective number of parties, one has to point out that it has systematically decreased at both electoral and parliamentary levels. Since 1993, the reduction of the number of parties in parliament has been considerable. On the other hand, the reduction of the number of parties entering into electoral competition became noticeable in 1997. The source of this discrepancy may have been ignorance on the part of the voters of the political consequences of the introduction of the 5 per cent threshold. In 1993 they did not take into account that their votes might be cast in vain, whereas in 1997, electoral behaviour was more sophisticated and strategic. What is more important is that the effective number of parties which was extremely high in 1991, is at the moment similar to those one may find in established democracies and even less than the average for Western Europe.

The decrease of the fractionalisation of the Polish party system has to some extent been slower than the decline in the effective number of parties. It currently stands at 0.78 and, in comparison with Western Europe, it is higher than the average value of the index (0,68). The evolution of the fractionalisation index and of the effective number of parties is shown in Table 5.4.

*Table 5.3* The strength of political parties in electoral and parliamentary arenas

| *The percentage of votes cast for:* | *1991* | *1993* | *1997* |
|---|---|---|---|
| The parties which entered parliament | 93.74 | 64.90 | 87.20 |
| The strongest party | 12.32 | 20.41 | 33.83 |
| The two strongest parties | 23.81 | 35.45 | 60.96 |
| *The percentage of seats*: | | | |
| Gained by the strongest party | 13.84 | 37.17 | 43.69 |
| Controlled by two strongest parties | 26.88 | 65.86 | 79.34 |
| The turnout | 43.20 | 52.08 | 47.98 |

*Source*: Calculations of the author.

*Table 5.4* The indicators of the stabilisation of the Polish party system

| *Date of election* | *1991* | *1993* | *1997* |
|---|---|---|---|
| Effective number of parties (electoral level) | 13.9 | 10.3 | 4.2 |
| Effective number of parties (parliamentary level) | 9.8 | 3.9 | 2.9 |
| Fractionalisation index | 0.92 | 0.90 | 0.78 |

*Source*: Herbut 1996; Antoszewski and Herbut 1997.

The third indicator of party system stability is the aggregation index. In 1991 its value was extremely low standing at 0.58. It is worth noting that in no West European country after the Second World War has it been lower than 2.0, and its average value is currently 7.47 (Antoszewski and Herbut 1997: 179). In Poland the level of aggregation increased to 6.19 in 1993 and to 8.74 in 1997. One should also mention that the aggregation of the parliamentary party system depends on the number of the parties represented in parliament. The number has decreased from twenty-four in 1991 to six in 1993 to five in 1997, as is illustrated in Table 5.5.

The fourth factor considered by researchers into post-communist party systems is the level of electoral volatility. As Toka points out, the apparent instability in party support and party identities may be the greatest obstacle in the establishment of a fully functional party system because it promotes intransigence on the part of political elites (Toka 1997: 9). Thus, the lowering of electoral volatility, reflecting the formation of 'strong party attachments', has been a symptom of the structurisation of the party system. For many reasons, the level of electoral volatility is rather high in the first phase of democratic transition. However, it is difficult to measure precisely the level of volatility because of the frequent splits and mergers that take place on the electoral and parliamentary levels (Gebethner 1993: 19). For example, there were four changes in the structure of the main political parties in the period 1993–7. We have already noted how in 1994 the UD and KLD merged to form the UW, and how two years later the

*Table 5.5* The number of political competitors and their strength

| *The number of the parties* | *1991* | *1993* | *1997* |
|---|---|---|---|
| Competing in the election | 111 | 25 | 22 |
| Able to register on the national list | 27 | 11 | 10 |
| Entering parliament | 24 | 6 | 5 |
| Aggregation index | 0.58 | 6.19 | 8.74 |

*Source*: Calculations of the author.

ROP came into being. In 1996 the KPN split into two factions, one of which entered the AWS. In turn, the AWS is a conglomerate of about thirty groupings. In such a situation the level of electoral volatility may be measured only approximately.

The level of electoral volatility is higher than in Western Europe, but 'there are not dramatic differences' (Raciborski 1997: 135–6). The same may be said if we compare the results of the first parliamentary elections in other European countries which have experienced democratisation in the post-1945 era. The data from Italy (after the Second World War), Spain, Greece, Portugal and Poland show us that there is no universal pattern in electoral volatility during the transition (see Table 5.6). The peak of volatility may be achieved in the second (Italy) and third elections (Spain) or even later (Portugal). It is uncertain whether the 1997 parliamentary election in Poland may be interpreted in terms of realignment or not.

All the data shown in the tables from 5.3 to 5.6 show us that Polish party system may be perceived as rather stable and, moreover, demonstrates that there is a *tendency* towards stabilisation. In 1997 it was also visible on the level of electoral behaviour. We have to point out that:

(1) The electorate of AWS is more or less the same as the electorate of the parties that came together in the AWS.
(2) The UW has gathered votes from former UD and KLD voters.
(3) The SLD has slightly increased the size of its electorate, mainly due to decline in support for the UP.

The 1997 parliamentary election also showed that further simplification of political competition took place. Although such competition was still multipolar, only two main political forces competed for victory and for the position of the formateur in the process of government formation. They were the right-wing and anti-communist AWS and, from the other side, the left-wing, post-communist SLD. Attitudes toward socioeconomic reform and to the past, formed the main dimensions of competition (Morawski 1998: 214). Despite the economic success of the post-communist coalition it was not able to defeat the integrated post-Solidarity camp. This shows that not only material questions have significance for the Polish electorate; it may indicate that competition over policies is accompanied, or even is

*Table 5.6* Electoral net-volatility in the first phase of democratic transition in selected countries

| *Country* | *Between 1st and 2nd* | *Between 2nd and 3rd* |
|---|---|---|
| Italy | 22.9 | 12.1 |
| Spain | 6.1 | 42.2 |
| Greece | 22.2 | 26.1 |
| Portugal | 11.8 | 9.8 |
| Poland | 23.0 | 19.0 |

*Source*: Morlino 1995: 318; Raciborski 1997: 135–6.

replaced, by valence competition (Markowski 1998). If this appraisal is correct, the further polarisation of the party system will be unavoidable, and the consolidation of democracy may be threatened, although as we have just noted there are plenty of indicators that stability is growing, giving cause for optimism about the future.

## Competition in the governmental arena

Analysis of the patterns of political competition in the governmental arena allows us to determine the coalitional potential of main political parties as well as their overall political relevance. In considering this question I have assumed that the main aim of political parties is to participate in formulating and implementing governmental policies. Thus, I have treated the parties as policy-seeking rather than office-seeking.

The fragmentation of the Polish party system, although decreasing, continues to result in the need for a coalition government. Since 1991, there has been no minority government in Poland. The examples of the Olszewski and Suchocka governments have shown that such a government has only a small chance of survival. Henceforth, only majoritarian cabinets have been formed. The strength and the composition of the Polish cabinets is demonstrated in Table 5.7.

*Table 5.7* Polish cabinets 1991–1997

| *Prime Minister* | *Durability (in months)* | *Number of parties* |
|---|---|---|
| J. Olszewski | 6 | 4 (PC, ZChN, PChD,PL) |
| H. Suchocka | 10.5 | 7 (UD,ZChN,KLD,PL,PChD,SLCh,PPG) |
| W. Pawlak | 16.5 | 2 (SLD, PSL) |
| J. Oleksy | 10.5 | 2 (SLD, PSL) |
| W. Cimoszewicz | 20 | 2 (SLD) |
| J. Buzek | n.a. | 2 (AWS, UW) |

*Source*: Calculations of the author.

*Abbreviations*: PChD: Christian Democratic Party; PSL: Peasant Party; SLCh: Christian People's Party; PPG: Polish Economic Programme.

## Conclusion

What then are the patterns of political competition in the Polish governmental arena? The most striking feature is the continuing inability of the parties deriving from the anti-communist opposition to co-operate with post-communist social democrats. In 1989 and 1991, the post-communists were generally perceived as exponents of the old regime and supporters of its restoration. They themselves were reluctant to participate in formulating policies that were at odds with their old ideas. Their return to power in 1993 resulted however, in their unrequited proposal to form an 'over-arching government', with the UD and UP. Similarly, in 1997 the UW refused an offer by the SLD to enter into coalition. In both cases, programmatic considerations played a minor role, with the political origin of the potential partners being the decisive factor. One has to point out, however, that in this respect Poland is not an exception among post-communist countries (only Hungary does not fit into this pattern). Thus, the coalitional potential of the SLD, and to a lesser less extent the PSL, remains low. One may also add that the KPN demonstrated low coalitional potential before its split in 1997. This is the only meaningful party that does not have its roots in either the Solidarity or (post-) communist camps. Because of its radicalism and a certain anachronism, it has not been taken into account by either major bloc as a possible coalition partner. These findings are important for another reason. They indicate that grand coalitions, which have been characteristic of several EU states, are unlikely to appear in Poland for some years to come. This in turn serves as another indication of the difference in party competition in Poland as opposed to the EU.

A second trait of Polish coalitions is that they are more or less syncretic. Some scholars characterise this phenomenon as typical for states experiencing democratic transition. For many reasons, it has led, however, to a certain incoherence of government policies. This was particularly visible after 1992. The cabinet of Hanna Suchocka included the pro-European and liberal (laissez-faire) UD and KLD, as well as the anti-European integrationist forces comprised of the strongly Catholic and populist ZChN, the Christian Democratic Party (PChD) and the Christian Peoples Party (SLCh). Between 1993 and 1997 the cabinet was comprised of the secular, pro-European SLD and the Catholic, eurosceptic, populist PSL. Once again, we are faced with another example of the difference that exists between party politics in Poland and the EU. Indeed, as the process of negotiation enters the final stage, such obvious tensions, which are replicated in the current coalition, are bound to come to the fore.

What is of most interest here is how parties with such radically opposing views on Poland's relationship with Western Europe in general and the EU in particular were able to enter into government with one another. Also of interest is the fact that elements of both the left, namely the PSL, and elements of the right, namely assorted christian democrats, both evince a hostility towards the idea of European integration. In other words, the issue of European integration cuts across both the class and clerical-religious cleavage. That parties which possess such contrasting views on such a fundamental policy area could enter into coalition with one another demonstrates two things about politics in Poland: the first is the validity of the findings presented in this chapter concerning the nature of cleavage and party competition in Poland today. The second is that, rhetoric to one side, in the early and mid-1990s, the question of Poland's relationship with the EU was not of fundamental concern to either parties or their supporters and voters.

Indeed, as negotiations with Brussels become ever more decisive, attitudes toward the 'European question' are likely to become of greater importance to both the electorate and the parties themselves. The AWS contains factions that, despite their claim to be representatives of post-1945 christian democracy, are in fact Catholic nationalist. In turn, the SLD contains individuals who on the grounds of ideology view the EU with deep-seated suspicion. Regardless of where such parties and individuals, together with the PSL, are positioned on the left-right ideological spectrum; they are above all in competition for the votes from small-town rural Poland, from church-going traditionalists, from the less well educated, from the elderly, and from among those who are still wary of or overtly hostile towards Germany.

This admittedly rather large caveat to one side, the most syncretic government is, however, the current AWS and UW coalition formed in 1997. Yet there are still many areas over which sharp controversies have appeared. In addition to monetary, education, and health policy and the issue of the complete decommunisation of the state, once again they include the question of European integration. We have already noted the fact there are serious divisions within the AWS over this matter. For its part, the UW, representing as it does economic and political liberalism and Poland's nascent middle class, is the only major party that is clearly and unequivocally committed to the European project. The extent to which coalitional coherence can be maintained as negotiations gather pace is open to question.

Given that it is a conglomeration of parties and factions, there is little agreement within the AWS itself as to the overall thrust of governmental policy. The political incoherence of the governing camp has been, of course, a source of hope for the opposition that it might regain power at the next election, even though surveys do not yet indicate major growth in support for the SLD, and especially for the PSL.

Our analysis of the political composition of Polish cabinets has demonstrated the relevance of nationalist, clerical and populist parties, as well as the parties perceived as post-communist, to both wider political life and coalition formation in Poland. The ZChN, PChD and Peoples Agreement (PL) have been represented in three cabinets. The SLD and PSL have enjoyed the same level of cabinet participation, albeit for a longer period of time than the parties of the first group. The parties of a liberal orientation have enjoyed shorter, more infrequent periods in power. The UD and KLD participated in two cabinets, although, as we have seen, the free market and pro-European policies of the UW are continually called into question, not only by the post-communist opposition but also by factions within the AWS.

The number of instances of the alternation of power may also measure the level of the competitiveness of the party system in the governmental arena. It is obvious that because of the shortness of the period under discussion, the conclusions to be drawn may be only tentative. What is worth noting, however, is that in Poland this alternation is frequent, as in other countries in the region. Every parliamentary election since 1989 has led to a change in government. This may be interpreted as an indicator of the high level of competitiveness within the party system. Yet there are signs that the current government may prove to be more durable than all of its post-1989 predecessors. If so, there is the chance for the right to dominate the political scene for a long time. I do not believe, however, that in the near future the traditional pattern of political competition between the strong united left and strong, although more fragmented, right, will be reflected in Poland. There is no political tradition for such a pattern and there are no strong incentives to 'Westernise' Polish politics because of the strength of the aforementioned nationalist current that opposes 'the imitation of foreign models'.

The main precondition of the 'Westernisation' of Polish political competition is the implementation of two important political tasks. One of them is the successful transformation of the economy from the centrally planned to the free market model. This requires that losers in the reform process obtain a certain degree of protection from the market via a limited amount of state intervention. Those parties which accept the need for a (strong) welfare state have a greater chance of attracting a majority of voters than those who extol the virtues of 'hard monetarism' and rapid marketisation. The second task lies in dealing successfully with the remnants of the nomenklatura. Until a common position on this question is achieved, the main axis of political competition will be the attitude to the past and its legacy. Nine years after the demise of the communist regime the evolution of this axis of political competition seems to be of the greatest significance to all concerned.

## Bibliography

Antoszewski, A. *Wybory parlamentarne 1993*, Wroclaw: Wroclawska Oficyna Nauczycielska, 1993.

Antoszewski. A. and Herbut, R. *Socjaldemokracja w Europie Zachodniej. Studium porownawcze*, Wroclaw: Wydawnictwo Uniwersytetu wroclawskiego, 1995.

—— (eds) *Demokracje zachodnioeuropejskie. Analiza porownawcza*, Wroclaw: Wydawnictwo Uniwersytetu wroclawskiego, 1997.

Bar, A. 1984. 'The emerging Spanish party system: is there a model?' *West European Politics* 7, 4, 128–53, 1984.

Bartolini, S. and d'Alimonte, R. 'Plurality, competition and party realigment in Italy: the 1994 parliamentary elections', *European Journal of Political Research* 29, 1,105–42, 1996.

Bartolini, S. and Mair, P. 'Policy competition, spatial distance and electoral stability', *West European Politics* 13, 4, 2–16, 1990.

Budge, I. and Farlie, D. *Explaining and Predicting Elections. Issue Effects and Party Strategies in 23 Democracies*, London: Allen & Unwin, 1983.

Cotta, M. 'New party systems after dictatorship: dimensions of analysis. The East European cases in a comparative perspective', *Universita degli Studi di Siena*, Working Paper 9, 1992.

Diamond, L. Linz, J. and Lipset, S. *Politics in Developing Countries. Comparing Experiences with Democracy*, Boulder: Lynne, Rienner, 1990.

Dudek, A. *Pierwsze lata III Rzeczypospolitej*, Krakow: GEO, 1997.

Enelow, J. and Hinich, M. *The Spatial Theory of Voting*, Cambridge: Cambridge University Press, 1984.

Gallagher, M. Laver, M. and Mair, P. 1992. *Representative Government in Western Europe*, New York: McGraw-Hill Inc, 1992.

Gebethner, S. (ed.) *Polska scena polityczna a wybory*, Warszawa: FIS, 1993.

—— (ed.) *Wybory parlamentarne 1991 i 1993*, Warszawa: Wydawnictwo Sejmowe, 1995.

—— (ed.) *Wybory 97'. Partie i programy wyborcze*, Warszawa: Elipsa, 1997.

Grzybowski, M. 'Poland: towards overdeveloped pluralism', in S. Berglund and J. Dellenbrant (eds) *The New Democracies in Eastern Europe. Party Systems and Political Cleavages*, Aldershot: Edward Elgar, 1994.

Herbut, R. *Systemy partyjne Europy Zachodniej. Ciaglosc i zmiana*, Wroclaw: Wydawnictwo Uniwersytetu wroclawskiego, 1996.

—— 'Systemy partyjne krajow Europy Centralnej i Wschodniej oraz wzorce rywalizacji politycznej', in A. Antoszewski and R. Herbut (eds), *Demokracje Europy Srodkowo – Wschodniej w perspektywie porównawczej*, Wroclaw: Wydawnictwo Uniwersytetu wroclawskiego, 1997.

Huntington, S. *Trzecia fala demokratyzacji*, Warszawa: PWN, 1995.

Ieraci, G, 'Centre parties and anti-system oppositions in polarised systems', *West European Politics* 15, 2, 17–34, 1992.

Kitschelt, H. 'European party systems: continuity and change', in M. Rhodes, J. Heywood and V. Wright (eds), *Developments in West European Politics*, London: MacMillan Press, 1997.

Klingemann, H. D. Hofferbert, R. and Budge, I. *Parties, Policies and Democracy*, Boulder: Westview Press, 1994.

Körösenyi, A. 'Stable or fragile democracy? Political cleavages and party systems in Hungary', *Government & Opposition* 28, 1, 87–104, 1993.

Laakso, M. and Taagepera, R. 'Effective number of parties: a measure with application to West Europe', *Comparative Political Studies* 12, 1, 3–27, 1979.

Laver, M. and Shepsle, K. *Making and Breaking Governments. Cabinets and Legislatures in Parliamentary Democracies*, Cambridge: Cambridge University Press, 1996.

Lijphart, A. 'Typologies of democratic systems', *Comparative Political Studies* 1, 1, 3–44, 1968.

—— *Democracies. Patterns of Majoritarian and Consensual Government in Twenty One Countries*, New Haven: Yale University Press, 1984.

—— *Electoral Systems and the Party Systems*, Oxford: Oxford University Press, 1996.

Markowski, R. 'Polski system partyjny w srodkowo-europejskiej perspektywie', *Studia Polityczne* 8, 8, 29–56, 1998.

Mayer, C, 'A note on the aggregation of party systems', in P. Merkl (ed.) *Western European Party Systems*, New York: Free Press, 1980.

Morawski, W. *Zmiana instytucjonalna. Spoleczenstwo, gospodarka polityka,* Warszawa: PWN, 1998.

Morlino, L. 'Political parties and democratic consolidation in Southern Europe', in R. Gunther, H. Diamandouros and J. Puhle, *The Politics of Democratic Consolidation. Southern Europe in Comparative Perspective*, Baltimore: Johns Hopkins University Press, 1995.

O'Donnell, G. 'Illusions about consolidation', *Journal of Democracy* 7, 2, 34–51, 1996.

Pehe, J. 'The consolidation of the party system in the Czech Republic', presented at the conference The Emergence, Development and Consolidation of Parties and Party Systems in East Central Europe, Leipzig, July, 1995.

Pedersen, M. 'The dynamics of European party systems: changing patterns of electoral volatility', *European Journal of Political Research* 7, 1, 1–26, 1979.

Raciborski, J. *Polskie wybory. Zachowania wyborcze spoleczenstwa polskiego*, Warszawa: Scholar, 1997.

Rae, D. *The Consequences of Electoral Laws*, New Haven: Yale University Press, 1971.

Sartori, G. *Parties and Party Systems. A Framework for Analysis*, Cambridge: Cambridge University Press, 1976.

Schumpeter, J. *Kapitalizm, socjalizm i demokracja*, Warszawa: PWN, 1995.

Toka, G. 'Political parties and democratic consolidation in East Central Europe, presented at the conference' The Articulation and Representation of Interests and the Party Systems in Central and Eastern Europe, *Duszniki-Zdroj*, 28–30 September 1997.

Wesolowski, W. 'The formation of political parties in post-communist Poland', in G. Pridham and P. G. Lewis (eds) *Stabilising fragile democracies. Comparing new party systems in southern and eastern Europe*, London: Routledge, 1996.

Wiszniowski, R. 1997, 'Wybory parlamentarne w krajach Europy Srodkowo – Wschodniej. Polityczne konsekwencje systemow wyborczych', in A. Antoszewski and R. Herbut (eds) *Demokracje Europy Srodkowo – Wschodniej w perspektywie porownawczej*, Wroclaw: Wydawnictwo Uniwersytetu wroclawskiego, 1997.

# 6 Parties and the Polish party system

## The process of structuring the political space

*Ryszard Herbut*

### Introduction

The focus of this chapter is upon political parties in Poland, and the way in which the party system in which they operate changed in the 1990s. In order to facilitate the analysis, a number of conceptual tools are employed. Particular attention is paid to the notion of 'political space', the characteristics of a party system during a time of regime transition, and the nature of sociopolitical cleavage. It is the contention of the author that the Polish party system will not develop according to the West European model because it lacks the cleavage structure upon which such systems were built. Instead, the Polish party system exhibits all the signs of having skipped this phase, and moved into a post-industrial phase of development, with uniquely Polish characteristics.

In order to understand what makes the Polish party system so unique, the reader is familiarised with the basis of post-communist party competition in Poland. The development of the two main political blocs is traced, and the paradoxes of what keeps the blocs intact, despite inner-bloc programmatic differences, are explored. In order further to clarify the situation for the reader, there is investigation of matters such as the changing nature of party organisation and campaigning in Poland. The piece ends with an examination of the problems that Poland's projected entry into the EU is causing among the parties and electorate in Poland.

### The dynamics of change

The consequences of the political changes that swept over Poland in the 1980s have given impetus to the search for new perspectives on the democratisation process underway in Poland and elsewhere in East-Central Europe. One of the main areas of study has been the dynamics of party and party system change. As Deschouwer and Coppieters suggest '. . . the uniqueness of the current process does not preclude thinking through analogies' (1994: 1). This means we should compare the experiences of East-Central Europe with those of the western half of the continent. Pre-existing explanatory models may be applied, but they have to be used carefully. Researchers must take into account the uniqueness of the changes in East-Central Europe and the specific parameters of the environment in which the development of the party system is taking place. It is necessary therefore to describe certain research assumptions important for the analysis in order to create a proper framework for the debate about the party and party system formation in Poland.

First, the transition towards democracy has been accompanied by the emergence of new societal structures, a new political culture and new patterns of political behaviour. Whereas political competition in Poland and other liberal democracies may be defined as a process of co-operation among the political parties engaged in the game of politics, the creation of a competitive party system in Poland entails constructing a new political space. The pattern of political competition as a fixed standard of co-operative behaviour among political parties means that they have to acquire specific programmatic, ideological and organisational identities. The process of shaping of political space is determined not only by parties acting as a group of select individuals with an interest in obtaining public office and political leadership. In addition they have to compete for votes. As Cotta says, the parameters of a new political space have to be defined both on the elite and mass level dimensions of politics (Cotta 1996: 69).

Second, when analysing political parties we should take into consideration at least two further interrelated perspectives. On the one hand, we have to examine parties as separate entities having some organisational and programmatic traits, and political strategies in the context of the current environment. This means parties have to follow some rules and characteristics contingent upon the social and political conditions which form their environment. The competition for votes puts them under continuous pressure to adjust their policies to the needs and values of society.

In Western Europe at least, parties have traditionally been viewed as the products of social cleavages. According to Stein Rokkan, mass politics (in Western Europe) has been structured by major societal cleavages. He attempts to explain the creation of parties as the products of these cleavage patterns, the parameters of which determine political alignment. Four critical junctures are claimed to have occurred in the historical development of West European society that produced particular societal and political cleavages. Parties, once constructed in their modern form, have the ability not only to passively or even actively adapt, they have the capacity to some extent create their political and social environment. Parties cannot therefore be treated as a simple expression of social forces. They are objects worthy of study in their own right. Attention may also be centred on political space and the party system itself. Whether it be for ideological, strategic or programmatic reasons, parties interact and compete with one another in some way in the political space available to them. The positions of parties are likely to vary considerably according to which dimensions of the political space are salient at any one time. The space between parties can be great or small, and such arrangements determine the degree of polarisation of the party system (Sartori 1976).

We may assume that such approaches encourage a more dynamic treatment of party systems. Some seek to identify changes in the party system that can be traced back to cleavages in societal conditions 'outside' the system. Others are complementary in laying bare the cross-pressures under which the party system operate. Either way, parties can try to shape or reshape voters' preferences by using their own resources of legitimacy or influence (the preference-shaping model) or pursue preference-accommodating strategies when voters' preferences are fixed and cannot be changed by the process of competition (Dunleavy 1991: 112–44).

We must also remember that it is impossible to propose a universal model of party systems that can be employed regardless of societal and organisational conditions. There are no parties 'suitable for all kinds of weather'. Rather, there are parties which are effective in fulfilling or otherwise, their functions within a concrete environment. The external environment delivers political resources of various kinds, such as economic, cognitive, cultural, and financial capital. A party can use these resources for its own goals by forming political strategies or creating the organisational structures in advance of taking political action. Political parties do not develop in an institutional or societal vacuum, and are influenced among other things by electoral laws (as the case of Poland clearly shows), social cleavages, the activity of other participants present in the political space, and the historical origins of political movements. With regard to Poland, we should also pay particular attention to the fact that party development is a continuous process, and one which is strongly goal-oriented. The factors facilitating effectiveness of that process derive from:

(1) Changes in the practice of politics in Poland that should be examined as part and parcel of the establishment of civil society;
(2) Changes in relations between parties that are strongly correlated with the process of the formation of political cleavages and political issues, and the primacy of politics in the stage of transformation;
(3) Changes to the state that are regarded by elite groups as a crucial point of reference in the process of embedding parties in new social conditions. For varying reasons, transformation has encouraged parties to anchor themselves within the state;
(4) Changes in the conception of democracy put forward by particular segments of the elite or political class as a whole, for instance toward a socially or market-oriented democracy.

## Party development in Poland

The Polish transition can be understood in fairly linear terms. Vigorous opposition under the banner of Solidarity managed to guarantee the reconstruction of civil society, compelling the communists to accept democratic reforms. Solidarity was active within the embryonic civil society of the 1980s, and negotiated a compromise with the regime that opened the way to the contestation of state power through parliamentary elections. Only the period of martial law could be regarded as having disturbed the logic of the Polish revolution. The revival of reformists in the Polish United Workers Party (PZPR) at the end of the 1980s consolidated the position of the anti-communist opposition. The Round Table Agreement of 1989 was the fruit of this process, and ensured some degree of political continuity in the transformative period.

Patterns of change and continuity have had an impact on the formation of those political parties that emerged immediately after 1989. Yet there is no single source of party identity. In general terms, we can draw a distinction between a 'historically-derived identity', comprised of ideological traditions and programmatic statements, organisational continuity and contemporary political appeals, put forward by a party at any given time as a means of making it a distinct actor within a party system (Sartori 1976: 171; Waller 1996: 24, 25). Thus, in the case of Poland, components of party identity associated with the past (both the post-democratic and the communist) and the present, combined with the impact of the national and international environment, coupled with organisational history, have formed the basis for constructing and for distinguishing individual party types present in the party system. In order to sharpen the focus of our analysis, let us examine the successive stages in development of parties in Poland since 1989.

### *Stages in the development of political parties*

Unlike in established democracies, attempting to define the parameters of parties and the party system within states experiencing a transition toward democracy is a complex task. According to Cotta this is a consequence of at least two factors characteristic of transition periods (Cotta 1996). First, the political space is still in a state of flux and, second, party identities are not yet strongly defined. 'As a consequence, problems internal to parties easily become problems of the party system and vice versa' (Cotta 1996: 71). Bearing this in mind, let us now examine the various stages in the development of the Polish party system.

The first stage began in 1988, and concluded with the Round Table Agreement and the 'contractual' or 'compartmentalised' election of 1989 (Olson 1993: 435). The two political forces, the PZPR and its allies and Solidarity, perceived one another as ideological rivals, and policy questions formed a mere backdrop to the real issue, which was in fact a plebiscite on the future direction of Polish society. Neither of the main protagonists can be viewed as having been parties in the classical sense of the word. Solidarity was a type of 'non-party' forum or 'party-movement'. As such, it acted as an umbrella organisation or specific grand coalition of the large majority of forces opposed to the communist regime. For most oppositional activists and their supporters, Solidarity was the natural vehicle through which to demand change, although as a political actor it had no specific orientation. In effect, during the 1989 election campaign, Solidarity did not advance any specific policies or (electoral) programme. Solidarity's prime goal was '. . . non-party mobilisation of public opinion in opposition to the communist regime' (Cotta 1996: 77). As the fight against the old regime was concentrated exclusively under the banner of Solidarity, so the new regime which appeared after the 1989 elections was superficially monolithic in character.

Solidarity was a mass organisation that under the cover of trades' unionism managed to construct a new regime. More importantly, with the coming to power of Solidarity, we witnessed not only the coming to power of a new government, but a change of political system. As a movement-oriented organisation, Solidarity was representative of the general will of the public, but it possessed few of the characteristics typically ascribed to political parties. For example, it had no stable and definite membership, a vague programme, and horizontal as opposed to vertical ties between members (Herbut 1998: 116). Solidarity was an organisation that derived its identity from the needs of the period of systemic change.

The second stage in the transformation process took place between 1990 and the mid-1990s. In 1990, differences within Solidarity became clear and a process of internal fragmentation began. Solidarity began to divide into several groupings, some of which appeared as significant players in the first fully competitive elections of 1991. These post-Solidarity parties included the Democratic Union (UD), the Liberal Democratic Congress (KLD), and the Christian-National Union (ZChN). The process of the institutionalisation of political parties had begun. We can identify at least three features of that process which mutually reinforced one another.

The first is that of 'overparticisation' (Agh 1998: 204, 205). There were so many parties, that in 1991 no party was able to secure more than a small fraction of the electorate, on average some 5.3 per cent. Most of these parties should be regarded as marginal phenomena, as there were too many parties for any of them to play a significant role in public life. Overparticisation signals that parties have started to be the main agents of political change and the dictators within the political system. Typical of this phase is the fact that such parties are very weak on the ground, although they are powerful actors in the distribution of resources.

The second ingredient was that of 'parliamentarisation'. Only parties represented in parliament may be counted as relevant. The process of parliamentarisation has had a great impact on structure and style of activity of the political parties. Their top-down character has been reinforced and, in effect, parties appear remote from the population as a whole. The gap between the narrow party elite, which consists of the party faction in parliament and party professionals based at the national headquarters (where such a distinction can actually be made), and the rank-and-file has increased. Thus, as soon as parties were successful in getting activists elected, they subdivided into electoral and government components, each of which maintained its own identity and leadership. They then began activity in the three following areas:

(1) At the parliamentary/governmental level, where office holders were prepared to enter into compromises even if that meant compromising on original principles.
(2) Party central offices also began to embark upon a series of activities aimed at creating and maintaining minimum levels of internal party consensus.
(3) Parties also began to organise themselves at the grassroots level (Katz 1996: 111).

We must remember that parliamentarisation leads to the creation of asymmetrical inter-organisational relations particularly in the public office arena. As a result, control mechanisms are instituted within political parties which involve a process of bureaucratisation. Such a process may be considered as normal in the development of parties. However, in Poland, bureaucratisation has appeared remarkably quickly for such a young party system. A clientelistic mode of operation has appeared in which internal power and decision-making criteria primarily derive from specific personal relations.

A third stage in the development of the Polish party system became apparent from the mid-1990s. In a sense, the process of the institutionalisation of parties has mainly been state-oriented. The state becomes a means by which parties can help ensure their own persistence and organisational continuity. Symbiosis between parties and the state should be regarded as an effect of forces in place during the transformation process. Parties have been forced to use the state and its institutions as a way of self-preservation. As a result, they have become rooted in society, but this has not been achieved through interaction with society, and the penetration of particular strata. There is prima facie evidence to suggest that a series of cartel parties has developed within the Polish party system (Agh 1998: 206). However, in the opinion of this author, this phenomenon does not yet exist in Poland. Thus, instead of the term 'cartel party', it is more appropriate to use the term 'cadre party of the transitional character'. Such parties may be on the way to cartelisation, and share some of the characteristics of cartel parties, but they still have some way to go.

## *The main types of parties in Poland*

In this section, a 'genetic' approach will be employed as a means of grouping parties according to their origins, roles and situation in party formation. Only those parties that have had a significant parliamentary presence in recent years will be considered. Ideological criteria will also be employed in order to place the parties in conventional party families.

*The post-communist parties*

1 The Democratic Left Alliance (SLD). This is an electoral coalition of leftist groupings the core of which is/was the Social-Democratic Party of the Polish Republic (SdRP). In 1999 the SLD created a separate party organisation. The SdRP was formed in 1990 following the dissolution of the PZPR. The SLD has assumed a modernising image and has promoted an 'ideologically free' pragmatic direction.

2 The Polish Peasants Party (PSL), which was formed in May 1990. This is the successor to the United Peasants Party (ZSL) of the communist period. It is an agrarian party and supports the idea of closer co-operation with the Catholic Church. As a party of farmers and rural Poland, the PSL gives expression to a commitment to a social welfarist model of the market economy. It also supports the continued existence of a comprehensive welfare state, and calls for a significant level of state intervention in the socio-economic spheres.

*The post-Solidarity parties.*

1 The Freedom Union (UW) was formed in April 1994 following the fusion of the UD and the KLD. The UW presents itself as a centre force that is ready to co-operate with both left and right. Pragmatism seems to be a main component of the UW's strategy, and it views itself as some kind of 'connecting road', which seeks to bind different factions together. The party programme is a mixture of right-oriented and (modern) social democratic postulates. In economic matters, the UW subscribes to the principles of the market economy, restricted interventionism, privatisation and so forth. Some elements within the party have supported separating church from state, and have opposed Catholic integralism. The leaders of the UW are very cautious on the issue of decommunisation. Value issues, for example attitudes toward religion and the past have constituted the main line of conflict between the UW and other post-Solidarity groupings, positioned further to the right.

2 Solidarity Electoral Action (AWS) was formed in July 1996 as a confederation of centre-right parties. The AWS is inspired by Polish Catholic values. As a right-oriented organisation it supports pro-market policies and privatisation but accepts limited state intervention as a method of regulating market forces in order to achieve social goals. Several tendencies have been identified within the AWS, ranging from centrist and

less ideological christian democrats, to those who favour 'national values' and some form of christian socialism. Within the AWS there are five major party or party-like organisations: the Social Movement AWS, the Conservative-Liberal Party (SKL) and the so-called Christian Democrats, the former Centre Accord (PC), the Christian-National Union (ZChN), and the Party of Christian Democrats (PChD).

## Modelling parties: some hypotheses and comments

Parties in Poland have had little opportunity to form stable relations with the electorate. They have had to approach a wide clientele of potential voters, rather than opt for support from well-defined segments of society. There are at least two reasons for this state of affairs having come to pass. The social experiment of the communist regime contributed to the creation of an undifferentiated or mass society. Therefore, economic and political interests are not rooted within specific groups as they are in Western Europe. Social groups do not exist as political entities which have specific political interests, and which act in a uniform way. There is no party that in reality could act as the representative of a particular socioeconomic group. As a consequence, parties lack the ability to segment the electoral market and to isolate particular target groups as the recipients of their manifestos.

We can expect that the amorphous structure of society will change and acquire a more differentiated, market-based composition. Yet this does not mean that a future model of electoral identification similar to that which appeared during the genetic phase of development in the western countries will appear in Poland. In the phase of post-communist reconstruction, collective interests have been subordinated to individualistic interests, and in line with this, Polish society is likely to continue to fragment in a manner typical of post-industrial societies. Parties will not be able to avail themselves of social cleavages in the classical sense of the word, simply because they will not appear. In such circumstances, parties will have no chance of assuming mass strategies because they will be unsuitable and outdated in the post-industrial individualistic environment.

In an open electoral market, floating voters will appear with quite pragmatic expectations with regard to electoral choice. Such voters are reluctant to identify with a particular party or even with a party's general platform. Parties are facing a volatile and transitory electorate, which is reluctant to enter into long-term identification with partisan symbols or ideologies. In such conditions, parties and voters have no real chance to form relatively stable forms of identification, based on traditional historic structures. Political parties do not represent particular social groups. We have to deal with the phenomenon of segmentation of society rather than with its pluralisation. In such a situation, parties have only slight chances of assuming control over social groups and representing them in an exclusive manner. In an open market, parties have to be orientated not only toward a particular clientele, but toward a broader potential electorate, and that means they will have to present appeals which cut across segmental boundaries. In the process of electorate creation, economic interests have a rather marginal significance, and at the top of the agenda, transitory factors or historical reasons appear, dictated by the existing state of affairs. The process of stabilisation of the electorate is feasible but there is no guarantee that it will follow the cleavage patterns identified by Stein Rokkan, Seymour Martin Lipset, and Derek Urwin.

### *The character of cleavages and the formation of party preferences*

So far we have established that the current nature of, and the antecedents to, societal cleavage in Poland is very different from that of the contemporary western democracies. It would, in fact, be very difficult to claim that there are cleavages in the sense of the word used by some authors. In Poland there are potential social cleavages but they are not institutionalised. Individual voters are members of such potential social groups, but they are not integrated into a set of relevant collective political identities. So instead of social cleavages there are very significant political cleavages, and that phenomenon is connected with the predominance of politics and political issues during the post-communist transformation. Political competition in Poland shows some degree of structure but only on the micro-level rather than on the macro-level. Citizens encounter too much uncertainty to identify precisely their economic interests, and how they should be persuaded to articulate them through consistent support of a single political party. Yet successive elections have given politicians and voters the opportunity to engage in a process of co-operation: 'of reciprocal signalling of political preferences and party programme that might facilitate the formation of alignments' (Kitschelt, Dimitrov and Kanev 1995: 145).

According to Meyer, three factors have had specific relevance in the process of formation of political cleavages and party preferences. The first is conflict arising from political issues, mainly to do with strategy and the direction and pace of transformation. The second involves a socioeconomic cleavage between the winners and losers from the transformation. And third, we have subjective features such as the motive for individual electoral decision conceptualised in terms of lifestyle, milieu or value orientation (Meyer 1997: 1).

In the subsequent attempt to capture votes, parties may actually seek to shape rather than reflect the attitudes of voters. Electoral preferences shown in public opinion research were disregarded by some parties in the electoral campaign of 1991. The immediate problems of decommunisation and privatisation were mentioned by only 2–5 per cent of respondents, an extremely small proportion when one considers the importance given to these problems by the parties themselves. Since then, voters have consistently shown themselves disinterested in decommunisation and the abortion laws, whereas many politicians have continued to focus upon these questions. In the electoral campaign of 1993, economic issues emerged as a main political division determining the pattern of electoral competition. Ideological conflicts continue to be largely confined to the elite level, and precisely because of this, have determined party politics and party competition. Elite behaviour is adversarial rather than consensual, and politicians have tried to inject their own ideological issues of the day to the societal level.

In the first phase of transition (until 1993), political conflicts/cleavages seemed to be more ideological in character than interest-specific. We must be aware that economic conflicts are less bargainable than ideological ones and sometimes it is difficult to reach a compromise. In the main, this is true of Poland. As we have already noted, developed cleavages did and do not exist in Poland, and the social structure is rather homogenous. Yet, the process of transition has been strongly ideologically motivated. Centrifugal rivalry at the elite level at least, should be treated as a confrontation between the 'old' and the 'new' political actors. The transition has provoked fundamentalist types of reaction at the level of the macro-system, as a reaction to the normative crisis of the state. As a consequence, conflicts have focused around the axiological base of the new order (Wnuk-Lipinski 1996: 249–51). In the political arena at least three pairs of fundamental dichotomies have appeared in reaction to the radical changes of the past few years. These are: the religious versus secular; nationalistic versus universalistic (pro-European integration) views; and a pro-welfare orientation and promotion of state-provided welfare versus support for a market-oriented state as a part of the liberal concept of the minimal state.

### *Party membership*

The membership of Polish political parties is low. Horizontal as opposed to vertical connections dominate Polish parties. Such a phenomenon seems to be a clear consequence of the state of society, and governs the way parties act in this field. First of all, parties do not depend on members for financial resources and instead rely on the state. The state provides subsidies to parties in the form of payment according to their electoral results and the number of seats they hold in parliament. In addition, parties represented in parliament receive extra funds in order to finance their parliamentary activities. State subsidies reduce the necessity of parties to find external sources of income, and in effect it is not necessary for them to create and maintain a complex system of funding organisations affiliated to the party.

Second, in Poland we can observe a popular fear or mistrust of parties. There is a traditional lack of interest in joining associations, as much as anything else in reaction to years of communist compulsion. Third, civil society is very weak, and pressure groups do not yet fully articulate sectional interests. Thus, there is a shortage of organisational resources that could be exploited for electoral gain. Pressure groups need access to decision-making processes and centres where the concentration of power lies. They need governmental parties as a focal point around which to structure their interests. Yet, given that cabinets and parties come and go, it is better for interest groups to avoid becoming too closely identified with any one single party. In contrast to Western Europe, where pressure group activity is differentiated, and where such groups seek to influence all parties represented in parliament, the attitude in Poland seems to be that as no one party holds the state in its thrall, there is no sound reason to cultivate specific parties (Kopecky 1995: 520). As we shall see, this has had an effect on the way in which Polish parties organise themselves.

### *Cadre type strategies*

When parties are unable to create stable forms of identification with the electorate through the control of some segments of society it means that, as nearly every voter is available to every party in an open electoral market, they have to find alternative ways of penetrating the electorate. In such a situation, the mass media provides a very effective channel of communication with society. The crucial role played by the mass media in mobilising supporters is likely to enhance the position of the upper echelons of the party (elite) and to diminish the role and utility of party membership. Generally, such a cadre strategy involves minimal organisation and is concentrated around candidates and those individuals which public opinion associates with a particular party (Herbut 1998: 121).

This modern version of cadre strategies allows politicians to use television and other electronic media as a means of mobilising substantial electoral support. We must be aware that this media-based cadre strategy is not in reality chosen by parties, but forced upon them owing to the lack of alternatives. Obviously, this strategy has an effect upon the conduct of election campaigns. They have become more professionalised and capital intensive. Such (expensive) campaigns tend to have the following features:

(1) They are centralised and the role of the local workers and volunteers is supplemented or replaced by the new professionals, consultants and agencies. These latter are guided from the centre, which leads to the so-called nationalisation of campaigns and standardisation of their agendas.
(2) Despite this greater use of specialists, the politicians are still in charge.
(3) Market segmentation appears, which means not only that catch-all strategies are employed, but that these strategies are combined with those aimed at specific target groups.

There is also increasing emphasis upon the role of party luminaries. This personalisation of campaigns can be seen as the by-product of the extremely strong position of elites during the process of democratic transformation. The focus upon party leaders may also to help stabilise political choices in the minds of the general public. Very often the attributes of the leadership is about the only thing parties can focus upon during campaigns. During the ongoing process of institutionalisation, two groups of individuals have played very important roles. They are the party leaders who play a role as 'visible assets' during the campaigns, and the 'invisible assets', comprised of consultants and specialists, responsible for the process of image formation and the selling of that image to the public.

Another major factor lying behind this personalisation of politics is the fact that, for the most part, there is little to focus on. We have already noted that Poland does not possess the cleavage pattern which up until recently, at least, characterised Western European societies. Neither are the issues that excite elites of paramount interest to the majority of voters. On top of that, policy differences between the major parties are not in fact that great in most areas. Within this context it is increasingly difficult to persuade voters to study and analyse manifestos in any depth. In such a situation, the personality of leaders is the only tangible evidence of difference that a voter can focus upon.

### *Patronage strategies*

This type of strategy is available only to those parties that have a reasonable chance of entering government. Such a strategy involves the trade of (government) jobs and services for votes. In order to effective, such a strategy requires that elected officers have control over appointments and the distribution of services. We must not overlook the phenomenon of patronage in post-communist regimes. The role that patronage plays in party politics is a function of the relationship between democratisation and de-bureaucratisation. In general, when democratisation precedes bureaucratisation, parties are able to co-opt the bureaucracy and use it to their own advantage. When the opposite is true, the bureaucracy is able to protect itself and politicians are forced to adopt strategies of another sort. The most efficient solution for dealing with the potential abuse of patronage comes where cadre parties are striving to gain support within the electorate and are faced with a relatively weak bureaucracy.

Polish parties are able to promote patronage strategies that are the by-product of the democratisation process. Bureaucratisation had in fact taken place decades earlier under the communists. When the political break-through of 1989 occurred it was in a situation where the bureaucracy was well entrenched. The PZPR had used patronage strategies in a global way and the state was in fact its creature. It would clearly be a matter of quite some time before the old guard could be sent packing. Nevertheless, the process of re-bureaucratisation has been conducted by all parties since 1989. Parties are once again trying to root themselves within the state and to take advantage of the spoils available. The politics of state may be new, started almost from scratch, but the rules are old.

## The emerging party system

The contemporary Polish party system is young, having come into being just after the 1989 Round Table Agreement and the so-called 'war at the top' initiated by President Lech Walesa in 1990. As should be clear by now, it is difficult to fit the Polish case to the complex models of party systems such as those devised by Giovanni Sartori or Gordon Smith. Having said that, there are signs of stabilisation, and we shall now vindicate that claim, through an examination of the various stages of development since 1989.

### *The first stage: 1989–1993*

When examining the first stage of development, we can identify some of the characteristics of the format and mechanism of party competition by examining the quality of interactions and by drawing attention to some significant trends. First of all, parties that were identified with the communist past were marginalised. This process of marginalisation referred to all parties of the socialist, social-democratic and even the left liberal type. The left wing was relatively unorganised and a majority of parties identified themselves with the right or centre of the spectrum. Anti-communism seemed to be a sufficient criterion in the formation of centre-right parties.

At least until 1991, there was a relatively strong and homogenous centre occupied by the Solidarity bloc. Within this bloc, centripetal drives eventually prevailed over centrifugal tendencies. In the immediate post-communist years, party politics was characterised by the domination of historically based cleavages, based, for example, on attitudes towards the past. Neither socioeconomic cleavages nor any other bundle of issues were of any real significance. Therefore, value dimensions, attitudes towards religion, and decommunisation or lustration, did not form the basis for conflict. The major political consequence of the lack of salience of questions based around socioeconomic issues was the failure of the political left.

After the 1991 elections, centrifugal tendencies among post-Solidarity parties appeared. Differences between them became obvious and the politics of confrontation came to the fore. That such a split could occur signalled that the decisive question of whether or not to move from a communist to a post-communist system had been solved. The question was now one of what kind of liberal democracy and market economy would be instituted. Socioeconomic issues started to play a significant role in party politics and the development of the party system, and divisions appeared not only between post-Solidarity and post-communist parties but also among parties that had originated within Solidarity. In addition, the value dimension began to assume a greater importance. Although the centre remained strong, ideological differences between the parties began to become more apparent. Yet, the appearance of such differences did not preclude the possibility of broad coalition formation. This was because centrifugal and centripetal forces existed side by side, and the former still dominated. The presence of cross-cutting cleavages also facilitated coalition formation.

Another characteristic of the immediate post-communist party system was its extreme fragmentation. A huge number of parties entered the competition for votes, and many succeeded in obtaining representation in the Sejm. Most of these parties were too small and narrow in outlook to aggregate the demands of significant proportions of the electorate into coherent policy programmes. Many of them were in fact more interest group than party. The centre-right wing was particularly over-crowded, and parties tried to outbid each other with immoderate programmes and slogans. In part, this fragmentation resulted not from cross-cutting cleavages but rather from personal animosities at the elite level. Extreme fragmentation was also a consequence of the novelty of the situation and the consequent lack of firm loyalties on the part of voters toward parties.

The post-Solidarity parties clearly possessed coalitional potential and each of them was practically indispensable in the process of coalition formation. Other parties possessed blackmail potential only. The main party of the left, the SdRP, was isolated and some politicians of the former anti-communist opposition viewed it as an anti-system party. Initially the PSL was similarly rejected, but eventually some post-Solidarity parties took advantage of the party's presence in parliament and entered into government with it. Lech Walesa played a role in bridging the gap between the PSL and parties from the Solidarity camp in order to create a 'presidential coalition' firmly under his control. He appointed Waldemar Pawlak, the leader of the PSL, to the post of prime minister even though many post-Solidarity parties opposed his mandate. Not only were they wary of the PSL, they were wary of Walesa's desire to turn Poland into a presidential republic.

During this period, coalition governments were the norm, as no party was able to secure a majority in the Sejm. In addition, successive governments were unable to form stable majorities. Even when the leaderships of governing parties reached compromise, there was no guarantee that resultant proposals would be adopted by the Sejm. During this period, Poland had four governments with anything from five to seven parties present in government. Post-Solidarity parties formed the core of the party system. Moreover, we can distinguish between two distinct groups of such parties. The first was the group of 'initiating parties', such as the UD and KLD, which took the leading role in the complex process of coalitional bargaining, and had the last word on the selection of the coalition partners. The second group was that of the 'supplementary parties', which commanded only a minority of seats in parliament but were from time to time necessary coalition partners. Such parties included the PChD and the Christian Peasants Party (SLCh).

In effect, there was a unipolar centre-right bargaining system. The post-Solidarity parties institutionalised a relatively clear pattern of party alignment based mostly on ideological lines, and on attitudes towards the past. A majority of post-Solidarity parties became more clearly identified with the politics of the right. Yet, bi-polar left–right competition appeared within the post-Solidarity bloc, together with a substructure of cleavage lines related to issues such as: the role of the president; the nature and scope of economic reform, and the salience of traditional values in modern Poland.

The majority of parties rejected the possibility of grand coalitions. Having said that, policy differences between most parties were relatively narrow and, with few exceptions, parties jockeyed for centrist positions, although there were of course differences between them. The first set of differences concerned attitudes towards the communist past. Some post-Solidarity politicians perceived the post-communist parties as dysfunctional to the new political system, whilst others did not. Yet, we must not interpret such attitudes as corresponding to the left-to-right dimension characteristic of Western Europe. The cleavage line was between the former ruling parties and the new parties with anti-communist origins. In turn, this cleavage was cut by one concerning value systems and attitudes toward the resolution of socioeconomic problems. No matter how the SdRP might change its policies, it was generally perceived by post-Solidarity parties as an unacceptable partner in the bargaining system

### *The second stage: post-1993*

Following the 1993 elections, a quite different pattern of political competition appeared. First of all there has been a consolidation in the number of parties represented in parliament. After the 1993 elections, the number of such parties was reduced to six and after the 1997 elections to five. Since 1993 Poland has had a two-bloc system, comprising of parties aligned into two rival alliances of the post-communist left and the post-Solidarity centre-right. After the 1993 elections the post-Solidarity leftist Labour Union (UP) played a pivotal role. However, the UP failed to win parliamentary representation in 1997, and since then, the PSL has attempted to fulfil this role with scant success. Parliamentary forces have divided into those who support and those who oppose the government. After the 1993 elections the former bloc was much stronger than was the latter, and the governmental parties had commanding majorities in both chambers of parliament. Since the 1997 elections, the balance of power in parliament is more symmetrical in character. One of the factors responsible for this is the active role of the president as an actor in inter-party bargaining. President

Aleksander Kwasniewski has exercised his constitutional powers on a number of occasions, presenting himself as a moderator. Of course some claim that his real intention in such interventions is to strengthen the hand of the SdRP. Whatever the case, in 1999, and with an eye on the forthcoming presidential elections, he reduced the frequency of such actions. Following the 1993 elections, only the SLD and PSL had coalitional potential. The situation changed radically after the 1997 elections, when the newly formed AWS entered parliament resulting in the UW gaining added coalition potential.

After the 1993 elections, the SLD did not have enough seats to govern on its own. It had little choice but to opt for coalition with the agrarian PSL. Although the coalition made sense because both were post-communist parties, there was little else that the two had in common. The SLD had established itself as a pro-market oriented party, but was compelled to co-operate with an old-style, conservative, clerical and agrarian party. As a result, it was a coalition more negative than positive in its programmatic character. Both the UD and the UP had temporary coalitional potential but the leaders of both parties did not want to take the risky step of entering into government with the post-communist SLD.

At the 1993 elections around 34 per cent of the electorate voted for parties which failed to gain parliamentary representation. Most of these wasted votes went to post-Solidarity parties. As a result, the Solidarity camp found itself grossly under-represented in parliament. Following the defeat of Lech Walesa in the 1995 presidential election, the post-Solidarity elite realised that their only chance of removing the governing parties and winning the next election would be through the formation of a centre-right coalition. During 1994 and 1995, five loose coalitions of post-Solidarity groupings had been established outside the parliamentary arena, such as the church-sponsored St Catherine's Convent. Finally, and building upon this work, in 1996 the AWS was founded as a grand coalition of post-Solidarity parties.

Following the 1997 elections, the post-Solidarity AWS and UW formed a new centre-right coalition. In reality it was the only coalition that was politically as opposed to technically feasible. To complicate matters, the AWS is in fact an electoral confederation of many parties with different programmes. So on most issues, the policy distance between the UW and sections of the AWS is quite large. The composition and the durability of both post-1993 two-party coalitions as minimal winning coalitions is strong evidence of the domination of the 'genetic matrix' in the process of structuring the pattern of competition within Polish politics.

During and subsequent to the 1993 electoral campaign, it seemed that the ideological–historical conflicts had weakened, allowing the socio-economic dimension to emerge as a main political division within the political sphere. Yet the 1995 presidential campaign and 1997 parliamentary campaigns contributed to the revival of old-style competition between the would-be supporters of the new regime and partisans of the old one. Although they remain the main representatives of both wings (left and right), the SLD and AWS remain coalitions of different groupings and parties, and a process of internal consolidation has been occurring. The SLD now exists as a party, and within the AWS, the Social Movement AWS, is emerging as the dominant player. These moves can be taken as evidence that Poland is firmly moving away from the period of post-communist transition.

### *The structuring of party alternatives*

In qualitative terms, the post-communist–anti-communist historical cleavage should be regarded as a factor that operates quite independently of other cleavage lines. This is clearly evident in the way parties act in the process of bargaining and coalition-building. On the socioeconomic dimension, the UW is much closer to the SLD than to other post-Solidarity parties, but the chances of co-operation between both parties are slender on account of genetic differences. With regard to the SLD and the PSL, once again genetic factors help explain why the two continue to co-operate with one another, just as much as they explain the continued alliance between the AWS and the UW.

If we employ a model of two-dimensional policy space we take into consideration two cleavages concerning the parties' socioeconomic policies and value orientations. At the moment a process of mutual re-enforcement is taking place, leading to the construction of political blocs. The process of structurisation of policy space in Polish politics has been dominated by two cross-cutting types of political conflicts.

The first of these occurs at the socioeconomic level, and occurs over issues such as market-oriented reform versus state intervention, and monetarist versus anti-monetarist ideas. The main dividing line is between parties which support the market economy, rapid privatisation and low inflation, and parties which represent the option of combining economic interventionism with a large-scale welfare state. In Figure 6.1, the horizontal socioeconomic dimension has been conceptualised as the space between the left pole, labelled 'economic etatism', and the right pole of 'economic liberalism'.

There is also a cleavage between those parties which accord primacy to the preservation of national identity and those that support liberal values. Parties' attitudes and policies in regard to the process of integration of Poland with the European Union (EU) have constituted one of the main lines of division within the cultural dimension. In the diagram, the value dimension (vertical line) has been conceptualised as the space within the upper pole called 'liberal cultural attitudes' and the lower pole entitled 'traditional cultural attitudes' (see Figure 6.1). There are four blocs of parties that represent four distinct political options (orientations):

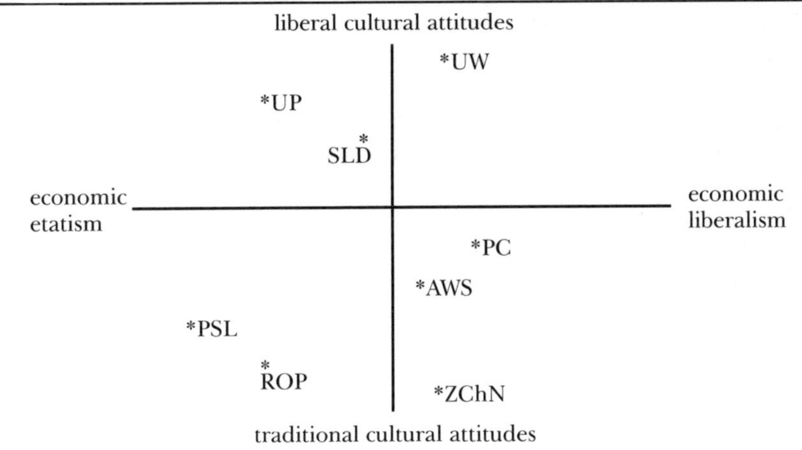


UP – Labour Union
SLD -Democratic Left Alliance
PSL – Polish Peasant Party
UW – Freedom Union
AWS – Solidarity Electoral Action
PC – Centre Accord
ZChN – Christian National Union
ROP – Movement for the Restoration of Poland

*Figure 6.1* Two-dimensional political space.

- the liberal (UW)
- the liberal-traditionalist (e.g. AWS)
- the traditionalist-etatist (the PSL and Movement for the Restoration of Poland (ROP)
- the liberal-etatist (SLD)

An interesting perspective on the degree of maturity of the parties and their long-distance strategies can be gathered from their attitudes towards the EU and the related process of integration. There are some data and information that provide us with opportunities to assess the overall stance of parties towards the membership, integration and specific policies associated with the process of 'Westernisation'. First of all, we must acknowledge that until the mid-1990s, there was a high degree of consensus among political parties in favour of Polish membership of the EU. Since then, there has, however, been some change in attitudes at both elite and mass levels.

There are pro-European parties that are more or less unconditional in their support of Poland's projected entry in the EU. The most important of such parties are the UW and the SLD for whom this has been a constant feature. The UW has been perceived as the most 'Euro-enthusiastic' party in Poland. The party supports the process of economic integration with the EU, and its programme concentrates primarily on the technical aspects of integration. For the SLD, Polish involvement in the EU remains an important issue. During the electoral campaign of 1997, the party employed the slogan 'Europe as Fatherland of Fatherlands'. In so doing it signalled its opposition to plans, no matter how tentative, to create a 'federal Europe'. Despite this difference, both parties perceive the issue of integration in national terms rather than in party political terms.

We then have parties such as the AWS and PSL, whose attitudes towards integration can be characterised as 'critical acceptance of the EU'. In general, the AWS supports the process of integration but the declarations of some politicians are cautious. It is clear that for both parties, the perceived national interest should take precedence over Europe. There is also considerable resistance to the surrender of national sovereignty, based on the belief that the moral obligation of Polish politicians is the preservation of the national and Catholic identity of the country. Given the PSL's constituency, the party argues that integration should take place on condition that the state undertakes to protect the (agricultural) 'internal market'. Some politicians from the PSL and the AWS claim that there is an 'asymmetry of benefits' in relations between the EU and Poland. In the words of the leading PSL politician and former prime minister, Waldemar Pawlak, 'either we will take care of our interests or we will be exploited; squeezed like a lemon'. The PSL and some politicians from the AWS have expressed the fear that integration would require a levelling-down of social benefits and that certain industries would require state protection in order for them to remain competitive. The PSL in particular is anxious about the future of Polish agriculture and the consequences of the opening of Polish markets to EU products. However, we must emphasise that occasional individuals to one side, both parties do not see any alternative to integration.

Only the small, so far marginal parties of the far left and right, such as the Federation of Polish Communists, can be regarded as explicitly 'anti-European'. Having said that, these forces are now seeking to consolidate. In April 1999 the Polish Agreement was founded by some conservative politicians as an alternative to the pro-European AWS. At the moment, the Polish Agreement represents an attempt by Catholic integralist groups, such as the National Party, Polish Family and Polish Youth, to raise their political profile.

The issue of European integration is tending to become more and more politicised in Poland, but there is no evidence at elite level that attitudes towards integration and Europe can yet be regarded as an independent cleavage line or dimension of competition within the party system. All parties represented in parliament, save the ROP, have agreed in substance that the issue of integration 'tends to be a valance, not a positional issue that divides parties'. Yet, as the negotiations move on to ever more substantive issues, the probability is that the situation could change, as there are signs that there is a process of polarisation of attitudes towards the EU at the mass level.

## Bibliography

Agh, A. 'The end of the beginning: the partial consolidation of East Central European parties and party system', in P. Pennings and J.-E. Lane (eds), *Comparing Party System Change*, London and New York: Routledge, 1998.

Bar, A. 'The emerging Spanish party system: is there a model?', *West European Politics* 7, 4, 128–55, 1984.

Cotta, M. 'Structuring the new party systems after the dictatorship', in G. Pridham and P. Lewis (eds), *Stabilising Fragile Democracies*, London and New York: Routledge, 1996.

Deschouwer, K. and Coppieters, B. 'A West European model for social democracy in East-Central Europe?', in M. Waller, B. Coppieters and K. Deschouwer (eds) *Social Democracy in a Post-Communist Europe*, London: Frank Cass, 1994.

Dunleavy, P. *Democracy, Bureaucracy and Public Choice*, New York: Harvester/ Wheatsheaf, 1991

Herbut, R. 'Partie polityczne i system partyjny', in A. Antoszewski and R. Herbut (eds) *Polityka w Polsce w latach 90. Wybrane problemy*, Wroclaw: Wydawnictwo Uniwersytetu Wroclawskiego, 1998.

Katz, R. 'Party organization and finance', in L. LeDuc, R. Niemi and P. Norris (eds) *Comparing Democracies. Elections, Voting in Global Perspective*, London: Sage Publications, 1996.

Katz, R. and Mair, P. 'Changing models of party organization and party democracy', *Party Politics* 1, 1, 5–28, 1995.

Kitschelt, H. Dimitrov, D. and Kanev, A. 'The structuring of the vote in post-communist party systems: the Bulgarian example', *European Journal of Political Research* 27, 2, 143–60, 1995.

Kopecky, P. 'Developing party organizations in East-Central Europe', *Party Politics*,1, 4, 515–34, 1995.

Meyer, G. 'New wine in old bottles?', paper presented at the conference on Articulation and Representation of Interests and the Party Systems in Central and Eastern Europe, Duszniki Zdroj, Poland, 28–30 September 1997.

Olson, D. 'Compartmentalized competition: the managed transitional election system of Poland', *The Journal of Politics* 55, 2, 435–41, 1993.

Sartori, G. *Parties and Party Systems: A Framework for Analysis*, vol. 1, Cambridge: Cambridge University Press, 1976.

Waller, M. 'Party inheritance and party identities', in G. Pridham and P. Lewis (eds) *Stabilising Fragile Democracies*, London and New York: Routledge, 1996.

Wnuk-Lipinski, E. *Demokratyczna rekonstrukcja. Z socjologii radykalnej zmiany spolecznej*, Warszawa: PWN, 1996.

# 7 The marketing of political parties in the 1990s

## A comparative study

*Robert Wiszniowski*

This chapter explores a number of themes and issues concerning the style of modern party campaigning in Poland. The main part of the analysis is constituted by an examination of the three general elections held during the 1990s. There is no doubt that political marketing can be viewed as one of the interpreters of party contests. Thus, party strategies and tactics during the parliamentary campaigns of 1991, 1993 and 1997 can be examined and assessed in terms of a marketing framework. The advantage of this approach is that it structures explanations of the modernisation of campaign procedures in Poland within a comparative perspective, which in broad terms is common to all European liberal democracies. In the light of this comment, this chapter also gives due attention to inter-country differences. For reasons of space, I am deliberately limiting the scope of my analysis to the impact of political marketing upon party strategies, and to parallel analysis of Polish party campaign styles and tactics vis-à-vis those encountered in European Union (EU) states. Within that analysis the growing influence of marketing techniques first adapted by parties within the EU will be evaluated.

### An academic approach to campaigning

Contemporary campaigning has come a long way from the campaign practices of old. As David M. Farrell and Martin Wortmann state: 'Party campaigns are becoming more professional' (Farrell and Wortmann 1987: 297). Thus the use of a political marketing framework to describe modern party election campaigns can be useful for comparison over time, as well as between and within countries. Numerous authors have in recent years devoted a great deal of attention to evident changes in election campaign styles and tactics in the context of new technological and structural changes in current American and West European politics. For example, Larry Sabato (1981) has discussed the increasing importance of political consultants in elections. William Crotty and Gary Jacobson (1980) have focused on the growth of Political Action Committees (PACs) and the concomitant 'decline' of American political parties. Robert Agranoff (1976) has analysed campaign changes under the rubric of 'new politics', comprising the employment of marketing experts, and increased emphasis on the use of the media. David M. Farrell (1996) has stressed technological developments, namely the television and telecommunications revolution, and pointed to the modernisation of political campaigns. Ian Budge (1996) and Richard S. Katz (1996) have described how organisational and functional changes within political parties have been stimulated by new technological developments. Ian McAllister (1996) has concentrated on a process of modernisation of political communications that is producing an increasing 'personalisation' of presidential as well as parliamentary campaigns.

It is appropriate at this point to provide a definition of campaigning. David M. Farrell suggests: 'Election campaigning is the process by which a campaign organisation, be it a party, candidate, or special interest organisation, seeks to maximise electoral gains. It consists of all those efforts, promotional or financial, made by the campaign organisation to meet that goal' (Farrell 1996: 161). Within such a context we can view campaigning as a process that requires organisational, promotional and financial resources. The extent to which such resources are available to a party has a great influence upon party strategies, which are formulated by using political marketing techniques in order to market the 'product'(McCarthy 1975).

## Factors that affect campaign strategies

Changes in campaign styles and party strategies generally relate to a composite of many key factors, such as greater use of the media; in particular, a growing emphasis on television, use of opinion polls, the employment of professional consultants, improved communications strategies, and party organisational processes. Before we attempt any description and classification of Polish campaigns, we need first to consider the context in which they occur. Context plays an important role in determining the nature of a party's campaign, for instance, as party-oriented or candidate-oriented, as 'defensive' or 'offensive', as 'traditional' or 'innovative', and as 'reactive' or 'proactive'.

Bearing these points in mind, it is appropriate for us now to analyse those environmental factors that significantly affect campaign strategies. First of all, we need to be aware of differences between and within political systems, i.e. between and within presidential or parliamentary systems (Butler and Ranney 1992). A popular view exists that presidentialism promotes candidate-oriented campaigning. In turn, parliamentarism, which is more typical of Western Europe, means that 'the modern campaign is manifestly a party campaign' (Bowler and Farrell 1992: 223). Yet it would be wrong to conclude that all European campaigns (in parliamentary states) are party oriented. If we select just one example, that of the degree of autonomy of organisation and self-reliance of the individual candidates, we find a number of European cases that reveal distinct candidate-based activities. For instance, the French, Finnish and, in a limited sense, Polish marketing strategies are consistent with the quasi-presidential nature of the political systems and the effects of electoral systems that in part focus attention on individual candidates.

The nature of a country's electoral law is another factor that must be taken into account (Katz 1980). It is commonplace that the electoral and party systems it helps to generate, play an important role in influencing the degree of campaign centralisation and which types of campaign practices and marketing techniques are applied. In that sense, list systems, such as that employed in Poland, where voters choose between parties and their programmes, tend to promote greater campaign centralisation than do plurality or single transferable vote electoral systems where voters are choosing between candidates. Also as Richard S. Katz shows, the availability of campaign finance makes a major difference to the nature of the campaign mounted by the parties and, in particular, to their degree of professionalisation:

> Elections vary in the degree to which party organisations recruit candidates and control access to the ballot; in the degree to which parties develop positions on issues to which all their candidates adhere; in the degree to which parties generate and channel the resources required for effective campaigning; in the degree to which voter choice is oriented toward party rather than individual candidate; and indeed in the degree to which it makes a practical difference which party wins.
>
> (Katz 1996: 107–8)

As Katz concludes, the degree of 'partyness' of elections also depends on, and is reflected by, the nature of the parties and the way in which the state regulates the campaign activities of candidates, parties, and their supporters (see Table 7.1).

Media systems, i.e. styles of media coverage, rules of election broadcasts, or the right to make use of television spots (Kaid and Holtz-Bacha 1995) are also of great importance. In today's world it is no longer a novelty for the vast majority of people living in democratic societies to experience election campaigns through the media. Media systems have a significant influence on the campaigning, whether it be at supranational, national, regional or local level.

The macro-level aspects of media systems are also of great importance, particularly when it comes to media presentation in the news (see Table 7.2). Four in particular are relevant. The first is the balance between public and commercial/private broadcasting. Second, we must consider the political autonomy of broadcasting from government and political parties. Third, the rules and traditions surrounding party access to broadcasting must be taken in to account. Finally, the extent of partisanship in the printed press must also form part of any analysis.

The nature or type of party systems, whether they be of the two-party or multi-party variety (Sartori 1976) is another factor in helping to determine marketing strategies. For instance, in a two-party system, such as in Great Britain, dominant parties tend to go for broke in their election campaigns, by trying to win elections outright. By contrast, in the multi-party systems of continental Western Europe the parties have to make allowances for possible coalition partners and so they temper their campaign messages appropriately. Neither must we forget that styles and modes of campaigning also vary across the different parties within each system (Bowler 1990). In some cases we can observe the role of challenging parties may be complicated by the degree to which the party space is crowded, and, especially in multiparty systems, challengers may spend as much time campaigning against other challenging parties as against incumbents. Smaller parties are more concerned with attracting new support than are larger parties, whose main aim is to maintain their vote share. According to David M. Farrell, another difference is that: 'Right-wing parties and "catch-all' parties find the abandonment of ideological baggage and the switch to greater reliance on leader image much easier to achieve than left-of-centre parties, which tend to have more complex–and potentially more restrictive–organisational forms' (Farrell 1996: 163–164).

It is clear from this brief discussion that campaign strategies can be greatly influenced by the context in which the campaign is occurs, and by the types of parties carrying out the campaign. Many of these environmental factors will be dealt with in more depth later in the text in our discussion of Polish campaign practices during the 1990s.

## Party and candidate strategies: the Polish and West European experiences compared

In the comparison of elections in the United States with those held in Western Europe, a distinction tends to be drawn between candidate and party-oriented campaigning. It is really rather easy to see how United States' elections can be characterised as candidate-oriented. As Richard S. Katz and Robin Kolodny put it:

> congressional elections are not primarily national contests between parties either, but (although either characterisation carried to its extreme would be an exaggeration) are better described as simultaneous constituency-level contests between pairs of candidates who incidentally have party labels and patronise a common core of purveyors of campaign services.
>
> (Katz and Kolodny 1992: 184)

Contrast this with the European situation where, as we have concluded, the campaign is more party than candidate-oriented, but recently has

*Table 7.1* Statutory control of campaign finances

| Country | Reporting | | | | | Audit of reports | Publicity | Limits on contributions | Limits on expenditures |
|---|---|---|---|---|---|---|---|---|---|
| | *Interval* | *By* | *To* | *Of* | *Disclosure* | | | | |
| Austria | Annual and prior to every campaign | Ps. | Government auditors | Expenditures | Details of income sources, and expenditures | Yes | Annual public statements | | |
| Germany | Annual and every campaign | P. | Speaker of the federal diet | Contributions, expenditures, assets, total campaign expenditures | Amount of contributions, donor's identity | Yes | | No | No, but implicit because grants have to be matched by party's private income |
| Greece | Annual and every campaign | C. and P. | President of parliament and minister of interior | Contributions and balance sheets, campaign expenditure | For donations greater than 200,000 drachmas, identity of contributor | Yes | Published in Athens newspapers | No | No |
| Italy | Annual and every campaign | P. | Minister or speaker of legislature | Contributions and expenses | Amount of contributions and donor's identity | Yes | Daily press, reports to legislature | No | No |
| Netherlands | No reporting | n/a | n/a | n/a | n/a | n/a | n/a | n/a | n/a |

| | | | | | | | | | |
|---|---|---|---|---|---|---|---|---|---|
| Poland | Annual and every campaign | Ps. | State election commission | Contributions, expenditures, and total campaign expenditure | For donations greater than 10 times of one prognoses “month salary” from budget sphere, amount of expenditure, details of income sources, and expenditures | Yes | Published in party’s newspapers, daily press, and other forms regulated by the State Election Commission | No, but excluding the foreign donations | No |
| Spain | Every campaign | Ps. | Election Commission | Contributions and expenses | Revenue and expenditures | No | Public inspection | On amount and source | On amount spent in each district |
| Sweden | Not mandatory | n/a | n/a | n/a | n/a | n/a | n/a | n/a | n/a |
| United Kingdom | Every campaign | C. | Returning Officers | Contributions and expenses | Details of expenditures, contributions from corporations and trade unions | No | Public inspection, report to legislature | No | On total amount if candidate accept public funds |

*Source*: LeDuc, Niemi and Norris 1996: 42–44 (Austria, Germany, Greece, Italy, Netherlands, Spain, Sweden, United Kingdom): Law on political parties, 27.06.1997/Dz.U. No. 98, poz. 604 (Poland).

*Note*: C: candidate; P. or Ps: party or parties; n/a: not applicable.

*Table 7.2* Media penetration and political controls on television

| | *Television and radio* | | | *Campaign regulations of TV coverage* | | | | *Newspapers* | | |
|---|---|---|---|---|---|---|---|---|---|---|
| *Country* | *Ownership: public or commercial* | *TV sets per 1,000 people, 1994* | *Radio sets per 1,000 people, 1994* | *Paid political aids* | *Free time to parties* | *Fair balance rules* | *Leader debate in last elections* | *Number of national dailies* | *Circulation per 1,000 people* | *Press freedom* |
| Austria | Commercial | 475 | 622 | Yes | Yes | Yes | | 34 | 358 | Free |
| Belgium | Commercial | 447 | 776 | No | Yes | Yes | Yes | 23 | 221 | Free |
| Denmark | Public | 528 | 1,012 | No | No | | Yes | 46 | 359 | Free |
| Finland | Commercial | 488 | 998 | No | No | Yes | Yes | 66 | 547 | Free |
| France | Public and commercial | 400 | 895 | No | Yes | Yes | Yes | 96 | 166 | Free |
| Germany | Public and commercial | 643 | 868 | Yes (not on public broadcasters) | Yes | Yes | No | 358 | 386 | Free |
| Greece | Public and commercial | 195 | 419 | No (not on state owned-stations) | | Yes | | 117 | | Free |
| Italy | Public and commercial | 423 | 794 | Yes | Yes | Yes | No | 73 | 105 | Free |
| Netherlands | Commercial | 485 | 902 | No | Yes | Yes | | 86 | 307 | Free |
| Norway | Commercial | 423 | 796 | No | No | Yes | Yes | 83 | 548 | Free |
| Poland | Public and commercial | 292 | 428 | Yes (50% lower price than commercial aids) | Yes | Yes | Yes | 45 | 181 | Free |
| Portugal | Public and commercial | 176 | 216 | | | | Yes | 28 | 83 | Free |
| Spain | Public and commercial | 389 | 304 | No | Yes | Yes | Yes | 102 | 82 | Free |
| Sweden | Public and commercial | 471 | 885 | Yes | Yes | Yes | Yes | 107 | 520 | Free |
| Switzerland | Commercial | 406 | 851 | No | Yes | Yes | | 98 | 496 | Free |
| United Kingdom | Public and commercial | 434 | 1,145 | No | Yes | Yes | No | 104 | 393 | Free |

*Source*: LeDuc, Niemi, and Norris 1996: 45–48 (Austria, Belgium, Denmark, Finland, France, Germany, Greece, Italy, Netherlands, Norway, Portugal, Spain, Sweden, Switzerland, United Kingdom); Law act on election rules to the lower house of Parliament, dated: 28.05.1993/ Dz.U. No. 45, poz. 205 (Poland).

become increasingly 'personalised' in character, partially as a result of the 'mediaisation' of politics. We can cite many examples that lend credence to such a conclusion, for instance, the growing significance of party leaders during the parliamentary campaigns. In principle, the basic point is that most campaigns are becoming more presidential, which means they are more personalised. Yet this is still far from saying that they are 100 per cent candidate-oriented. Within this context we have to remember the leading candidates in West European elections are strictly connected with individual parties, or alliances, or even parliamentary factions. In other words, candidates who have been selected by the party subsequently may be dropped, and whoever campaigns on behalf of a party, and is therefore associated with its standpoints and ideology, cannot disregard the party patrons.

It would of course be facile to assert that only environmental factors determine the context of campaigning. Candidate-oriented campaigning can in some ways be a product of unstable, unpredictable, economic, or socio-political situations that arise during campaigning, or just before it starts. Candidates may also be forced to rely on their own individual means. In some ways, candidates have little chance to present themselves as primarily candidates of a party, because, on the one hand, their party may be negatively assessed by a great number of voters and, on the other hand, party competition is constrained by so-called 'anti-party' campaigning rules. The Finnish national election of 1995 provides us with an appropriate example. The election campaign was strongly focused around the Centre Party (KESK) prime minister, Esko Aho, and Paavo Lipponen, leader of the Social Democratic Party (SDP). During the election period, Finland was in the midst of its deepest economic crisis ever, with an unemployment rate close to 20 per cent, a rapidly growing budget deficit, and all time high interest rates. It was the economic crisis and how to solve it which dominated the campaign for all eighteen parties which contested the election (Sundberg 1996: 325). We have already noted how Paavo Lipponen, as leader of the main opposition, was given much attention in the mass media. He took full advantage of four years in opposition and attacked the Centre Party which, in his view, was primarily responsible for the economic crisis. The parliamentary campaign to the unicameral Finnish parliament shows how environmental factors (economic and political) determine the nature of political party strategies in the electoral arena. In the Finnish case, we have a clear example of how such campaigning in most instances produces an 'anti-party' oriented campaign, where the political position of party leaders plays a significant role in reproving the whole party.

By way of contrast, the Polish parliamentary election of 1997 shows how crucial and important political marketing techniques, especially television, produce strongly candidate-oriented campaigns. In most cases, the Polish parliamentary elections were strictly connected to party leaders, 'candidate and [the] party leader's personality play a tremendous role and become a particular argument of all competing parties as the way for maximising electoral gains' (Herbut 1998: 122). For instance, the campaign of the Movement for the Restoration of Poland (ROP) could be analysed as an appropriate example in the context of the personalisation of party strategies. As Janina Paradowska states, the ROP did not produce a broad team of party leaders. Indeed, in the electoral arena only one party leader, Jan Olszewski of the ROP (prime minister between July 1991 and June 1992), chose to focus on his personal achievements as prime minister (Paradowska 1997: 6). Yet, we have to remember, as Ian McAllister has observed: 'increased coverage of party leaders in political communication does not necessarily mean that leaders have therefore become more important than parties or issues in voters' choices' (McAllister 1996: 281). However, there is no doubt that the process of modernisation of political communication has produced an increasing personalisation of politics, even in the strong parliamentary systems of Western Europe.

## The professionalisation of campaigning: the Polish case

The object of this section of the chapter is to attempt to locate Polish campaigning practices within the framework of political marketing techniques and demonstrate how campaigning in Poland has changed over time. Concepts devised by David M. Farrell (1996) and Pippa Norris (1997) are useful in drawing a distinction between Polish and West European campaigning. Taking into account their suggestions, we have a large matrix within which we can categorise and analyse Polish campaigns in comparative perspectives. Changes in campaigning, historically, and technically, have a substantial impact on the institutional context of election campaigns, such as the structure of communications. As Pippa Norris states: 'The focus is upon the key actors in the election-leading politicians, professional consultants and commentators-the battle to dominate the campaign agenda, and the process of electoral communications' (Norris 1997: 194–5).

We can build on this foundation in order to come to understand Polish elections as a dynamic interaction between three agencies: the electorate, the parties and the media. Each part of this so-called trinity can be seen to play a distinct role in constructing the meaning and determining the outcome of campaigns (Norris 1997: 195). We can analyse parties as organisations that seek to attract, reinforce and mobilise supporters. The electorate may be considered to be a structural and very often, politically indifferent group, but one which is nevertheless actively engaged in the campaigning process. In turn, the media provides the essential linkage function allowing parties and voters to communicate with each other (see Table 7.3).

When we strip away the nuances of individual arguments, despite the varying emphases of the different campaigners, the single theme they all share in common is one of change, of Polish campaigns becoming enormously more

*Table 7.3* Professionalisation of campaigning

| | *Pre-modern* | *Modern* | *Post-modern* |
|---|---|---|---|
| Campaign organisation | Local and decentralised | National and centralised | National co-ordinated, but locally – operational autonomous |
| Preparation | Short-term action and ad hoc prepared | Long-term action and "stable" prepared | Permanent campaign and "still" prepared |
| Agencies, consultants | Minimal use | Greater use | Even greater use of consultants |
| Central co-ordination | Party leaders | Party leaders and consultants | Consultants as campaign personalities |
| Feedback | Local canvassing | Opinion polls | Opinion polls, focus groups, Internet web sites |
| Use of media | Direct and indirect Direct=national and local press, posters, meetings, direct mail Indirect=radio leadership speeches | Indirect and direct Indirect=television broadcasting through national channels and major territorial Direct=national and local press, party press, posters, billboards, meetings, press conferences | Direct and indirect Direct=television narrowcasting through fragmented channels (cable TV), targeted ads, direct mail: e-mail and video-mail, virtual-conferences (meetings) – political cyber-space |
| Campaign events | Local public meetings, whistle-stop leadership tours | TV debates, press conferences, "Pseudo-events", billboard wars | More "mediatised" and locally fragmented |
| Costs | Labour intensive, low budget and local | Labour and capital intensive, higher costs for TV programmes, and for PAC(s) | Capital intensive, highest costs for TV ads, and for consultants, professionals |
| Targeting of voters | Social class support base (specific social categories of voters) | Catch-all (all categories of voters) | Market segmentation (specific categories of voters) |

*Source*: Farrell 1996: 170; Norris 1997: 196.

professionalised. The inaugural fully free parliamentary election took place in 1991 (Antoszewski 1998: 79–93). The second competitive election came in 1993, and the third in 1997. To put it another way, Poland held three general elections within a very short space of time. Quite remarkably, each successive campaign was clearly more 'Western' in style than the one that preceded it. Two aspects of this Westernisation, or modernisation should immediately be stressed. The first aspect is strictly connected to the vital role of televisual technology. There is a general opinion that usage of television provides a good indicator of the level of professionalisation of campaigning in the country. Television's influence on campaigning attracts key attention in election studies and it is generally at the centre of debates over what exactly is 'new' about contemporary campaigns. Many scholars who analyse the role of mass media in society point out that television has contributed to the nationalisation of campaigning, in the sense that everything is focused on one leader, one party, one set of common themes (Farrell 1996: 172–3).

The second aspect is more technical/organisational in nature and linked to the expansion of political consultants and agencies which specialise in political campaign management in East-Central European countries. We have many examples of parties and presidential candidates who have employed marketing firms, and technical advisors. For instance, in 1993 Saatchi & Saatchi prepared the parliamentary campaign for the Liberal-Democratic Congress (KLD). During the Polish presidential campaign of 1995 the media professional, Jacques Séguéla, who played a dominant role in François Mitterrand's presidential campaign in 1988, advised Aleksander Kwasniewski, the eventual winner of the presidential campaign (Ulicka 1996: 159–60).

When we asses the Polish parliamentary elections, it is worth mentioning that in 1991 at the beginning of the post-communist era, campaigning should be classifying as having been pre-modern. Use of this term signifies that in many cases the preparations for the campaign were *ad hoc*, and generally unstructured. The main features of pre-modern campaigning are summarised in the first column of Table 7.3. Yet, we have to remember the first fully free election should also be analysed as a great victory for the idea of democracy. Political parties acted spontaneously, principally in order to achieve their own political ends, without any principled party alliances, rather than as well-organised and rational political institutions. A common picture that emerges from an examination of the 1991 parliamentary election is of the huge number (111) of parties that contested the election. In 1993 the number was reduced to twenty-five, with a further reduction to twenty-two taking part in 1997. The reductions were, of course, due in part to changes in the electoral system (see Table 7.4), as well as the reconstructed processes of party strategies. Preliminary forms of strategic marketing management appeared during the 1993 campaign. Modernisation was also connected to changes in the law regarding public subsides for those parties present in the electoral and parliamentary arenas (see: Table 7.5),

*Table 7.4* The electoral systems to the *Sejm* 1991, 1993 and 1997

| | *Year of election* | *Electoral system in Lower House (Sejm)* | *Formula for Lower House* | *Threshold for Lower House* | *Closed, preferential, or panacharge list for Lower House* | *Maximum years between elections for Lower House* |
|---|---|---|---|---|---|---|
| Poland | 1991 | Proportional representation | LR-Hare-Niemeyer | n/a | Preferential | 4 |
| | 1993 & 1997 | Proportional representation | D`Hondt | 5% of the district vote (for parties) 8% of the district vote (for coalitions)<br><br>7% of the national vote (both for parties and coalitions) | Preferential | |

*Source*: Data of the author.

*Note*: LR – Largest-Remainders electoral formula; n/a– Not Applicable.

and on television advertising (see Table 7.6). There were also changes concerning the regulation of TV debates and access to airtime. These changes were complemented by more public meetings, at which party candidates and leaders spoke, and circulated party manifestos and candidate biographies. Billboards, posters and newspaper advertisements were all more noticeable than they had been in 1991.

In 1997 television played the main role. This in turn resulted in greater centralisation and massification of the campaign. The campaigning directed more attention on direct forms of marketing techniques than previously. The leaders of the larger parties were presented to the public at organised rallies, parades and pop concerts. For example, the Polish rock group Lady Pank promoted the Freedom Union (UW), and the disco Polo group Bayer Full lent its support to the Polish Peasants Party (PSL). What was really novel about the campaign was that, for the first time, some campaign material was available on the Internet. Internet usage took another step forward at the beginning of the 1997 campaign, when the main parties, the AWS, SLD, UW, PSL, ROP and Labour Union (UP), engaged in an on-line debate with one another (Ociepka 1999: 159). There were even open primaries on the Internet before election day, in which a total of 867 people took part. The results of this virtual election were not, however, a useful predictor of the eventual outcome, especially for the UW, which

*Table 7.5* Public subsidies to parties and candidates

| | *Direct Subsidies* | | | | | |
|---|---|---|---|---|---|---|
| *Country* | *Recipient* | *Interval* | *Basis* | *Eligibility* | *Specific grants or Services* | *Indirect Subsidies* |
| Austria | Parties, parliamentary groups | | Per vote | | Billposting broadcasting, printing ballots, party oundations, press and publications, women's and youth organisations, education and information | |
| Belgium | No direct subsidies | n/a | n/a | n/a | Broadcasting, encouragement of voting | |
| Denmark | Parliamentary groupspress | Annual | Per seat | | Broadcasting, and publications, women's and youth organisations | |
| Finland | Parties | Annual | Per seat | | Billposting, broadcasting, press and publications, women's and youth organisations | |
| France | Presidential candidates | Election | | | Billposting, broadcasting, printing ballots, press and publications | Kickbacks of deputy salaries |
| Germany | Parties | Election | Per vote | 0.5% of votes for national party lists of candidates, or 105 of first votes cast in constituency if no regional list has been accepted | Broadcasting, subsidies to party foundations | Tax deductions |

*Table 7.5* (continued)

| | *Direct Subsidies* | | | | | |
|---|---|---|---|---|---|---|
| *Country* | *Recipient* | *Interval* | *Basis* | *Eligibility* | *Specific grants or Services* | *Indirect Subsidies* |
| Greece | Parties | Election | Equal distribution of 10% of flat rate, then per vote. If coalition, amount divided by agreement among parties involved | Participated in last election and got at least 3% of votes. Has a list of candidates in at least 2/3 of the electoral districts. If a coalition: received at least 5%–6% of votes, depending on coalition status | | |
| Ireland | No direct subsidies | n/a | n/a | n/a | Broadcasting | |
| Italy | Parties and parliamentary groups | Annual, every election | Per vote | Parties presenting candidate lists in more than 2/3 of constituencies and obtaining no less than 300,000 votes or 2% of total amount of votes | Broadcasting (according to guidelines of Parliamentary Committee), women's and youth organisations, education and information | Kickbacks of deputy salaries |
| Netherlands | No direct subsidies | n/a | n/a | n/a | Broadcasting, encouragement of voting, party foundations, women's and youth organisations | Tax deductions |
| Norway | Parties, parliamentary groups | Annual | Per seat | | Broadcasting, nomination costs | |

*Table 7.5* (continued)

| | *Direct Subsidies* | | | | | |
|---|---|---|---|---|---|---|
| *Country* | *Recipient* | *Interval* | *Basis* | *Eligibility* | *Specific grants or Services* | *Indirect Subsidies* |
| Poland | Parties, parliamentary groups | Annual, every election | Per seat, per vote (but each party must submitted | Party must be registered with National Election Commission | Broadcasting of each party(s) electoral committee (law act regulation), political TV aid (the cost: 50% less than commercial aid), subsidies to party foundations, public subsidies, economic activity, but without any National Treasury connections | Tax exemp-tions and deduc-tions |
| Spain | Parties | Annual, every election | Per vote | Party must have won at least one parliamentary seat (which requires at least 3% of the national vote) | Broadcasting, free space for posters, use of public halls, reduced postal rate for campaign mail | |
| Sweden | Parties, parlia-mentary groups | Annual | Per seat, per vote | Party support: obtained at least 2.5% of votes in last two elections. Basic support: party obtained over 4% of the votes. Supplementary support: based on number of parliamentary seats won by each party | Publication, voting, encouragement of voting, broadcasting, women's and youth organisations | |

*Table 7.5* (continued)

| | *Direct Subsidies* | | | | | |
|---|---|---|---|---|---|---|
| *Country* | *Recipient* | *Interval* | *Basis* | *Eligibility* | *Specific grants or Services* | *Indirect Subsidies* |
| Switzer-land | No direct subsidies | n/a | n/a | n/a | | |
| United Kingdom | Parliamentary groups | Annual | | | Publications, mailing broadcasting, free use of public halls | Gifts to parties exempt from inheri tance tax |

*Source*: LeDuc, Niemi, and Norris 1996: 38–41 (Austria, Belgium, Denmark, Finland, France, Germany, Greece, Ireland, Italy, Netherlands, Norway, Spain, Sweden, Switzerland, United Kingdom); Law act on election rules to the lower house (*Sejm*) of Parliament, dated: 28.05.1993/ Dz.U. Nr 45, poz. 205 and Law act on political parties, dated: 27.06.1997/ Dz.U. No. 98, poz. 604 (Poland).
*Note*: n/a: Not Applicable.

*Table 7.6* Television penetration as an indicator of campaigning modernity

| *Pre-modern Campaign (labour intensive)* | *Modern Campaign (labour and capital intensive)* | | *Post-modern Campaign (capital intensive)* |
|---|---|---|---|
| | 251–450 | 451+ | |
| | Belgium | Austria | |
| | France | Denmark | |
| | Ireland | Finland | |
| | Italy | Germany | |
| | Norway | Netherlands | |
| | Poland | Sweden | |
| | Spain | | |
| | Switzerland | | |
| | United Kingdom | | |

*Source*: Farrell 1996: 174 (Austria, Belgium, Denmark, Finland, France, Germany, Ireland, Italy, Netherlands, Norway, Spain, Sweden, Switzerland, United Kingdom); Law act on election rules to the lower house (Sejm) of Parliament, dated: 28.05.1993/ Dz.U. Nr 45, poz. 205 (Poland).

*Note*: Cases where television spots are permitted are in bold.
*Statistical data*: Television sets per 1,000 people in 1994.

polled 41.5 per cent on the Internet, and 13.37 per cent in reality, or the Democratic Left Alliance (SLD), which gained 8.87 per cent on the Internet as opposed to 27.13 per cent of the real votes. On the other hand, it is worth mentioning that Solidarity Electoral Action (AWS) obtained 33 per cent of the Internet vote, only 0.83 per cent less than its actual total. What these results tell us about those who were regular on-line subscribers at the time is of course self-evident. All in all, there was plenty of evidence to show that the 1997 parliamentary election combined even more elements of modern campaigning than did its predecessor in 1993.

## Political parties in the context of applied political marketing techniques

In general, analysis based on political communications suggests that the major transformation in election campaigns has come less from long-term structural trends or changes in party strategies, than from the system of political communications employed in modern campaigns. As we can see from Table 7.3 there is a minimum of nine categories that explain party strategies in the campaigning process. The Polish parliamentary elections of the 1990s have contributed to the overall consolidation of democracy. After the collapse of the communist regime, the parliamentary arena, together with the party system, was drastically and immediately re-shaped. Initially it emerged fragmented and unstable, full of inexperienced political actors very often concerned with a whole range of novel issues. These themes included the construction of new party elites: ideological traditions and the creation of a new party system; and devising ways of making contact with desired target groups.

For many observers, Polish party competition is viewed as being truly modern, with distinct 'West European' tendencies being evident in the process of electoral communication. In other words, the pattern of electoral competition is not much different from that experienced in the EU in particular and Western Europe as a whole. The real question concerns the degree to which Poland corresponds to West European norms. It is beyond all doubt that Polish political parties employ those marketing techniques used by their EU counterparts. Polish politicians behave in the same manner as do politicians in EU member-states. They use the media, opinion polls and public relations tools as proffered by professional consultants. Although understanding and recognising the use of such methods aids our understanding of Polish politics, the reality is that neither political parties nor the electorate at large has reached the level of democratic consolidation to be found in Western Europe. We have to be aware that although television, computerised and satellite communications in some sense contribute to a globalisation of politics, the regional impact of this phenomenon is varied.

Such 'universal information' may be congruent with the level of political debate in the EU, but it is not necessarily relevant or applicable to a fairly new democracy such as Poland. This is beyond all doubt. For example, marketing techniques that were commonplace in Western Europe and North America in the 1950s, were not used in Poland until the early 1990s. The same applies with regard to structural issues of party organisation. In Western Europe most parties have long-standing organisational cultures, and long ago created links with relevant sections of the electorate. In

Poland, on the other hand, social alignments are still unclear, and the parties still do not possess structures which fully correspond to those of their counterparts in Western Europe. Thus each of the three general elections held in Poland during the 1990s were characterised by a dynamically developing interaction between three fairly new agencies: the electorate, the parties and the media. Each part of this triad continues to play a significant role in constructing the meaning and nature of modern campaigning. The fact that the process of campaign modernisation in Poland has a completely different background to that which exists in the EU/Western Europe cannot be stressed enough. The reasons for this discrepancy include the fact that Poland has only recently rid itself of de facto one-party rule. Second, the experience of party competition is novel in itself. Third, the electoral systems employed have been as new to the electorate as have been the parties. Finally, the media has played a disproportionate role in shaping and creating the images of party leaders. This situation may in fact carry nearly as much danger as it does promise. Many party activists and politicians seem to believe that the road to electoral success lies primarily through the development of the most sophisticated marketing techniques. The roots of this belief seem to rely in the misperception of the nature of political competition in the EU/Western Europe, and the application of marketing techniques in those states. Most Polish parties, including the Eurosceptic PSL and ROP, are greatly enamoured by Western marketing techniques, regardless of their applicability to Poland.

The various national, regional and local elections held in Poland during the 1990s have deepened the process of internal democratisation as well as having led to a real modernisation of campaign styles and strategies. There has also been an explosion in expenditure on elections. The three largest parties, the AWS, SLD and the UW spent over 29,000,000 Zloty, or US$7,000,000 between them in the 1997 campaign. The fact that these parties had such relatively large funds at their disposal helps to explain the success of these parties, and the failure of others. It is, of course, a truism that money can help to buy success. However, there is a danger that in Poland money and expenditure of funds on marketing techniques can cause disruption as well as bring advantage. Key sections of the electorate may find themselves beyond the reach of the marketing men, and may ultimately be effectively disenfranchised. It could be argued that Poland is simply standardising its political marketing practices according to West European norms. This may well be the case. However, it is not healthy if parties and voters simply interact with one another through the judicious application of marketing techniques.

From such a perspective, the conditions and factors of the process of transition and democratic consolidation involves more than the progressive removal of basic uncertainties about the prospects for system survival. Party strategies and images designed for use in election campaigns seem to be moving closer toward to EU patterns, but as Andrzej Antoszewski argues elsewhere in this volume, they are governed by differently defined dimensions and are not at the same level of evolution as in the EU. Given their increasing importance, measuring the degree to which electoral campaigns have become professionalised is a vital task. As Danilo Zolo states:

> the elaboration of a 'theory of political communication' would be far more relevant. Such a theory would need to take account of the new morphology which the communication processes are currently acquiring within political systems subject to the information revolution.
>
> (Zolo 1992: 161)

We need to explore these points in order to specify the actual role of political parties in contemporary democracies. Ian Budge defines parties, as 'very much multi-level and multi-faceted organisations, centred around ideology and policy, but also characterised by candidates, personalities and organisations' (1996: 126). The question is perhaps, whether or not the increasing influence of campaign professionals vindicates or invalidates Budge's assertion.

## Conclusions

By now it should be clear that modern electoral campaigns are conducted in Poland. However, we need to be aware of subtleties of nuance. In general, when we compare Polish parliamentary campaign practices in the 1990s with those encountered in the EU, we asses them as continuously moving away from pre-modern to modern styles, as is witnessed by increasing use of the television and the Internet. There are also grounds to believe that like so much else in Poland the process of campaign modernisation will be telescoped. However, a too rapid process of modernisation can generate negative outcomes. It is difficult to construct appropriate organisational and structural links within the party system given that the electoral arena is still quite unstable. Those elements of instability are connected to voter perception and public reception of the political marketing techniques used by parties and by individual candidates. For instance, in 1993 controversies abounded when the KLD employed Saatchi & Saatchi to design its campaign. Many commentators criticised the KLD and its campaign on the grounds that it had rather too rigidly attempted to implant the American/European experience: 'In Poland the politics is associated with the battle, blood, and solemn slogans that are connected to romantic heritage. Thus, Poles cannot accept joyful decorations and rock concerts which determined the image of the KLD' (Janicki and Peczak 1995: 4).

There is another aspect of the Polish political system that is worth mentioning before we conclude. As Ryszard Heburt explains in this volume, Polish parties do not operate within stable social alignments. West European party systems were created upon pre-existing societal cleavages. In contrast, in Poland the question of the final structuring of such cleavages by parties is still to be achieved. Cleavages, such as they are in Poland, exist in radically different way from those upon which the West European party systems were built. Thus, in the absence of an obvious body of support, political parties in Poland have to try to adopt political marketing techniques that will appeal to a huge swathe of the electorate. In such a context political marketing is playing a dominant role in the maximisation of party profits in electoral arena.

It has to be accepted that in Polish parliamentary elections we can observe the whole spectrum of political marketing techniques. In other words, Poland uses the same marketing techniques as are employed in Western Europe. Crucially, however, they are operating in a different context of structural relations. There is clear evidence that the composition of marketing techniques in particular countries can be greatly influenced by the institutional context in which the campaign occurs, as well as depending upon a party's experience and organisational, or structural, links. In Poland, as elsewhere, the expectations of the public as voters have an important role to play in shaping the matrix of forces which help to decide which marketing techniques are the most appropriate.

## Bibliography

Agranoff, R. (ed.) *The New Style in Election Campaigns*, Boston: Holbrook Press, 1976.

Antoszewski, A. 'System wyborczy i wybory parlamentarne po 1989r.', in A. Antoszewski and R. Herbut (eds) *Polityka w Polsce w latach 90. Wybrane problemy*, Wroclaw: Wydawnictwo Uniwersytetu Wroclawskiego, 73–93, 1998.

Bowler, S. and Farrell, D.M. 'The contemporary election campaign', in S. Bowler and D.M. Farrell (eds) *Electoral Strategies and Political Marketing*, New York: St Martin's Press, 223–34, 1992.

Bowler, S. 'Voter perceptions and party strategies: an empirical approach', *Comparative Politics*, 23, 1, 61–83, 1990.

Budge, I. *The New Challenge of Direct Democracy*, Cambridge: Polity Press, 1996.

Butler, D. and Ranney, A. (eds) *Electioneering: A Comparative Study of Continuity and Change*, Oxford: Clarendon Press, 1992.

Crotty, W. and Jacobson, G. *American Parties in Decline*, Boston: Little, Brown and Co., 1980.

Farrell, D.M. 'Campaign strategies and tactics', in L. LeDuc, R.G. Niemi and P. Norris (eds) *Comparing Democracies: Elections and Voting in Global Perspective*, Thousand Oaks, London and New Delhi: Sage Publications, 160–83, 1996.

Farrell, D.M. and Wortmann, M. 'Party strategies in the electoral market: political marketing in West Germany, Britain and Ireland', in *European Journal of Political Research* 15, 3 , 297–318, 1987.

Herbut, R. 'Partie polityczne i system partyjny', in A. Antoszewski and R. Herbut (eds) *Polityka w Polsce w latach 90. Wybrane problemy*, Wroclaw: Wydawnictwo Uniwersytetu Wroclawskiego, 115–38, 1998.

Janicki, M. and Peczak, M. 'Wojna na miny czyli polityk jako towar', *Polityka* 41, 2006, 4–6, 1995.

Just, M. *et al.*, *Crosstalk: Citizens, Candidates and the Media in a Presidential Campaign*, Chicago: University of Chicago Press, 1996.

Kaid, L. and Holtz-Bacha, C. *Political Advertising in Western Democracies: Parties and Candidates on Television*, Thousand Oaks: Sage Publications, 1995.

Katz, R.S. *A Theory of Parties and Electoral Systems*, Baltimore: Johns Hopkins University Press, 1980.

—— 'Party organizations and finance', in L. LeDuc, R.G. Niemi and P. Norris (eds) *Comparing Democracies: Elections and Voting in Global Perspective*, London-New Delhi: Sage Publications, 107–33, 1996.

Katz, R.S. and Kolodny, R. 'The USA: the 1990 Congressional campaign', in S. Bowler and D.M. Farrell (eds) *Electoral Strategies and Political Marketing*, New York: St Martin's, 183–201, 1992.

LeDuc, L., Niemi, R.G. and Norris, P. (eds) *Comparing Democracies: Elections and Voting in Global Perspective*, London-New Delhi: Sage Publications, 1996.

McAllister, I. 'Leaders', in L. LeDuc, R.G. Niemi and P. Norris (eds) *Comparing Democracies: Elections and Voting in Global Perspective*, London: Sage Publications, 280–98, 1996.

McCarthy, J. *Basic Marketing: A Managerial Approach*, Illinois: Homewood, 1975.

Norris, P. *Electoral Change in Britain since 1945*, Oxford: Blackwell Publishers, 1997.

Ociepka, B. 'Wplyw nowych technologii na komunikowanie masowe', in B. Dobek-Ostrowska (ed.) *Studia z teorii komunikowania masowego*, Wroclaw: Wydawnictwo Uniwersytetu Wroclawskiego, 149–68, 1999.

Paradowska, J. 'Jak to sie stalo: Twarze i maski, *Polityka* 39, 5–6, 199, 1997.

Sabato, L. *The Rise of Political Consultants: New Ways of Winning Elections*, New York: Basic Books, 1981.

Sartori, G. *Parties and Party Systems: A Framework for Analysis*, Cambridge: Cambridge University Press, 1976.

Semetko, H.A. 'The media', in L. LeDuc, R.G. Niemi and P. Norris (eds) *Comparing Democracies: Elections and Voting in Global Perspective*, London: Sage Publications, 254–279, 1996.

Sundberg J, 'Finland', *European Journal of Political Research*, 30, 3–4, 321–30, 1996.

Ulicka, G. 'Wplyw marketingu politycznego na zmiany w zyciu publicznym panstw demokratycznych', in T. Klementowicz (ed.) *Trudna Sztuka Polityki: Szanse, Ryzyko, Blad*, Warszawa: ELIPSA, 157–67, 1996.

Zolo, D. *Democracy and Complexity: A Realist Approach*, Cambridge: Polity Press, 1992.

# 8 The Europeanisation of government in Poland in the 1990s

*Andrzej W. Jablonski*

## Introduction

The aim of this chapter is to examine the evolution of governmental and constitutional structures in Poland in the 1990s from the perspective of their convergence with the institutional patterns of Western Europe. In the view of this author, this process of 'Europeanisation' may be viewed as two-dimensional and having encompassed two phases. The first dimension and phase occurred as part of the general transition to liberal democracy and a market economy, as experienced by all of the countries of East-Central Europe since the fall of communism. The second dimension and phase constitutes a process of the harmonisation of norms, institutions, procedures and policies within the *acquis communitaire* of the European Union (EU). This latter process also embraces the other countries of East-Central Europe just as it does Poland, but whereas the first phase may be viewed as having been a generic experience, the second has dealt with issues specific to Poland. So, whilst EU members have been seeking to create institutions and policies which facilitate the process of deepening and widening, the associated countries such as Poland have been consolidating their domestic institutions with a view to eventual membership of the union.

Since the collapse of communism, Poland, together with several other countries in the region, has undergone a comprehensive reform process designed to create a modern liberal democratic political system. The transition towards the West European model of government has been conducted in an evolutionary manner. Systemic reforms have been undertaken on two main levels: at the level of representative institutions and the rule of law, and through the establishment of a liberal democratic state based on the rule of law. They have also included the establishment of political pluralism, free elections, the creation of a democratically elected parliament and an independent judiciary. These reforms have in turn been complemented by reform of the political executive; including the re-establishment of a directly elected presidency, and the establishment of legitimate and effective centres of government. There have also been reforms aimed at creating a modern civil service, and in the spheres of the system of local and regional government in accordance with the European Charter of self-government. Having outlined the main areas in which reforms have taken place, this chapter will examine the evolution of the Polish political system since the commencement of the post-communist transition focusing upon the areas highlighted in the previous paragraph.

## Europeanisation as a guideline for constitutional reform

In Poland, during the first stage of democratic transition between 1990 and 1991, the attention of the new policy-makers was focused on dismantling the communist constitutional system and the instalment of political institutions of a liberal democratic nature. Having said that, some measures of reform relating to fields such as the internal structures of the cabinet and the state bureaucracy were postponed to the second half of the decade. The earliest regime changes were implemented by the amendments to the communist constitution on 7 April 1989 following the Round Table agreements. The amendments agreed upon at the Round Table restored parliamentary bicameralism, re-invigorated the presidency and opened the legal way to the partially free elections of 4 June 1989. The second series of fundamental amendments to the constitution came on 29 December 1989. These amendments separated the state from the communist party and instituted a republican form of government. This involved embarking upon a series of measures aimed at restoring the sovereignty of the nation, the rule of law, a (partly) representative lower chamber of parliament the Sejm, and a fully representative upper chamber, the Senate.

The model of government created by the Round Table was that of a semi-presidential regime, with strong presidential authority modelled on the French Constitution of 1958. The president was to be elected by a joint convention of the Sejm and Senate for a six-year term, with the option of standing for a second term. As guardian of the post-communist constitution, the president had the right to dissolve parliament in the event of it being unable either to form a government or to enact legislation (Garlicki 1995: 82). A further amendment to the constitution in September 1990 strengthened the presidency by providing for the popular election of the Head of State. This, and other latter changes to the political regime, had been brought about through the passing of the 'Small Constitution' on 27 October 1992. This temporary document established a 'rationalised' parliamentary system, consisting of the dual executive president and the Council of Ministers, and a dual legislature, the Sejm and Senate. Unfortunately, the competencies of the cabinet ministers and the president in the areas of foreign, internal and defence policy overlapped and contributed to years of conflict between the two offices. The 'Small Constitution' changed the balance of power between the organs of state: it strengthened the powers of the government to the cost of parliament and the president. For example, a 'constructive vote of no confidence' was added to the constitutional order. The newly weakened president could no longer dismiss the government as easily as before, and he found it more difficult to intervene in the work of cabinet ministers. The president's real power over the government was now dependent upon the political composition of the Sejm. The presidential veto could be an effective tool of control over legislative policy only when the incumbent government had a small majority or was riven by factionalism. When ruling coalitions were stable and possessed clear majority support and/or the two-thirds of seats necessary to override the presidential veto, the cabinet had almost supreme authority in the policy process.

The 'Small Constitution' was, however, simply intended to be a stop-gap until agreement could be reached on a full post-communist constitution. The factionalisation within the Polish polity meant that it would take a further five years before a full post-communist constitution could be presented to both government and the people. This constitution, which was ratified by parliament on 2 April 1997, and approved by the public in a referendum on 25 May 1997, came into force on 16 October 1997. It institutionalised relationships between the main organs of state on the lines of a presidential–parliamentary model. The dual executive model was sustained, but the range of presidential competencies was further curtailed. Presidential veto power was weakened by the insertion of a clause that reduced from two-thirds to three-fifths the parliamentary majority necessary to overcome the presidential veto. The constitutional ambiguities concerning the presidential competencies in security, defence and foreign policy were eliminated, with these ministries being clearly placed firmly within the jurisdiction of the cabinet.

The constitution of 1997 has broadened the competencies of the prime minister at the cost of the cabinet as whole. Now the prime minister alone has the power to countersign acts of the president. According to one expert, this constitution 'stresses the leading role of the prime minister in the government . . . and makes him stronger in relation to the president' (Garlicki 1995: 85). An innovation of the 1997 constitution is that it allows for a constructive vote of non-confidence in the prime minister. Article 158 states that 'the Sejm shall pass a vote of no confidence by a majority of votes of the statutory number of deputies, on a motion moved by at least forty-six deputies and which shall specify the name of the candidate for prime minister' (The Constitution of the Republic of Poland 1999). The effective power of the president in dealing with the cabinet depends on the internal cohesion of the latter and its ability to gain support by the strong majority of deputies. To overcome the presidential veto over the cabinet's bills, the latter needs slightly more than a three-fifths majority of the deputies in the lower chamber, which given the complexity of Poland's party system is not necessarily a straightforward task (Antoszewski 1998: 112–13). The relatively strong position of the president within the structure of the organs of state stems from his popular mandate. The evolution of the constitutional government of Poland during the 1990s has resulted in the political system being classified and labelled in many different ways. Some have characterised it as a 'rationalised parliamentary system', others as one of 'partial semi-presidentialism' or 'presidential-parliamentary' government (Crawford 1996: 290). The mode of argumentation that lay behind the process of constitutional reforms was political as well as pragmatic. There was a common perception in Poland that liberal democratic norms could be best secured through the establishment of a form of rule based upon a dual executive. This model, as opposed to a pure presidential or pure parliamentary model, would, it was hoped, provide political stability and institutional mechanisms for the effective governance of the country. In other words, Poland was having to learn which aspects of the liberal democratic model best suited local conditions.

Another important step in this process of institutional learning was the change to the electoral law in 1993. Through the introduction of a 5 per cent threshold for all parties, bar those representing ethnic minorities, and an 8 per cent threshold for coalitions, the party system was to a large degree consolidated. In turn, it became possible for (relatively) stable majorities to emerge in both chambers of parliament. It was this consolidation of parliamentary political forces that helped facilitate the subsequent constitutional changes of 1997, which moved Poland farther away from a system of semi-presidential to a form of parliamentary regime. They did so by strengthening the position of the prime minister in relation to the president and to other members of the cabinet. It is now easier for the prime minister to replace a member of his cabinet than it was under the 'Small Constitution'. The prime minister can now replace ministers without having to consult with either the Sejm or the president. Article 161 of the constitution states that: 'The President of the Republic, on request of the Prime Minister shall effect changes in the composition of the Council of Ministers' (The Constitution of the Republic of Poland 1997). Thus in 1999, Prime Minister Jerzy Buzek was able to replace four members of his cabinet with a minimum of fuss. Had he tried such a move in 1991 he would have needed the consent of the Sejm and in 1994 he would have had to have entered into a time-consuming bargaining process with the president (*Gazeta Wyborcza*, 10 June 1999). As a result of this process of incremental constitutional reform, the current legal framework within which policy-making is carried out has become more conducive to stable and effective governance (*Gazeta Wyborcza*, 10 June 1999). The process of rationalisation of the constitutional order has brought positive results in terms of the consolidation of democracy. It has also created a safer institutional framework for the political executive, within which it can implement reforms of state and economy, as well as in terms of its EU integration policy. The constitution of 1997 also laid down the legal grounds for the Europeanisation of the sources of law in Poland. Thus Article 90 of the constitution states:

> 'The Republic of Poland may, by virtue of international agreements, delegate to international organisations or international institutions the competence of organs of State authority in relation to certain matters. . . . A statute, granting consent for ratification of an international agreement . . . shall be passed by the Sejm by a two-thirds majority vote in the presence of at least half of the statutory number of Deputies, and by the Senate by a two-thirds majority vote in the presence of at least half of the statutory number of Senators . . .'.
>
> (The Constitution of the Republic of Poland 1997)

Importantly, as part of the overall attempt to gain legitimacy for such a fundamental change to Polish political practice and tradition, the population at large may also become involved in this process. Under Article 25 of the constitution of 1997, the granting of consent for ratification of such agreements may also be secured by nation-wide referendum (The Constitution of the Republic of Poland 1997). So far, neither provision has had occasion to be tested.

The conduct of the executive since the parliamentary elections of 1997 has proved that the continued existence of a watered down dual executive may be not so dangerous to the political stability and efficiency of government in Poland as some politicians expected. The 'cohabitation' type of intra-executive relationships formed after this election, where the post-communist president has had to govern in tandem with a post-Solidarity prime minister and cabinet, has in fact worked relatively smoothly, and without serious constitutional setbacks. Although the president has on occasion exercised his right of veto, such as on the issue of the reform of local and regional government (see below), he has on the whole used this power sparingly.

## Reforming the cabinet

The earliest reforms to the central political executive in Poland focused on the restructuring of those departments most clearly linked to the operational structures of the former socialist regime. Reorganisation of the former Ministry of Internal Affairs and restoring political control over the security and police forces was one of the first reforms conducted by the first non-communist government. The institutions of economic policy-making were also radically rebuilt after the abolition of the socialist system of central planning and the commencement of large-scale privatisation. The new Ministry of Privatisation was quickly incorporated into the structure of central government. In addition to changes in the internal practices of the cabinet, many central offices, state agencies and foundations were created to deal with different issues related to the emergence of a market economy. The most important examples include the Office for Fair Competition and Consumer Protection, the Agency for the Restructuring and Modernisation of Agriculture, the Agency for Military Property, and the National Fund for Environmental Protection (*Rzeczpospolita*, 22 March 1999).

Although by the mid-1990s Poland had made great strides in the arena of institutional reform, there was still plenty of scope for change. Especially if the country's rulers were to be taken seriously in their claim that membership of the EU was Poland's stated destination. The Polish executive was and is facing problems common to many governments elsewhere in Europe, where governments struggle to meet common objectives. The first arises from the need to ensure that different parts of the governmental machinery work together. The second is the attempt to ensure that policies have the desired impact.

A comprehensive reform package concerning the internal structures of central government was devised by the government of Hanna Suchocka in 1992–3. However, the instability of her coalition meant that the government lacked the majority necessary to get the legislation through parliament. Nevertheless the package of bills adopted by her administration between January and September 1993 was an important step forward in the process of the development of a new legal framework in this field. The conception of reform was informed by the following principles:

(1) Administrative reform is conceived of as the precondition necessary to enhance the efficiency and legitimacy of the state executive and public administration.
(2) The establishment of a cohesive centre of government, capable of developing and defending the public interest is a necessary precondition of good governance.
(3) Any increase in the legitimacy and efficiency of the political and administrative system requires the implementation of comprehensive reforms to the system of local government, and the creation of a tier of local government in the vacuum (which existed until 1999) between the central state apparatus and the *gminy* (communes).
(4) A small number of large regions should replace the current forty-nine *voivodships* (provinces), in order to meet the imperatives of regional economic development and co-operation with similar units of territorial administration in neighbouring countries.
(5) The establishment of a modern civil service, employing professional, politically neutral corps of clerks should be a prime objective of the government (Wiatr 1995: 156).

Since the nineteenth century, these ideas and principles have constituted an integral part of the institutional frameworks of West European states. However, for reasons of history and geopolitics, it was not until the 1990s that Poland was presented with its first ever opportunity to implement such measures. As we are about to see, whereas all the leading players agreed with the proposition that reform should proceed in accordance with the principles outlined above, as usual the devil lay in the detail.

The parliamentary election of September 1993 saw power pass into the hands of the post-communist Democratic Left Alliance (SLD) and Polish Peasant's Party (PSL). Nevertheless, the process of administrative reform continued. In August 1996, after three years of legislative wrangling, a package for the new structure of central government was passed by the Sejm. The new law retained most of the clauses proposed earlier by the post-Solidarity government of Hanna Suchocka. However, the new law focused primarily only on the reform of the nerve-centres of government, namely the structure of the cabinet and central agencies, and did not provide for the further decentralisation of the territorial structure of the state. The primary objective of the new law was the elimination of a main flaw of the Polish governmental system: namely a lack of co-ordination between different ministries and agencies, which had led to chaotic decision-making and the government being labelled a 'confederation of ministers'. The prerogatives of different ministers were restricted by statutes to narrowly defined sectors of policy. Some argued that the system was unable to produce rational solutions to many socioeconomic problems, many of which were too complex to be solved by a single ministry. For example, the inception of a project partly financed by foreign capital may give rise to questions concerning such diverse policy areas as energy, transportation, the environment, telecommunications, and even internal security. The ongoing competition between different ministers over budgetary resources has eroded the power and prestige of the political executive. Bureaucratic politics revolving around the distribution of funds across ministries and central agencies has weakened the ability of the central leadership to cope with the completion of the programme of legal and economic reforms necessary prior to the admission of Poland to the EU. It has even been argued that:

> The system of joint decision making in Poland displays in an extreme and enlarged form all the problems of ministerial collegial government which can also be found elsewhere. The Council of Ministers is obviously too weak in order to act as an integrating force, and the same is true for the president and the parliament, which has not been able to tip the balance to either advantage . . . this is *afortiori* true for Polish government where the informal culture and routines of consensual politics and administration have had no time to develop.
>
> (Toonen 1993: 160)

One of the aims of new legislation adopted in August 1996 was to overcome precisely these problems through strengthening the policy-making abilities and cohesion of the cabinet as a whole, as well as the power of the prime minister within the cabinet. The Act on the Cabinet Ministers of 1996 defined the prime minister as the decisive power broker and co-ordinator of the work of other ministers, except for the Minister of Defence and Minister of Internal Affairs whose duties continued to be prescribed by separate statute. The regulation which stated that the 'minister supervises over the particular sector of administration' was revised and more power passed into the hands of the prime minister (*Rzeczpospolita*, 7 November 1997). The new regulations were aimed at stimulating teamwork within the cabinet, and at improving government performance, especially in the area of economic and social policy. The Office of the Prime Minister was created in order to provide insitutional support to the prime minister. Importantly, it is the prime minister who nominates its head. The Office of the Prime Minister comprises a complex structure consisting of the Deputy Prime Ministers, Secretaries and Under Secretaries of State, the Director General, and the Secretary of the Council of Ministers. The new legal statutes also included a clause preventing ministers from evading the doctrine of collective responsibility for jointly taken decisions. In sum, an attempt was made to adapt and apply to Poland the principles of cabinet government as practised in Western Europe.

Another of the main aims of this reform package was to consolidate into the hands of a single Minister of the Economy, those policy-making institutions responsible for the conduct of macro-economic policy. This new organ, established as part of the above-mentioned legislative package, assumed the duties of three former separate economic ministries: the Ministry of Trade and Industry, the Ministry of Foreign Economic Co-operation, and the Ministry of the Regional Economy and Housing. The integration of several ministries into a single Ministry of the Economy was forced by the need to increase the state's capacity to steer the course of economic transformation and to improve the performance of the Polish economy in the European market. Another ministry created under the above reform package was the Treasury. The main role of this ministry is to supervise the administration of remaining state assets. The scope of jurisdiction of the Finance Ministry was narrowed to one of supervision of the fiscal and budgetary policy of state and the control over the budget. Some of the prerogatives of this formerly powerful ministry have been passed to the Ministry of the Economy and to the Treasury. Further reform came on 1 January 1997, when the new important new Ministry of Public Administration and Internal Affairs commenced its formal existence. It is responsible for supervising the work of a number of agencies of central government, including the police, border security forces, the central fire department, and civil defence.

In sum, the new formal structure of government administration established in 1996 resulted in the closure of five ministries and two central agencies and established two new ministries and five lower rank governmental organs. The new ministries and central offices created in 1996 included the following: the Ministry of Public Administration and Internal Affairs, the Ministry of Economy, the Office of Prime Minister, the Centre of Strategic Studies, the Committee of European Integration, and the

Office of Housing and the Development of Cities. They in turn replaced the following former ministries and central offices: the Ministry of Internal Affairs, the Ministry of the Ownership Transformation, the Ministry of International Economic Co-operation, the Ministry of Trade and Industry, the Ministry of Construction, the Office of the Council of Ministers, and the Main Office of Planning (*Rzeczpospolita*, 31 December 1996).

The main idea driving these reforms was a growing belief that Poland needed a stronger and more cohesive executive in order to improve governmental performance in strategic areas of state policy. The reformers were seeking to establish a more rational organisation of the cabinet. During the period of implementation, public opinion on the whole believed that the reform of central government would bring about an improvement of the policy capacity of the state. According to one opinion poll, 76 per cent of respondents believed that the reform of central government would improve the quality of government performance (*Rzeczpospolita*, 25 September 1996).

In the second half of the 1990s, the prospect of accession by Poland to the EU became a new important factor to be taken into account by the reformers of central and local government. On 8 August 1996, in order better to co-ordinate the policies of the various organs of public administration involved in the arena of European integration, parliament established a Committee of European Integration. At the head of the committee stands the prime minister. Its membership consists of the Ministers of Foreign Affairs, Internal Affairs, Economy, Finance, Environmental Protection, Labour and Social Policy, Agriculture and Justice. The heads of various other ministries and agencies may also participate according to case. Crucially, the chief Polish negotiator with the EU is attached to the Office of the Prime Minister, which gives him regular access to the premier and the Minister of Foreign Affairs, who exercise ultimate responsibility for the conduct of the accession negotiations. Despite the establishment of this committee, a problem of co-ordination of responsibilities for conducting Polish integration policy has been not resolved and several crises of competence erupted in 1996 and 1997. As a consequence of these disputes and the ongoing debate on accession, a further reconfiguration of responsibilities cannot be ruled out.

The reform of central government in 1996 constituted an important step forward in the process of the reconstruction of the political executive and in the creation of agencies competent to handle the process of negotiation with the EU. Unfortunately, elements of the reform package have still not been fully implemented. For example, the Act on the Council of Ministers, which came into force on 1 April 1999, is still questioned by many high-ranking officials. The critics of this law believe it gives too much power to the prime minister. Some politicians and parties within the governing coalition are hesitant to accept the position of the premier as 'first among equals' within the cabinet. In short, some elements within the political parties are not interested in further weakening their hold on their nominees to the executive (*Rzeczpospolita*, 17 May 1999). After much dispute, the Act finally passed through the Sejm on 12 July 1999. The prime minister was given power to reshuffle the cabinet in response to changing priorities (*Rzeczpospolita*, 12 July 1999). The new law allows for greater flexibility in the operation of government, based on the practice of cabinet government in the United Kingdom.

## The bumpy road to modern bureaucracy

The poor performance of administrative personnel has long been a hallmark of East Central-European administrative systems, especially when compared to that of their counterparts in, for example, the United Kingdom, where from the middle of the nineteenth century a tradition and a code of behaviour slowly developed which formed the hallmark of the whole civil service and not just of any one department or any one grade (Chapman and O'Toole 1995: 8). The administrative cultures and *modus operandi* of civil servants in Poland and her neighbours remained static throughout the nineteenth century, whereas in Western Europe the modern nation-state was coming into existence.

The bureaucracies of East-Central Europe were heavily affected by a culture of patronage, low professional competence, a weakly developed work ethic, a lack of civic responsibility, arrogance and corruption. If such a legacy continues to be a part of administrative behaviour in today's Poland, it may hamper the emergence of a mature democratic society. Especially important for the development of democratic pattern of relationships between the state and civil society is the administrative culture of street-level bureaucrats working in such areas as the housing departments of municipalities, tax offices, unemployment agencies, and social security offices. The nature of the relationship between the citizen and administrative personnel depends on the work ethic, cultural habits, levels of remuneration, transparency of decision-making procedures and reasonable legal rules. The cultural and legal conditions necessary for the creation of a modern bureaucracy in Poland can be achieved only through the evolutionary growth of economic and political stability.

Changes based on the West European model entered the reform agenda soon after the change of regime in 1989. Under the socialist regime, the key personnel recruitment in the administrative system had been controlled by the personnel departments of the communist party. High-ranking administrative officials from all levels of government constituted a part of the nomenklatura. The bureaucratic party-state of 'really existing socialism' was the employer of an army of bureaucrats who were in charge of all the sectors of the economy and most other spheres of society's life. It was therefore imperative that the power of these officials be decisively broken, and it is a testimony to their power that reform of the civil service in post-communist Poland was commenced relatively late.

Eventually, on 14 June 1996, the Sejm passed the Civil Service Act, which created a new category of public employees, that of civil servants. An editorial in a popular daily proclaimed the passing of this law to be 'one of the most important reforms of the state, which clearly divides administrative positions from political ones and protects civil servants against party control. Without this Act all other political and economic reforms would have been useless' (*Gazeta Wyborcza*, 15–16 June 1996). According to the law of 1996, the employees of government departments and agencies became members of the corps of civil servants. The recruitment of candidates to the category of public officials should be conducted according to formally defined and transparent criteria, such as possession of a university degree, high ethics and, for the most senior of grades, prior administrative experience of a minimum of seven years. Given that just about the only people with such experience were in fact members of the former nomenklatura, this last criterion was highly criticised by the post-Solidarity bloc of parties. With some justification, the then governing SLD and PSL were accused of attempting to colonise the machinery of state. According to the legislation, recruitment would be conducted by a special state commission consisting of independent high-ranking officials. These, then, were the provisions which were supposed to create a new civil service corps independent of the political parties.

In practice, the enactment of this legislation was very uneven. Unsurprisingly, when the post-Solidarity Electoral Action (AWS) and the Freedom Union (UW) assumed power in October 1997, the implementation of the civil service law was suspended and placed under review. The only institutions installed by the SLD–PSL government were the General Director of Civil Service, the administrative secretaries of the ministries and the General Directors of the regional executives.

The consolidation of a fully professional civil service, when it finally arrives, will be achieved only if the legacy of a tradition of patronage and of conceiving public administration as the electoral reward of the victorious parties is overcome. The joint inheritance of the authoritarianism of the inter-war period and the communist party/state have not yet been fully eradicated in the new Poland and continue to exercise a negative impact on the prospects for the emergence of an impartial public administration. It is difficult problem across the whole of the region. In the words of one observer of the scene:

> the pursuit of particularistic party interest within the context of administrative reforms will replicate rather than repress the patterns of neo-traditionalism and fragmentation inherited from the past. Unfortunately this type of centralisation via the appropriation of power by a single party is likely to dominate efforts aimed at administrative reform throughout the region.
>
> (Cirtautas 1995: 300)

This dominance of particularistic interests over the common good may obstruct the efforts of the reform-minded leadership to establish an impartial civil service. In Poland, shortly after the adoption of the new legal statute on civil service, it turned out that the recruitment process to the newly established posts of the General Directors in the *voivodships* (provinces) conformed to old rather than new norms. According to press reports, a number of freshly nominated civil servants were recruited from the ranks of former officials of the SLD and PSL. The speedy nomination of 'new civil servants' had put in doubt the impartiality of the recruitment processes and the good intentions of the incumbent government to apply rules of transparency and equal opportunity in the selection of civil servants. As we have previously noted, the situation altered after the change of government in the autumn of 1997. The new AWS and UW government formally suspended previous nominations and moved to revise the procedure. On 18 December 1998, a new Civil Service Act was passed by the Sejm. The president (who was opposed to the new legislation) then sent the bill to the Constitutional Tribunal in order to test its legality. In the meantime, many administrative officials were replaced by the nominees of the new government (*Rzeczpospolita*, 14 May 1999). The Constitutional Tribunal found the new Act to be valid, and it formally came into force on 1 July 1999 (*Gazeta Wyborcza*, 1 July 1999). From that date, all employees of the central government administration obtained the status of civil servants. New candidates to the civil service corps will have to take part in open procedures of recruitment based on merit. The highest ranks in the new bureaucratic hierarchy are to be filled in by the winners of transparent competition, from among rank-and-file civil servants. Prime minister Jerzy Buzek subsequently confirmed that the overriding objective of the Act was to separate the civil service from the political parties: 'We want the civil servants to be the best, not ours' (*Gazeta Wyborcza*, 13 April 1999).

The adoption of the second Civil Service Act has established a civil service whose procedures are closely modelled upon the practices of West European states, particularly the United Kingdom. However, the traditional roles of administrative personnel in Britain and many other countries of Western Europe have over the past decade undergone evolution towards the model of so-called 'new public management'. Polish legislators seem not to have noticed this change, and that may evoke problems in the near future.

## The evolution of relations between central and local government

The democratisation of society following the fall of 'really existing socialism', necessitated the imposition of legal constraints upon the almost unlimited power of the former party/state. In Poland the postulate of dismantling the bureaucratic party/state had been clearly articulated in the underground political writings of the anti-communist opposition. This idea was anchored in the tradition of autonomous local government, with its historic roots in the seventeenth century. It survived in the political culture of Poland as a reaction against the centralist doctrine of the communist state and was used for manipulative purposes by the party and state authorities during the political crises of 1956, 1970 and 1980. In the period 1980–1 the idea of a 'self-governing republic' was at the centre of Solidarity's image of a post-communist Poland. In the struggle to establish a democratic and pluralist society this programme was to play a crucial role in the dismantling of the centralist party/state. The concept of a 'self-governing republic' conceived of the devolution of power as constituting a panacea against the bureaucratic system of the communist state (Pokladecki 1995: 70). The legislative bills containing the proposals for the decentralisation of the territorial structures of government were placed on the political agenda at the earliest stages of the post-communist transition.

The idea of decentralisation of the state was discussed during the Round Table talks between the ruling coalition and Solidarity from February to April of 1989. The first and most important step of reform was implemented by the first non-communist cabinet headed by Tadeusz Mazowiecki (Kallas 1997: 456). The adoption of the Territorial Self-Government Act in March 1990 had established the legal framework for the establishment of autonomous local councils at the level of the *gminy* and had cleared the way for the first free elections to these bodies in May 1990. Public opinion saw this reform as somewhat revolutionary precisely because it re-created democratic politics at the local level after half a century of 'democratic centralism'. Elected communal councils and their executives have become vital institutions of representation for the interests of both urban and rural populations. Many of them are active agents of local development, participants in European aided projects, borrowers on the capital markets, and members of domestic and international associations of municipalities.

As elsewhere in Europe, the main problem for Polish local government has been one of finance. Their share of public revenues is too small to cover statutory expenses. Inevitably, this has led to a growing dependence on subsidies from central government on the part of local authorities. This has given rise to concerns that despite best intentions, Poland could be witnessing the re-centralisation of the Polish system of public finance at the very least (*Rzeczpospolita*, 2 March 1999).

One of the main obstacles against continuing with the process of decentralisation in Poland between 1991 and 1996, was the distinct lack of a political consensus concerning the degree of devolution deemed to be necessary and efficient, and the lack of a coherent vision of the state. The reforms of 1990 had embraced only the lowest level of local government. Attempts to embrace the intermediate levels of public administration proved much more difficult. Throughout this period, the political elite and academic experts were engaged in a series of debates concerning the most appropriate model for the future shape of Polish regional and local government. The initial conclusion was that there did indeed need to be a further reform in the nature and scope of territorial division and administration of the state. The reforms of 1990 were judged as being far too modest for a state that hoped to become a member of the EU.

Once this consensus was achieved, debate focused upon two main themes. The first was restoration of local government at the level of the *powiaty* (counties), and reform of the *voivodships* into regions similar in terms of size and competencies to those to be found in some EU countries. The two issues were inextricably linked to one another. The re-establishment of the *powiaty* was designed to fill the gap between the central state apparatus and the *gminy*. The reintroduction of the *powiaty* would mean a return to the three tier administrative system that existed in Poland prior to the last major reorganisation of local and regional government in 1975. Prior to the reorganisation of that year, Poland had been divided into seventeen large *voivodships* and roughly 300 *powiaty*, which in turn had been further subdivided into a series of *gminy*. The administrative reform of 1975 eliminated the *powiaty* and created forty-nine small and weak *voivodships*, all of which were easily controlled by the party/state apparatus. The facade of democratic accountability existed within these units, but real power resided in the headquarters of the party bureaucracy.

After 1989, the same *voivodships* obtained the status of territorial units of central administration. The chief executives (*voivods*) were responsible for the implementation of central governmental policy in the *voivodships* and were the nominees of the prime minister. Hamstrung by the lack of any real autonomy, these units were in addition too small to fulfil the tasks of regional development and co-operation with the outside world. Most of them lacked the necessary infrastructure and resources to deal with growing problems of economic and technological transformation, unemployment, environmental problems and so forth. With the downfall of the communists, the bulk of the population was supportive of the idea of recreating the *powiaty* within a system of consolidated *voivodships*. The intended reforms would, in addition, broaden the scope of local government in Poland, and make Polish practice more consistent with the models of government prevalent in most of the EU.

The 'Small Constitution' of 1992 included a section on local government that described the *gminy* as the legitimate basis of local government in Poland. However, this constitutional provision was not subsequently incorporated into the new (temporary) constitutional code. The incorporation was only achieved with the enactment entrenching of the principle of autonomous local government into Poland's political and constitutional system, and as such reflected the growing impact of 'Europe' on the thinking of Polish political elite. In February 1993, the Polish envoy to the Council of Europe signed the European Charter of Territorial Self-Government. In so doing, Poland adopted the full contents of the Charter and declared its readiness to obey its regulations.

The constitution of 1997 provided a stimulus to the cause of local government reform. Included within it were a set of clauses that clarified the notion of self-governance and opened the way to the next steps in local government reform. Of principle interest to students in the field were:

(1) The Preamble to the Constitution which emphasises the principle of subsidiarity as one of the leading components of the constitutional order of Poland.
(2) Article 164 which states that: 'other units of regional or local self-government shall be specified by statute.
(3) Article 165 which requires that: 'units of self-government shall possess legal personality. They shall have rights of ownership and other property rights . . . the self-governing nature of units of local governments shall be protected by the courts.
(4) Article 167 which confirms that: 'units of local-governments shall be assured public funds adequate for the performance of the duties assigned to them.
(5) Article 172 which holds that: 'a unit of local-government shall have the right to join international associations of local and regional communities as well as to co-operate with local and regional communities of other states.' (The Constitution of the Republic of Poland 1997).

The aforementioned constitutional regulations all served to entrench the constitutional position of local self-government and cleared the way for further decentralisation of state powers beyond the level of the *gminy*. Such ideas began to take shape in the second half 1998 when, after much wrangling between the president and the government, splits within the AWS, and various regional campaigns aimed at persuading the government to take local sensitivities into account, new legal statutes establishing the new structures came into effect. These acts opened a new chapter in the history of the Europeanisation of government in Poland. The implementation of the new territorial structure of local and regional administration has completed the process of convergence of Polish local government structures with the 'European model'. The administrative map of Poland resulting from the 1998 reform comprises sixteen *voivodships*, and almost 400 *powiaty* and very nearly 2,500 *gminy*. The new *voivodships* have a dual structure of authority: the self-government segment consists of elective councils, and the governmental segment is headed by the *voivod* who in turn still represents the central government in the region.

This most recent phase of reform may be conceived of as an important step towards the Europeanisation of Polish local and regional government. It was inspired by the salient principles directing the evolution of many West European states over the past two decades: decentralisation, internationalisation, supranationalism, competition, co-operation and development. The desired aims are common to those pursued by many West

European states, and are designed to create more effective institutional conditions for the development of national economies within the framework of the Single European Market and the creation of an ever closer European union. The completion of this 'European type framework' of territorial government has created better conditions for regional and local development. It has also made possible the closer engagement of the new Polish regions in the emerging European-wide network of development projects, investment grants, structural funds and the like. Prior to the implementation of these reforms, some of these activities were possible only at the level of the *gminy*. The former *voivodships* had not fulfilled the European criteria for regional government, and could undertake international co-operation only at the narrow executive level. The new *voivodships* have obtained the statutory right to engage in collaborative links with outside regions and other units. What is more important, the *voivodship* councils have become important actors in the construction of regional policy and in the emerging network of supranational intergovernmental relations. The EU's pre-accession strategy enhances this process by offering financial grants for projects submitted jointly by central and regional governments. This policy accentuates trends toward the different tiers of government, establishing horizontal as well as vertical links. Spurred by these changes, Poland is currently working on its first national development plan since 1989. To be eligible for funding, it has to be congruent with the programme of the EU. The national plan for development will consist of the sixteen regional plans devised by each of the *voivodships* and six sectoral plans prepared by the ministries of Agriculture, Fishery, Regional Development, Social Policy, Environmental Protection and Transportation. In order to facilitate the implementation of policy initiatives in these fields, legislation has recently been passed allowing ministries to develop regional policies. The relevant ministry will have the task of co-ordinating such initiatives and ensuring that the *voivodships* and centre speak with one voice (*Rzeczpospolita*, 12 July 1999 )

## Concluding remarks

Throughout the 1990s Poland has made enormous progress on the road to the Europeanisation of its institutions of government but the reform programme is still not fully implemented. The most important achievements comprise the passage of the constitution of April 1997, the completion of the decentralisation programme, and the reform of the civil service and the executive. Yet, the continuing debate concerning central–local relations indicates that the division of powers between centre and periphery has not yet been fixed.

Poland is now facing several challenges that are forcing political elites to make a more coherent policy about the strategy of development. The first challenge is the declining competitiveness of national industry and agriculture partly caused by the slow pace of economic reforms. The second is the low take-up rate by central and local government of pre-accession assistance grants offered by the EU. The ability of local authorities in particular to obtain development grants has been so far very modest. This may be because the centre insists on involving itself in the process. Bids for projects have been assessed by the ministries according to functional criteria. Lack of expertise on the part of the administrators of grant-aided projects and poor communication between the centre and periphery has contributed to Poland obtaining only a small percentage of the Polish–Hungarian Assistance for the Economy (PHARE) grants for which it has applied. The capacity of all public institutions to make use of these programmes must be improved. Decentralisation, if successful, will provide an opportunity to overcome institutional obstacles to development.

At the time of writing (August 1999), and in the wake of the radical reconstruction of central, regional and local government in the 1990s, Poland has entered a phase of transition where the problems which remain to be solved are more or less comparable with those which exist among her West European counterparts. With the completion of the Europeanisation of the constitutional order, the main challenge which Poland now faces is the completion of the process of economic reforms and the harmonisation of Polish law with the *acquis communitaire* of the EU.

## Bibliography


Antoszewski, A. 'Instytucje wladzy ustawodawczej i wykonawczej', in A. Antoszewski and R. Herbut (eds) *Polityka w Polsce w latach 90.Wybrane problemy*, Wroclaw: Wydawnictwo Uniwersytetu Wroclawskiego, 95–114, 1998.

Chapman, R. and O'Toole, A. 'The role of the civil service: a traditional view in a period of change', *Public Policy and Administration* 10, 2, 3–19, 1995.

Cirtautas, A.M. 'The post-Leninist state: a conceptual and empirical examination', *Communist and Post-Communist Studies* 28, 4, 381– 92, 1995.

*The Constitution of the Republic of Poland*, Warsaw: Sejm Publishing Office, 1999.

Crawford, K. *East Central European Politics Today*, Manchester University Press, Manchester, 1996.

Garlicki, L. 'The presidency in the new Polish constitution', *East European Constitutional Review* 81–89, Spring /Summer 1997.

*Gazeta Wyborcza*, various issues, April 1999–July 1999.

Jablonski, A.W. *Rzad i administracja publiczna: Polityka w Polsce w latach 90. Wybrane problemy*, Wroclaw: Wydawnictwo Uniwersytetu Wroclawskiego, 1998.

Kallas, M. *Historia ustroju politycznego Polski X-XX* Wroclaw: Wydawnictwo Naukowe PWN, 1997.

Kulesza, M. 'Options for administrative reform in Poland', *Public Administration* 71, Spring /Summer, 33–40, 1993

Laver, M. and Shepsle, K. 'Cabinet ministers and parliamentary government', ECPR Joint Session of Workshops, Limerick 1991, unpublished manuscript.

McGregor, J.P. 'Constitutional factors in politics in post-communist Central and Eastern Europe', *Communist and Post-Communist Studies* 29, 2, 147–60, 1996.

Pokladecki, J. 'Demokratyczny system kreacji wladzy a elity lokalne', in P. Dobrowolski and S. Wrobel(eds) *Wladza i spolecznosci lokalne a reforma samorzadowa w Polsce,* Katowice: Wydawnictwo Uniwersytetu Slaskiego, 69–79, 1995.

*Rzeczpospolita,* various issues September 1996–July 1999.

Taras, W. 'Changes in Polish public administration', *Public Administration,* 71, Spring /Summer, 13–32, 1993.

Toonen, T.A.J. 'Europe of the administrations: the challenges of '92 (and beyond)', *Public Administration Review,* 52, 2 , 227–34 1992.

—— 'Analysing institutional change and administrative transformation: a comparative view', *Public Administration* 71, Spring/Summer, 151–68, 1993.

Ustroj administracji publicznej, *Zbior najnowszych przepisow*, Wydawnictwo Prawno-Ekonomiczne INFOR, Warszawa 1999.

Wiatr, J. 'The dilemmas of reorganizing the bureaucracy in Poland during the democratic transformation', *Communist and Post-Communist Studies* 28, 1, 153–60, 1995.

# 9 The reform of Polish local government, and the Europe of the Regions

*Wieslaw Bokajlo*

## Introduction

The Maastricht Treaty tied the process of the enlargement of the European Union (EU) to a deepening of its structures. In other words the pursual of 'an ever closer union' is now explicitly linked to the accession of countries of East-Central Europe. It is to hoped that eventual inclusion within a single economic and currency zone will have a positive impact on the countries of East-Central Europe. Whatever the case, engendering such a situation will be a challenge for current EU as well aspirant member-states, of which Poland is one.

Since the signing of the Association Agreement of 16 December 1991, Poland has focused its political strategy upon the challenges it faces in the implementation of the said agreement, as well as the wider challenges associated with Polish accession to the EU. Poland, along with all other applicant states, was obliged to satisfy three fundamental prerequisites of the Association Agreement: (a) the establishment of a market economy (b) the completion of the process of internal democratisation, and (c) the creation of a political and legal system that protects the rights of minorities, in particular national minorities. In other words, the objective was to ensure that as far as possible, domestic law was not in conflict with the EU's *acquis communitaire*.

Then in June 1993 the Copenhagen meeting of the European Council offered a totally new interpretation of the integration process. The EU confirmed its readiness to admit countries that were party to the afore-mentioned European Agreement. However, the Council added that further economic and political criteria concerning democracy, the rule of law, human rights and respect for and protection of minorities, the existence of a functioning market economy, as well as the capacity to cope with competitive pressures and market forces within the EU, should be met.

In order to help aspirants to meet all of these objectives, the EU has established various funds and funding agencies. For Poland, the most important is the Polish Hungarian Assistance for Restructuring of the Economy (PHARE) programme. According to the terms of PHARE, the EU has agreed to part-finance nine schemes designed to support the process of restructuring the most important sectors of the Polish economy. The objectives of the European Agreement are also implemented under this programme. They include measures to improve cross-border co-operation, improvement in the economic infrastructure of depressed regions, and improvements to transportation and communication links on the Polish–German border and along the Baltic littoral. The PHARE programme has also supported initiatives aimed at developing modern and democratic structures of local and regional government. It is to this process we shall now turn.

## Democratisation and decentralisation of the state

The selection of the appropriate institutional and political solutions in countries undergoing a political transformation is a key problem of the state. Poland started to implement the requirements of the EU's regional policy in keeping with the concept of the Europe of the Regions with the Amendment to the Constitution of the Polish People's Republic of 7 April 1989 and the Constitutional Act of 17 October 1992, otherwise known as the 'Small Constitution'.

The central government's special unit for dealing with issues of regional and local self-government is the Committee of European Integration, which is headed by a Minister Without Portfolio of cabinet rank. The government's Centre for Strategic Studies also plays a significant part in formulating regional policy at the national and sub-national levels. At the suggestion of the present cabinet, in September 1999 this centre will be probably converted into the Governmental Office for Regional Policy.

Since the implementation of a full post-communist constitution in the summer of 1997, Poland has attempted to do more than simply tailor its internal reforms to the model established by the EU. In addition, Article 90 of the 1997 constitution provides that: 'The Republic of Poland may, by virtue of international agreements, in relation to certain matters delegate to an international organisation or international institution the competence of organs of state authority' (The Constitution of the Republic of Poland 1997). This is a significant step, and illustrates the extent to which Poland's integration into the EU is a process that involves major change in several aspects of national life, especially those that are related to Poland's ability to meet the so-called Copenhagen criteria. The country has undertaken major projects pertaining to the solidarity of civil society, the development of the economy and of economic competitiveness, as well as strengthening its administrative capacity.

In the 1980s, the population at large believed that democracy would open up new opportunities and possibilities, especially through the erection of democratic institutions that protect individual civil liberties, and limit or exclude partisan political influence from matters of state. Unfortunately, it was forgotten that the transition from authoritarian to liberal democratic rule is a very complex process which would liberate forces which might prove to be very difficult to control. To cut a long story short, the process of democratisation unleashed a vigorous debate on the future shape and direction of the Polish state and society. We shall now turn directly to the specific question of reform to the structures of local and regional government.

## Polish reform of the local and regional self-government

Traditions of local autonomy in Poland originated in the Middle Ages. In the period 1569–1794, the Republic of Nobles was a de facto federation of two national states: the Polish Kingdom and the Grand Duchy of Lithuania. This Commonwealth was composed of three autonomous provinces, which possessed their own legal codes, official languages, legislative, executive and juridical powers as well as their own armies. The example of the Polish–Lithuanian Commonwealth allows contemporary politicians to demonstrate that Poland has not always been a centralised state. To some extent, they are also able to refer to the case of Silesia and its traditions of autonomy. Strong traditions of self-government were present in Silesia to the extent that it, in effect, opted out of the Polish orbit in the middle of the fourteenth century, until being annexed from Germany in 1945. Yet despite these antecedents, for various reasons the modern Polish nation-state founded in 1918 was not characterised by any meaningful level of decentralisation, Upper Silesia and Volhynia aside: a trend which the communists re-enforced (Bokajlo 1998).

After the initiation of reform in the wake of the semi-free elections of 1989, the Polish state embarked on the systematic institutional reform, with the overall aim of democratising public administration. The first stage of reform commenced with the Law of 8 March 1990, which brought into existence autonomous and self-governing communes. Under the 'Small Constitution' of 1992, a two-tier unitary state consisting of two levels of administration was established. At base, communes or *gminy* representing towns and villages came into existence. Above the communes the forty-nine *voivodships* (provinces) remained in place pending envisaged further reform. Each *voivodship* was possessed of an assembly of delegates, the *Sejmik Wojewodzki,* which although bereft of decision-making powers acted as a consultative body for the administration of the region, and were directed by a *voivod* (*chief executive*) who, in Napoleonic fashion, was in fact the appointee and representative of Warsaw.

In turn, the 1997 constitution strengthened the principles and guidelines concerning decentralisation, re-affirmed that the *gminy* formed the basis for local government in Poland, and in effect paved the way for a second stage of reform instituted in 1998. On 5 June of that year, three new statutes were issued concerning regional and local government. A statute of

16 July 1998 defined the electoral law to be used in future elections in local and regional elections, and on 24 July 1998 two further statutes were issued. The first divided Poland into sixteen *voivodships* comprised of 373 counties (*powiaty*) and 2,489 *gminy*. The second was designed to clarify the division of labour between central government and the various tiers of regional and local government. The legislative process was rounded-off by a statute issued on 24 November 1998 which sought to define the revenues of local authority bodies for the financial year 1999–2000. With all the legislation in place, the new authorities began to function on 1 January 1999. However, as we are about to see, not only did the government fail to achieve some of its original objectives, the debate on reform exposed deep fissures within the ruling coalition.

## Political parties and the reform of the territorial structure of the state

With regard to the government's original proposals, there were claims that at the micro level the division of labour between Warsaw, the *voivodships*, county boroughs, counties, and communes was unclear. There was also a suspicion in some quarters that Warsaw was seeking to divest itself of powers in order to escape responsibility for difficult areas of policy-making. For its part, the government claimed that a reduction in the number of *voivodships* from forty-nine to twelve would aid the process of recovery in economic black spots. The government also claimed that the plans would enable it to carry out strategic reforms to the health and education sectors, the administration of which was to be transferred to the *voivodships*, along with responsibility for the environment and transportation infrastructures.

Unfortunately, the governing Solidarity Electoral Action (AWS) found it difficult to maintain internal party discipline and cohesion on the matter. The interests of its various factions came to the fore, and representations from towns which were to lose their status as provincial capitals led some AWS politicians to demand that the new structures should in some way 'protect' by enhanced electoral representation, the interests of *voivodship* capitals and smaller communities. The government countered its internal critics by arguing that enhanced representation for some could only be achieved at the expense of the many. Thus, any 'protection' that might be needed by former *voivodship* capitals was purely a financial matter, and should be the concern of the newly constructed units.

For its part, the AWS's smaller left-liberal coalition partner, the Freedom Union (UW), was consistent in its approach. They supported the AWS's original programme on a far more consistent basis than did many members of the AWS itself. The main concern of the UW was that the legislation be transparent and that the division of labour between centre and periphery be clear.

Complaints were voiced about the nature of the proposed boundaries, with demands being made, particularly in the north of the country, that the proposals take into account economic and historical ties. For example, in the northern city of Bydgoszcz a cross-party alliance of opponents of the proposals was able to ensure the continued survival of the *voivodship*. The various regional interests that came to the fore during this time often united the politicians of different political ideologies. This trend was particularly observable in the Opole *voivodship*, where a cross-party inter-ethnic alliance was developed, and in the Czestochowa *voivodship*. In the latter case, SLD deputies and the subprior of the Jasna Gora monastery acted together to promote the idea of unifying the former Czestochowa, Radom and Kielce *voivodships* within a single new *voivodship*. There were objections from the capitals of the *voivodships* scheduled for abolition that their status would be diminished as a result of demotion to county borough status.

The debate also centred on the rationale of the reform, and it was here that the fragility of the consensus within the AWS was exploited by its opponents. Although the AWS presents itself as being a mainstream christian democratic organisation, elements of it whilst being Catholic are intensely nationalistic and hostile to 'foreign forces'. According to the analysis pursued by AWS dissidents, the Polish Peasants Party (PSL), and various small right-wing parties not represented in parliament, such plans for decentralisation were by their very nature dangerous. They represented not a chance for Poland to re-join Europe, but rather an attempt and opportunity on the part of Poland's enemies once again to destroy the fabric of the Polish nation and state. For such people, the EU represents at best a desire to create a federal Europe of which Poland should steer well clear. At worst, the EU represents a Masonic, atheist conspiracy and, in addition, is but the latest incarnation of the eternal German desire to subjugate the Polish people.

Similar attitudes are exhibited by both the parliamentary and extra-parliamentary right in all European countries, and are not unique to Poland. What is worrying about the Polish example is that such attitudes appear to be more mainstream than in many other European states, and that sections of the clergy, through newspapers such as *Slowo* (The Word) and *Radio Marjya*, have lent credence to such arguments. However, we should not allow ourselves to be come overly despondent. As we move into our study, it will become clear that although such attitudes are fairly commonplace among some sections of society, the Europhobes are in fact firmly in the minority. Let us now turn to our account of the fate of the government's proposals, by showing how the main opposition party played a key role in determining the eventual shape of the new structures

The post-communist Democratic Left Alliance (SLD) claimed that although in coalition with the PSL, they had wanted to pursue reform in this area, and that their priority had rightly been reform of central government and its administrative structures. It stressed that whatever shape reform eventually took, the central government, by virtue of its superior economic resources, would remain the major player. Having said that, the SLD constantly declared its support for the principle of reform. It did so not on the grounds of strengthening the principle of subsidiarity but on those of pragmatism, and efficiency. The SLD also argued that the new units be endowed with administrative structures which would ensure effective government, and allow them to develop the infrastructure of the territory over which they exercised responsibility. They were particularly concerned that the *gminy* would be too weak to raise any substantive funds of their own, and prey to the mercies of higher tiers of government, particularly the centre in Warsaw.

The opposition presented itself simultaneously as the party of Europe, the party of reform, and the party which was most sensitive to regional needs. In its righteous anger against the government, the SLD managed successfully to dodge the issue of why it had failed to reform local and regional government when it had been in power during the course of the previous parliament. This seeming paradox to one side, the SLD was extremely successful in exploiting the weakness of the governing coalition and of the AWS in particular.

Given the outcry which accompanied publication of the proposals, not least within the AWS itself, the whole process had become badly bogged down. The elections, which were originally scheduled to take place in June 1998, had to be postponed to October. Apart from the public protests and the SLD's ultimately successful campaign to force change upon the government, the PSL also got in on the act. In their attempt to present themselves as the defenders of 'traditional Polish values', they made it clear that their opposition to the government was fundamental in nature.

The PSL dominates the Polish countryside as the party which claims to represent the interests of farmers, peasants, and all of those involved in agro-business. Recently, the PSL has had to face competition from the even more conservative and overtly anti-EU Polish Agreement, although it is still too early to tell whether this latter organisation is anything more than a mere flash in the pan. The PSL was and remains a consistent opponent of the government's programme for reform of regional and local government. They were in favour of maintaining the original forty-nine *voivodships* and proposed they be strengthened by the creation of 2,483 powerful *gminy*. They were also in favour of the central government continuing to provide the lion's share of financial resources for local and regional government (*Salzburger Nachrichten*, 13 July 1998). The vote in the subsequent elections for the PSL-led Social Alliance showed that such populism may have managed to reverse the seepage of support away from the party.

Eventual defeat in parliament in June 1998 of the original proposals prompted something of a crisis within the ranks of the governing coalition. Forty-one members of the AWS and eight from its coalition partner, the

UW, voted with the opposition. Although most of this group of defectors did so out of concern for the fate of their regions, there was a hard-core of AWS members whose opposition was based around the premise that the government was in effect promoting the re-Germanisation of western Poland, and of Opole Silesia in particular. To its credit, the AWS then expelled the two most voluble purveyors of this view, a move which forced the resignation of a further six of such like-minded MPs (*Frankfurter Rundschau*, 8 June 1998).

With its proposals for twelve *voivodships* now in tatters, the government attempted to cobble together a compromise solution with the SLD. The result was that in July an amended bill was passed which provided for the introduction of fifteen *voivodships*, 308 counties, 65 county boroughs or *powiaty*, 2,489 communes or *gminy*, giving a total of over 63,000 seats to be filled in the scheduled elections (Central Europe Online, 4 January 1999). However, President Kwasniewski correctly sensed that he could wring further concessions from the government, given that the necessary three-fifths majority to override his presidential veto could not be found. So he vetoed the compromise and informed parliament that he would not lift it unless two additional *voivodships*, one in the north-west and another in south central Poland, were created. In the event, the government conceded the point on the southern (Swietokrzyskie) *voivodship*, and the legislation finally came into law. It was also claimed by both the president and the opposition that these opposition-inspired amendments went a long way to satisfying the objections of people who did not want their regions subsumed within over-large *voivodships*.

## The dual nature of public administration and the distribution of powers

Despite these changes, it is important to remember that the constitution of Poland still defines the country as a unitary state, in which public power is decentralised. The public administration of the state is divided vertically, between the centre in Warsaw and the various tiers of local government. According to the constitution, the central government shall: 'conduct the affairs of state not reserved to other organs or local self-government' and 'manage the government administration'. As head of the executive, the prime minister exercises, within the limits and by the means specified in the constitution and statute, supervision of local self-government. Actions carried out by regional and local authorities are subject to review by the prime minister and *voivods*, who are now appointed in consultation with the directly elected *Sejmiks* (regional assemblies), and with regard to financial matters by regional audit chambers.

The overall system of government is based on the separation of powers between the legislative, executive and judicial branches of the state. Poland has a two-chamber parliament: the Sejm which is composed of 460 deputies, and the senate composed of 100 senators. According to the constitution, the members of both chambers are elected by universal, direct and secret ballot for a term of four years. Members of the Sejm are largely elected by proportional representation within multi-member constituencies. On the other hand, senators are elected under the simple-majority system within *voivodships*, but are not viewed specifically as representatives of the region, unlike their counterparts in the German Bundesrat.

We have already noted how the basic territorial division of the state is determined by statute. The statutes, in turn, allow the various local and regional councils the capacity to develop autonomous social, economic and cultural ties, as well as giving them the ability to carry out their general duties. This operationalisation of the principle of subsidiarity is expressed in Article 163 of the constitution, which states that: 'Local authorities shall perform public tasks not reserved by the constitution or statutes to other organs of public administration'. Therefore, public duties aimed at satisfying the needs of a self-governing community are performed by units of local government. If the fundamental needs of the state require it, the centre may instruct the periphery to fulfil other essential tasks. In addition, regional and local authorities possess individual legal personality and status; they have rights of ownership and other property rights. Finally, we need to note that the self-governing nature of these units is protected by the courts.

Before examining the operational structures of each of the three tiers it would be as well to describe the competencies of each. In that way, we will be in a position better to understand some of the problems and issues which have arisen since the reform took place in 1998. Competencies are delegated according to the principle of subsidiarity. A good example of how this works in practice is the educational sector. The *voivodship* is responsible for the grammar schools. The *powiaty* have responsibility for secondary schools, and the *gminy* take responsibility for the primary schools. As we are about to see, education is by no means unique in terms of the application of the subsidiarity principle.

If we now examine each tier in turn, we find that the voivodships are responsible for areas which are clearly regional in character and cannot be executed by either the *powiaty* and the *gminy*. These include the construction of a regional development strategy, regional spatial planning and development, rural modernisation, economic innovation, transportation infrastructure, cultural and environmental protection, and some social and health services. Defining and developing a regional development strategy is seen to be among the most important tasks of the *voivodships*. Education and health care are also deemed to be of great importance and, as we shall see have proven to be bones of contention.

In turn, the *powiaty* are responsible for such areas as the police, some social services, building regulations, environmental protection, sewage disposal, consumer affairs, road and bridge maintenance, and consumer protection. Finally, the *gminy* are left with those matters of a local significance not reserved for either of the other two levels, central government, or other para-state agencies. Thus they maintain responsibility for local public transport, some health care services, road and council housing maintenance, water supply, environmental protection and land management.

According to statute, in the *voivodships* the administration of designated competencies is conducted by a number of bodies. They include organs of central government; the *voivod* him or herself, the organs of the *voivodship* itself, and a range of ancillary organisations. Functional responsibility is divided according to the nature of the legislation under which a policy is being implemented.

The *voivod* is still the single most important person in a *voivodship's* administrative hierarchy. Unless explicitly excluded by statute, s/he has the final say in determining which policies can be implemented within the *voivodship*. Not only that, as the representative of the central treasury, the *voivod* controls the *voivodship's* purse strings.

In turn, the *voivodships* possess a number of organs which are designed to facilitate the execution of their tasks. The most important are the *Sejmik* which possesses a dual legislative and supervisory role, and the administrative board, both of which are subordinate to the *voivod*. In theory, there is strict demarcation between the competencies of the *voivodships* and those of the *powiaty* and *gminy*, and the *voivodship's* administrative organs do not perform any supervising or controlling functions with respect to either of the aforementioned levels of authority.

The *Sejmik* is exclusively responsible for, among other things, the enactment of local legislation, planning a regional development strategy, the improvement of agriculture, and *voivodship* budget, the allocation of funds, defining and discharging local taxes, ensuring where necessary that the *powiaty* and *gminy* discharge their duties, entering into co-operation with foreign companies, governments and regional and local authorities and managing the property of the *voivodship*. In essence, the *powiaty* perform exactly the same functions in the areas of responsibility delegated to them, as do the *gminy*.

Moving onto the *powiaty*, we have already noted that they may take the form of either conglomerations of *gminy*, or of county boroughs. Like the *voivodships*, the *powiaty* also possess a dual administrative structure, namely the district council and the district board. As its name suggests, the council is a legislative and controlling organ, whereas the board is an organ of administrative power.

The ruling body of the *powiaty* is the district management board, which is presided over by an elected representative (*starosta*). In the communes, the council chooses a chairman and deputy chairman from among its members, and appoints, not necessarily from the midst of the council, a communal board which in small towns is presided over by a chief officer, and in large towns and cities by a mayor or president. In the *gminy*, commune heads, who may bear any one of a variety of titles, are the chief executives of the communes, and are elected from among the ranks of the councillors.

To repeat, according to the constitution, the *gminy* form the basic unit of local self-government. The *powiaty* form a second intermediate tier of local government, which may be constituted either as a set of communes or as a county borough. The highest and largest tier, the *voivodships* are understood as regional self-governing communities, which are constituted by the inhabitants of the *voivodships* by legal force. In order to fulfil its duties, a *voivodship* forms regional self-governmental units and may enter into a contract with other subjects in law. It is interesting to note that despite these reforms, the new *voivodships* still have a dual governmental structure consisting of the *Sejmik* and a *voivod* as representative of central government. Until the office of the *voivod* is either abolished or downgraded in structure it is difficult to envisage Poland evolving a federal structure of government.

## Electoral procedures and constituencies

Each level of regional and local government possesses directly elected assemblies. Elections take place every four years according to universal suffrage and are conducted by secret ballot. Not only are political parties free to contest the elections, citizens committees may be formed for that purpose, and individuals may stand as independents.

At all three levels, a variant of the party list system in multi-member wards is employed. Although in the larger communes single-member wards replace multi-member wards. An unusual feature of the elections was that in communes of fewer than 20,000 inhabitants, the panacharge system was used, thereby enabling voters to select candidates from one or more lists. Things were somewhat simpler at the level of the *powiaty* and the *voivodships*. Here, voters could vote for candidates under an open party list system. At all levels, a 5 per cent threshold was utilised in order to promote a degree of consolidation. *Powiaty* assemblies are composed of no fewer than twenty and no more than sixty members according to population size. With regard to the voivodships, the size of the assembly is determined by the size of the population. Those voivodships with fewer than 2,000,000 inhabitants have forty-five members, increasing by five members per additional 500,000 inhabitants.

In terms of composition of the executive agencies of the various authorities, the procedures are: members of the management boards of the various municipal authorities are elected by the full council, by simple majority, and on condition that at least half the councillors are present. In the *gminy*, the chief officer is elected by an absolute majority of the council. The same arrangements apply for the election of mayors in small towns and presidents in the 104 largest towns and cities. In the *powiaty* the *starosta* is elected by an absolute majority of the votes of the elected members. The president of a *voivodship* governing board, as well as the vice-president and other members of the *voivodship* executive, is elected by an absolute majority of councillors. The *voivod* is nominated (and can be dismissed) by the prime minister of the Council of Ministers.

From a formal–legal point of view, the Polish reform of territorial self-government seems to be able to accommodate the notion of a Europe of the Regions. However, this reform has met with a number of difficulties, some of which shall be outlined below. We have already noted that there were complaints that some aspects of the primary legislation were in places unclear. This has led to disputes over which authorities have competence for which areas. This has been the case especially with regard to the regulations which determine the financial resources of the three tiers. In general, the issue revolves around the extent to which subsidies from central government can be withdrawn and replaced by internally generated funds. Given the shortfall of capital in Poland, this is a particularly thorny issue. In turn, this problem is exacerbated by the fact that the privatisation process has not been completed, and that neither the central government in Warsaw, nor the *voivodship* administrations wish to subsidise loss-making state industries, chiefly mining and metallurgy. The question of agricultural subsidies and who should pay them to Poland's huge number of largely inefficient farmers, is an even more delicate and potentially explosive issue. In theory it would be simple to introduce market-oriented reforms in this sector. In reality, in the short and medium term, it would do nothing more than release a huge number of ill-educated and highly aggrieved people onto the labour market.

The depth and extent of these economic and financial issues is the chief reason why a large number of social groups, including the trades unions, seek to influence every branch of the administration. A combination of lack of clarity over (financial) responsibilities and capabilities, and a history of centralised rule, have combined to revive an attitude among those hurt by (potential) reforms that the state should continue to provide subsidies indefinitely and should continue to provide a cradle-to-grave welfare system. It is far too early to tell how these problems will be resolved. Of decisive importance will be the degree to which changes in Polish political culture show themselves to be fundamental as opposed to superficial. If a decisive change is underway, then the new structures are likely to take root. Alternatively, if the government backs down in the face of demands that it should continue to be the distributor of largesse, then the whole project is likely to flounder, as pressure groups by-pass the new units of local and regional government and continue (successfully) to lobby the centre.

## Political parties and interest representation

According to the constitution, all units of local government have the right to associate with and join international associations of local and regional communities. On this legal basis, numerous non-partisan and non profit-making associations of local and regional authorities have been created in recent years. They include: the Association of Polish Towns, the Union of Small Polish Towns, the Union of Polish Metropolitan Areas, the Union of Rural Communes, the Union of Polish Districts, and the Association of Polish Communes and Regions. These associations may also, on request from any of their members, intercede with either the Sejm, the Senate or the government itself. In addition, representatives of these associations are consulted by the government within the framework of the Joint Committee of Central Government and the Local Authorities. In addition, both houses of parliament possess cross-party regional lobbies.

The constitution allows all citizens the right to submit petitions, proposals and complaints in the public (national, regional, and local) interest, in his or her own individual interest or with the appropriate consent, in the interests of another person. Such petitions may be presented to the relevant organs of the public administration, as well as to other organisations and social institutions which perform duties prescribed within the field of public administration. Most importantly, in theory at least, citizens have the right to use petitions to initiate demands for legislative change. To stand any chance of success, a petition must contain the signatures of at least 100,000 registered electors. So far, no substantive changes have resulted from this mechanism. However, the point, within the context of this chapter, is that the possibility for citizens to band together outside the framework of the political parties, and effect change, does exist.

With regard to perceptions on the part of the general public, Tables 9.1 and 9.2 show that two months before the local and regional elections of 1998, the electorate was divided on the proposals very much according to ideological persuasion. It is also clear that large sections of the electorate did not care one way or the other. The acceptance of the reform package was related to the attitude of the then cabinet, where, in fact, almost half of the ministers opposed the proposals. They, in turn, were backed by around one-third of the coalition's parliamentary membership, which was hostile to the reforms in varying degrees. The government could take small comfort that a bare majority of its supporters supported its plans.

In part, the strategies of the various parties in the subsequent elections was determined by the electoral law and regulations. The UW attempted to be a pioneer in this field, having already taken regional variation into account during the 1997 campaign. Already during the 1997 general election, the UW paid attention to the fact that the debate on regionalisation was intensifying. However, the UW lacks a substantive grassroots organisation, particularly in eastern Poland. As a result, it was often forced to field candidates whose lack of political experience became evident during the campaign (*Zycie*, 6 April 1997). The conservative Movement for the Reconstruction of Poland (ROP), mindful of the 5 per cent clause, allowed its local branches to enter into alliance with whichever

*Table 9.1* Government's proposals for administrative reform?

| | *Do you support the government's proposals for administrative reform? (in %)* | | | |
|---|---|---|---|---|
| *Political orientation* | *Yes* | *No* | *Indifferent* | *Undecided* |
| Leftist | 28 | 57 | 10 | 6 |
| Centre | 34 | 52 | 9 | 5 |
| Rightist | 51 | 32 | 10 | 7 |
| Undecided | 24 | 36 | 25 | 15 |

*Table. 9.2* Governmental project of the administrative reform?

| | *Do you support the governmental project of the administration reform? (in %)* | | | |
|---|---|---|---|---|
| *Potential electorate* | *Yes* | *No* | *Indifferent* | *Undecided* |
| AWS | 56 | 29 | 10 | 5 |
| UW | 53 | 40 | 2 | 5 |
| UL | 46 | 42 | 12 | 0 |
| ROP | 41 | 44 | 14 | 2 |
| SLD | 27 | 61 | 8 | 5 |
| PSL | 23 | 62 | 5 | 10 |
| Uninterested in the election | 27 | 43 | 20 | 11 |

parties they saw fit. As a result, they had several hundred candidates elected to various lists drawn from the AWS, the Homeland Patriotic Movement, and various citizens' committees. As a glance at the appendices shows, the major parties dominated the electoral process at *voivodship* level, but in the *powiaty*, and more especially the *gminy*, the citizens' committees were the real winners.

Consequently, at *voivodship* level, the SLD, AWS, UW and the PSL-led Social Alliance dominate. The major exception is to be found in the Opole *voivodship* where the German minority obtained 21 per cent of the vote, and formed a coalition with the AWS and UW. The Homeland Patriotic Movement coalition of small right-wing populist parties failed to achieve its hoped-for breakthrough (its best result of 7 per cent in the Lower Carpathian *voivodship*). Similarly, the Catholic nationalist 'Polish Family' list did badly (with a best result of 7 per cent in the Lower Silesian *voivodship*). Differences in voter support were noticeable between regions, between urban and rural areas, and according to the order of the election. Thus, in the cities, the national political parties are of the greatest relevance, and civil movements and associations are less relevant. The main exception to this rule is the city of Wroclaw, where the citizens' committee Wroclaw 2000 holds sway.

The results from the Ozimek commune in the Opole *voivodship* serve as a characteristic example of the problems that the political parties faced at *gminy* level. The communal council is composed of twenty-eight members. The greatest number, twelve, belongs to the German minority list. A further thirteen councillors are drawn from a variety of local civic associations: the Civic Committee for the Defence of the Opole-region (six); Agreement and Dialogue (six), and the Alliance for the Ozimek Commune (one). Only one nation-wide political party, the SLD, has any representation at all (three). Under these circumstances the search for coalition partners becomes both necessary and inevitable. In this case, the SLD holds the balance of power, and the mayor was selected from among the Agreement and Dialogue group.

## Territorial reform and the policy process

When introducing the package of reforms to local and regional government, its proponents underlined that these changes constituted a necessary base from which to launch other key reforms, particularly in the areas of a national insurance system, health care, and taxation. Having said that, during the implementation phase, these other issues tended to become submerged within the overall debate on the primary reform.

That the taxation and revenue gathering system has still not been reformed properly is evidenced by the fact that the revenues of the various sub-national units are insufficient to their needs, mainly due to the incompleteness of privatisation, and the fact that locally generated revenue simply does not cover operating costs. Therefore, the local and regional authorities are beholden to central government for financial subvention. The situation is further complicated as a result of a (theoretical) legal requirement upon these authorities to perform only those tasks which they can finance. The situation is particularly severe in the *voivodships*, who have at their disposal only 1.5 per cent of personal income tax and 0.5 per cent of company taxes. In theory, the *voivodship* is supposed to fill the deficit through income generated by its own activities.

The lack of attention to detail in this field is particularly incomprehensible as the whole issue is also tied to that of reform within the primary and secondary educational sectors. The opposition has been able to point out that failure to reform the tax system properly has not only led to general problems of the financial sustainability of the new tiers of local and regional government, but has in addition led to the less than perfect implementation of primary school reform in the *gminy*, and secondary school reform in the *powiaty*.

The same applies to the reform of health care. The opposition once again has pointed out that without basic changes to the taxation system, the *voivodships* cannot possibly hope to perform the health care responsibilities they assumed as a result of the reforms. This issue has proven to be so serious that it has provoked strikes by nurses and doctors. Interestingly enough, the strikes have been directed above all against the Ministry of Health, as opposed to the *voivodships*, who in law are their employers. Whether this is because the medical profession still 'thinks centrally', or because it realises with whom fault lies, and who wields real power, is an interesting question.

The new territorial division has also led to renewed debate on the national electoral law. The debate is not drawn across ideological lines, and unites different interests within the AWS, UW, SLD and PSL. Discussion on reform of the electoral law centres around to what extent, if any, the new *voivodships* and *powiaty* should form the basis for new parliamentary constituencies. At present the country is divided into fifty-two constituencies each of which return between three and seventeen MPs. Cynics argue that what is at stake here is not increasing the profile of the regions at national level, but the desire of those parties currently represented in parliament to maintain their grip on power.

The fact that national parliamentary constituencies were drawn-up in the early 1990s with reference to the old *voivodship* boundaries is considered to be the main disadvantage of the present electoral law. So far, no one has actually formally proposed that the current sixteen *voivodships* form the primary base for new parliamentary constituencies. To do so would call into question one of the fundamentals of Polish parliamentary democracy, namely that the national parliament represents the nation as in its entirety, and not as a series of regions. A possible alternative would be to re-model the Senate on the lines of the German Bundesrat. However, once again this has not been formally suggested, and given that Poland is not a federal state, the German model is not necessarily appropriate.

On the other hand, there does appear to be general agreement that constituency boundaries need to be in some way re-drawn. One scheme would involve creating fifty-two multi-member constituencies, each of which would return an equal number of MPs to the Sejm. Each of these new constituencies would be more or less equal in terms of population size. The advantage of such a reform would be that as no major legislation would be needed, it might actually get through parliament. Given the cross-party support that exists for such a measure, it may safely be assumed that the cynics have a point. All the main parties calculate that such changes are likely to accrue more benefits than costs, and are likely further to promote the homogenisation of the party system.

## EU regional policy and regional and local elites

Results of opinion polls confirm that the aforementioned problems notwithstanding, by and large the general public, particularly in Silesia, still supports the principles that lay behind the reforms. There is also evidence that the councillors and their officials are reasonably satisfied with the way in which things are progressing. Results of polls conducted by the Institute of Political Science at the University of Wroclaw, provide a useful snapshot of these attitudes.[1] They also give us some idea of the attitudes exhibited by actors in local politics in Poland toward the idea of the Europe of the Regions. The polls were conducted (primarily among councillors) in the communes of Ozimek, Glogowek and Glucholazy of the Opole *voivodship*, and in the Boleslawiec commune in Lower Silesia *voivodship*. The results from the Glucholazy and Boleslawic communes which are inhabited almost exclusively by ethnic Poles, may be compared with those of the surveys from the Ozimek and Glogowek communes, which have a large number of declared Germans. It is also worth mentioning that the Ozimek commune comprises of twelve villages and is of an industrial–agricultural character. The Glogowek commune (twenty-three villages) is primarily agricultural in character, the Glucholazy commune (seventeen villages) is of an agricultural–touristic character, and the Boleslawiec commune (twenty-nine villages) has an agricultural–industrial character.

In terms of geographical location, the Glucholazy commune borders the Czech Republic, the Boleslawiec and Glogowek communes are close to the border with Germany, and the Ozimek commune lies about fifty kilometres north of the Czech border. With regard to the two communes with a large German population, we find that the Germans are concentrated in the rural periphery. In the case of the Ozimek commune, around 41 per cent of the population regards itself as German, whereas in Glogowek, the Germans form a slight majority of the population with 51 per cent of the inhabitants claiming to be German. In both communes German social-cultural associations are exteremely active.

In all the communes, respondents showed themselves to be familiar with the idea of a 'Europe of the Regions'. Above all they share the hope that it will help to bring political decision-making closer to citizens. The results from Ozimek showed 45.5 per cent of councillors shared this belief. The comparable results from Glogowek, Glucholazy, and Boleslawiec were 85.7 per cent, 40 per cent, and 40 per cent respectively. Similarly, the councillors believed that a Europe of the Regions would deliver them greater competencies. The respective figures were: Ozimek 42.6 per cent, Glogowek 71.4 per cent, Glucholazy 60 per cent, and Boleslawiec 83.4 per cent. The respondents also tended toward the view that the development of a Europe of the Regions would provide a degree of protection from attempts by the (Polish) state to recentralise. In Ozimek, 27.2 per cent, in Glogowek, 57.1 per cent, in Glucholazy, 60 per cent, and in Boleslawiec, 83.4 per cent of respondents were of that view. In Ozimek, 40 per cent, in Glogowek, 71.4 per cent, in Glucholazy, 20 per cent, and in Boleslawiec, 50 per cent of those interviewed believed that a Europe of the Regions would be helpful in reducing the salience of national boundaries. Only 10–16 per cent of councillors in all the communes believe that the creation of a Europe of the Regions would make European politics more, as opposed to less, complex. Whether a *gminy* was mono or multi-ethnic appeared to be a factor in assessments of whether the formation of regional authorities will eventually lead to increased interference by Brussels in the internal affairs of Poland. In Ozimek no one (Pole, German or Silesian) was of that view, and in Glogowek, only 14.3 per cent agreed with the proposition. On the other hand in the ethnically homogenous communes of Boleslawiec and Glucholazy. 66.7 and 80 per cent, respectively were of the opposite view

All, or almost all, of the councillors of the 'Polish' communes, together with a majority of the councillors in the 'German' communes, shared the view that after Poland accedes to the EU, Polish local and regional authorities would have a distinctive influence on its decision-making processes. Only a minority of German councillors felt that the opposite was more likely. Among the councillors, and irrespective of ethnicity, there exists a marked divergence in opinion on whether insufficient financial resources will continue to be a basic problem for Polish local and regional government in terms of interest articulation in Brussels. All councillors in the Ozimek commune, but only one-fifth in the Glucholazy commune, were of this opinion. It is difficult to determine the difference in views here, but it is reasonable to assume that once again they are a reflection of the difference in ethnic make-up between the communes, and the different agendas and perceptions which stem from that fact.

Taking into consideration the fact that in recent years Poland has entered into inter-regional as well as cross-border co-operation within the Euroregion programme, it was no surprise to learn that the councillors recognised types of co-operation as the most effective strategy for the consolidation of Polish regional and local authorities within the EU. Understandably in the two communes with a large German population, there was greater interest in the possibility that the creation of a Europe of the Regions would lead to enhanced rights for ethnic minorities. In Glogowek 86 per cent of those polled were of this view, and in Ozimek the figure was 64 per cent. Interestingly, in the two mono-ethnic communes, councillors were keen to underline that such matters were primarily the affair of the Polish state. All the respondents were, however, united in the belief that in a Europe of Regions there would be a 'deepening of democracy and development of civil society'. They also shared the belief that developments in this direction would contribute positively in a number of other areas. These included the consolidation of regional and structural policy (Ozimek 45.5 per cent, Glogowek 85.7 per cent, Glucholazy 40 per cent and Boleslawiec 50 per cent). The figures were similarly positive with regard to environmental protection: Ozimek 58.3 per cent, Glogowek 100 per cent, Glucholazy 80 per cent and Boleslawiec 83.7 per cent; and also with regard to hopes for improvements to the transportation infrastructure (Ozimek 54.5 per cent, Glogowek 85.7per cent; Glucholazy 40 per cent, and Boleslawiec 100 per cent).

Interestingly enough, although there was great enthusiasm among respondents for the creation of a Europe of the Regions, as we shall discover shortly, this enthusiasm was also tinged with realism. The circumstances whereby the current Committee of the Regions may come to perform not only consultative and advisory functions but transform itself into the EU's third arm, have not yet arisen. On the other hand, the Committee is supposed to form one of the main planks upon which the Europe of the Regions will be built. At present, many EU politicians either reject outright the creation of such a framework, or steer clear of any substantive discussion of the issue. Those interviewed in our survey proved to be no exception to this general rule. In Ozimek, 30 per cent of respondents ranked the Europe of the Regions in third place behind identification with the nation-state and the EU respectively. The comparable results for the other *gminy* were Glogowek 29 per cent, Glucholazy 40 per cent and Boleslawic 50 per cent.

As if by way of confirmation of these reservations, most councillors assessed their knowledge about the role and activity of the EU Committee of the Regions as either being average or weak. Only in the Boleslawiec commune did a majority of councillors (67 per cent), estimate their knowledge as being high. Then again, although the Committee was formed on 9 March 1994, polls indicate that as many as 70 per cent of EU citizens have never even heard of it. The councillors' hopes concerning this institution speak volumes with regard to devoting greater resources dedicated to improving knowledge of the concept. The respondents themselves were convinced that the inter-institutional role of the Committee is very important (Ozimek 50 per cent, Glogowek 100 per cent, Glucholazy 80 per cent and Boleslawiec 50 per cent). Whether or not such hopes are misplaced, remains to be seen.

## Conclusion

In this chapter we have surveyed the process of the reform of local and regional government in Poland. It should be clear from the above analysis that this process of reform is dynamic and is still not yet complete. It is also clear that in some quarters, at least, the process has not yet gone far enough, and that more needs to be done in order to dovetail Polish structures within the broader federalist project. Considering that it is only just over ten years since the transition from authoritarianism began, in general, Polish democracy works remarkably well. Poland has gone some way to preparing itself for a Europe of the Regions should such a structure ever arise. The political culture of Poles, attitudes toward the idea of regional autonomy, and the general development of civil society may all help to popularise the vision. In his 1998 book, *Recreating Europe. The European Union's Policy towards Central and Eastern Europe*, Professor Alan Mayhew examined the problems faced by the applicant countries in terms of accession. Fiscal redistribution, institutional reform, environmental repair, the restructuring of heavy industry and agricultural concerns are, of course, serious issues which need to be settled. However, we cannot argue with his conclusion that enlargement is not only necessary but that it will bring major gains to the whole continent. It is to be hoped that this chapter has clarified some of the issues involved.

# Appendices

*Appendix 9.1* Results of the Polish Communal Elections: October 1998

| *Party* | *Total Number of Seats* | *Share of Vote* |
|---|---|---|
| Solidarity Electoral Action (AWS) | 7,141 | 13.57 |
| Democratic Left Alliance (SLD) | 5,686 | 10.81 |
| Social Alliance | 3,153 | 5.99 |
| Freedom Union (UW) | 699 | 1.33 |
| Homeland Patriotic Movement | 206 | 0.39 |
| Polish Family | 136 | 0.26 |
| Citizens' Committees | 35,599 | 67.65 |
| Totals | 63,765 | 100.00 |

*Appendix 9.2* Results of the Polish County Council Elections: October 1998

| *Party* | *Total Number of Seats* | *Share of Vote* |
|---|---|---|
| Solidarity Electoral Action (AWS) | 3,130 | 30.42 |
| Democratic Left Alliance (SLD) | 2,825 | 27.45 |
| Social Alliance | 1,341 | 13.02 |
| Freedom Union (UW) | 371 | 3.61 |
| Homeland Patriotic Movement | 48 | 0.47 |
| Polish Family | 14 | 0.14 |
| Citizens' Committees | 2,561 | 24.89 |
| Totals | 10,290 | 100.00 |

*Appendix 9.3* Results of the Polish *Voivodship* Elections: October 1998

| *Party* | *Total Number of Seats* | *Share of Vote* |
|---|---|---|
| Solidarity Electoral Action (AWS) | 342 | 40.00 |
| Democratic Left Alliance (SLD) | 329 | 38.48 |
| Social Alliance | 89 | 10.41 |
| Freedom Union (UW) | 76 | 8.89 |
| Homeland Patriotic Movement | 2 | 0.24 |
| Polish Family | 1 | 0.11 |
| Citizens' Committees | 16 | 1.87 |
| Totals | 855 | 100.00 |

## Note

1 Piotr Bogucki, Marek Cynk, Andrzej Krasicki, Monika Miller.

## Bibliography

Bajor, H. 'National minorities in the transformation process', in C. Bryant and E. Mokrzycki (eds) *Democracy, Civil Society and Pluralism in Comparative Perspective: Poland, Great Britain, and the Netherlands*, Warszawa: IFiS Publishers, 1995.

Bokajlo, W. (ed.) *Federalism. Teorie i Koncepcje*, Wroclaw: Wydawnictwo Uniwersytetu Wroclawskiego, 1998,

Bryant, C. 'Civil society and pluralism', in E. Wnuk-Lipinski (ed.) *Sisyphus. Social Studies*, 1, 8, 1992.

Bryant, C. and Mokrzycki, E. (eds) *Democracy, Civil Society and Pluralism*, Warszawa: IFiS Publishers, 1995.

Central Europe Online, www.centraleurope.com/ceo/news/03.html, 4 January 1999.

*The Constitution of the Republic of Poland*, Sejm Publishing Office, Warsaw, 1999. *Frankfurter Rundschau*, 8 June 1998.

Jednaka, W. *Proces kształtowania sie systemu partyjnego w Polsce po 1989 roku*, Wroclaw: Wydawnictwo Uniwersytetu Wroclawskiego, 1995.

Mayhew, A. *Recreating Europe. The European Union´s Policy towards Central and Eastern Europe*, Cambridge: Cambridge University Press,1998.

Michta, A. 'Democratic consolidation in Poland after 1989', in K. Dawisha and B. Parrott (eds) *The consolidation of democracy in East-Central Europe*, Cambridge: Cambridge Universiy Press, 1997.

Müller-Graf, P. and Stepniak, A. (eds) *Poland and the European Union-Between Association and Membership*, Baden-Baden: Nomos Verlag, 1997.

Przeworski, A. 'The choice of institutions in the transition to democracy: A Game Theoretic Approach', in E. Wnuk-Lipinski (ed.) *Sisyphus Social Studies* 1 8, 1992.

Pudlo, K. 'Zmiany w statusie i warunkach dzialalnosci mniejszosci narodowych oraz etnicznych w Polsce w latach 1989–1994', in: A. Jablonski, K. Paszkiewicz and M. Wolanski (eds) *Studia Politologiczne*, Wroclaw: Wydawnictwo Hector, 1995.

*Salzburger Nachrichten*, 13 July 1998.

*Zycie*, 6 April 1997.

# 10 Poland, *die Vertriebenen*, and the road to integration with the European Union

*Tadeusz Lebioda*

## Contexts and controversies

'The road of Poland to the European Union leads through Germany', is a phrase which gained common currency in Poland during the 1990s. The grounds for such a belief lay in the positive evaluation by the German government of Poland's application for membership of the European Union (EU), as evidenced in Article 8, paragraph 3 of the German–Polish Treaty on Good Neighbourly and Friendly Co-operation of 17 June 1991. They also lay in the rapid development of diplomatic, trade and cultural relationships between the both countries following the collapse of communism. There is no doubt that since 1989, Germany has played the part of unofficial spokesman of Poland's interests in its efforts to join the European structures. Additionally, for historical reasons, the German political elite also feels itself in some way obliged to improve the lot of Poland and its people. The progress made since 1988, when the process of internal transformation finally got underway in Poland, can scarcely have been imagined by those courageous individuals who began the dialogue.

The acceptance by the majority of Polish society that Germany and the Germans should play such a role would have been equally difficult to imagine. Prior to the transformation, for most Poles, especially those with direct memories of World War Two, the picture of Germany and the Germans continued to be shaped by that tragedy and its consequences. During the period of communism the negative perception of Germany by the average Pole became fixed in the social consciousness. Only with the fall of the Iron Curtain and the end of the Cold War did it become possible to hold an open and honest debate about a whole host of bilateral issues.

Undoubtedly one of the key issues, which after 1989 was subjected to serious re-evaluation on the Polish side, was the problem of the mass expulsion of Germans from former German territory between 1945 and 1949. As a result of decisions taken on 2 August 1945 at the Potsdam conference, about 114,000 square kilometres of German territory east over the rivers Oder and western Neiße was either acquired by the Soviet Union or placed under Polish administration (pending the conclusion of a peace treaty). At Potsdam it was also decided that the majority of Germans living in those areas who had not already fled or been thrown out, were be to 'transferred to Germany in an orderly and humane manner'. In sum, approximately 3,150,000 inhabitants of Silesia, together with about 2,000,000 inhabitants of Pomerania, 2,000,000 inhabitants of East Prussia and 350,000 Germans from the Free City of Danzig, or almost 7,500,000 people in total lost their homes, property and, in tens of thousands of cases, their lives. During the period of communist rule, in the eyes of Poles, the expellees embodied the fears, prejudices and antipathy toward all things German. To understand the changes that have taken place since 1988 in the Polish perception of this issue and how the process of integration with the EU has influenced the debate, it is first necessary to delve into history.

## The historical legacy

Polish perception of this issue was the product of three elements: the anti-German attitude of the majority of Polish society as determined by its experience of German occupation, the circumstances under which the communists had come to power in the late 1940s, and the use by the communists of the 'German threat' as a means of bolstering their internal legitimacy. The wartime experience shaped the perception of at least two generations of Poles toward Germany and the Germans. The draconian police and administrative methods, the ruthless struggle against the Polish resistance, the extermination of the Jewish population, and the mass enslavement of around 2,000,000 Poles in German-occupied Poland successfully inculcated feelings of hatred and vengeance not only toward Nazis but towards all Germans (Kersten 1994: 52–3). The aggressive nationalism articulated after the defeat of Germany influenced the behaviour of Poles towards Germans before and after Potsdam. Almost all Germans were held personally responsible for the policies of the Nazi party, and the fate of expellees was perceived as the legitimate consequence of a war started and lost by Germany.

This attitude helps to explain the huge general levels of violence, especially in 1945 and 1946, against the remaining German population, which was devoid of any means of self-defence. Official propaganda was marked with virulence and hatred toward all things German. Such a statement finds confirmation not only in the words of communist activists of that period but also in the opinions of many of the representatives of the opposition and the Catholic Church. As the leading opposition politician and president of the Polish Peasants Party (PSL), Stanislaw Mikolajczyk, expressed it in 1946: 'If someone is German, his place is in Germany, not in our country'.

Once the expulsions were completed, the general mood and attitude of Poles towards the expellees quickly became a tool in the hand of Polish communists, who used it to broaden the level of identification of society with the new regime. The communist government, supported as it was by the Red Army, the Soviet secret police, terror and propaganda, sought to legitimise itself through anti-German propaganda in the absence of any democratic mandate. That is why the Polish Workers' Party (PPR) paid so much attention to the newly labelled 'Recovered Territories'. Former German areas were even given their own ministry when, on 13 November 1945, vice prime minister Wladyslaw Gomulka became Minister for the Recovered Territories. Gomulka was anti-German by conviction and allowed his animosity to colour his political behaviour until his final fall from power in December 1970. Gomulka sought to transmit his anti-German phobia to almost the whole of society, and to present the communist party and its Soviet allies as the sole guarantor against attack by a vengeful Federal Republic. As Minister for the Recovered Territories, Gomulka was both thorough and enthusiastic. He believed that his first priority was to rid former German areas of all Germans, saying that: 'We do no want to have enemy and foreign German elements in our country.' (Gomulka 1968: 100). There was to be no place for Germans in the mono-ethnic state which the Polish communists were trying to create. Gomulka continually preyed upon Polish fears of Poland playing host to a fifth column, reminding the population at large of allegations that Poland's pre-war German minority had been almost universal in its admiration for Hitler. In short, Gomulka sought to strengthen and legitimise communist rule by enhancing anti-German sentiment in Polish society.

It has to be said that this strategy captured the popular mood of the day. However, it is a fundamental misapprehension that is still shared to this day by many Poles and Germans, to believe that all Germans were in fact expelled from Poland. After October 1945, former German nationals, whom the Polish government claimed merely to be superficially-Germanised Poles, were usually allowed to stay after submitting to a so-called 'verification procedure'. This involved a bureaucratic process for the applicants, most of whom had already been incarcerated in concentration camps for having been German. An analogous process of rehabilitation was instituted for Germans who had been citizens of pre-war Poland. In total, approximately 1,017,000 persons were eventually granted Polish citizenship, which became obligatory (without consent) on 8 January 1951. The majority, some 815,000, were to be found in Upper Silesia, with around 80,000 resident in the Olsztyn *voivodship* in Masuria. (Ziolkowski 1959). To this number must be added the designated German minority of approximately 250,000 that was largely concentrated in the industrial centres of Lower Silesia. Crucially, neither (former) German inhabitants of Upper Silesia and Masuria, nor (former) German citizens of pre-war Poland were allowed to manifest any sign of German culture.

Gomulka was keen to complete the expulsion process for another reason. This was the need to re-house millions of Polish refugees and internally displaced persons (Gomulka 1968: 100). The national census of 1950 showed that there were 4,550,000 incomers to the Recovered Territories. They were comprised of 2,8000,000 migrants from central Poland, 1,550,000 repatriates from the *kresy* of eastern Poland, which had been annexed by the Soviet Union in 1939, and around 150,000 returnees from a variety of other countries (*Narodowy Spis Powszechny* 1955). Naturally enough, the authorities sought to create a bond between the incomers and the areas in which they now found themselves living, and, wherever possible, economic incentives were offered in order to help individuals and families prosper. Migration, forcible (as it often was also for the incomers) or otherwise, provided opportunities to achieve a higher standard of living. Such policies went hand-in-hand with a continuation of anti-German rhetoric aimed at re-enforcing dependence upon and identification with the state. The population was constantly 'reminded' that the Federal Republic was full of vengeful people who, if it were not for the vigilance of the communist party, would surely attempt to re-gain their homes and property in a typically German manner. An assessment of the extent to which such sentiments were widespread in post-war Germany is beyond the scope of this chapter. However, the activities of the refugees and expellees associations, inadvertently or otherwise, for years added grist to the communist propaganda mill.

Between 1948 and 1950, various such associations came to be formed in the Federal Republic. Eventually, in October 1957, an umbrella organisation, The Union of Expellees (*Bund der Vertriebenen*, BdV), was created. In addition, a refugees' party, which in the late 1950s had limited electoral success, came into being, and a minister with responsibility for refugee questions was appointed. Despite their lack of substantive electoral success, the refugees were successful in creating an effective network of lobbyists, and in establishing a large number of cultural and social associations. For decades the leaders of those organisations, such as Herbert Czaja (a pre-war christian democrat) and Herbert Hupka (whose Jewish mother was murdered by the Nazis), were portrayed as the greatest enemies of Poland. In addition, a crude historiography was created which presented Polish–German relations as having been a pattern of heroic Polish defence against naked German aggression led by, among others, the Teutonic Knights, Frederick II and Otto von Bismarck. Inevitably, the BdV was presented as the latest incarnation of intrinsic German evil, and the alliance with the Soviet Union being the only means of keeping them out.

## The years of glacis

On 6 September 1945 a decree on agricultural reform in the Recovered Territories gave title, but crucially not ownership (see below), of former German lands to the new Polish inhabitants. This and the unceasing propaganda portrayal of the Recovered Territories, created the image in the public mind that the area was Poland's promised land. Throughout

1945 there was a steady stream of applications from people willing to take over German retail outlets, industrial plants, workshops and former German property in general. The change in sovereignty received further domestic legal sanction through a law of March 1946. The BdV has never accepted that either Act has validity in international law.

The whole issue of property ownership and residual uncertainties concerning its status, albeit much more so in Poland than in Germany, has to this day contributed to a residual feeling that somehow these questions are still open. In the 1950s in particular, many people in both countries believed, and in a majority of cases hoped, that somehow the territorial status quo could once again be altered. That expellees should have desired this, should come as no surprise at all. Interestingly enough, this seems to have been the attitude of a majority of those Poles who had been re-settled from the *kresy* to the Recovered Territories. The air of uncertainty, which given geopolitical realities and without wishing to be callous, was largely self-induced, contributed to a feeling among the newly established Polish population and their descendants, that they were somehow only temporary migrants. Official propaganda concerning the ever present German threat, continued to re-enforce such fears, which of course was exactly its objective.

The communists also used hatred towards all things German to eliminate domestic opposition and to strengthen their power. The referendum of 30 June 1946 contained a question which asked the voter to assent to the post-war border changes with Germany. The flood of anti-German propaganda which accompanied the referendum vote was used to weaken support for the PSL and its leader, Stanislaw Mikolajczyk. He was accused of supporting the view of the United States and the United Kingdom that all that had been agreed at Potsdam was that German territory be placed under Polish administration, pending the conclusion of a peace treaty. Although the American and British governments were correct, Mikolajczyk's position was in fact little different from that of his communist opponents. Either way, the communists received the approval they sought, and Mikolajczyk's position was further weakened.

The issue of attitudes towards the expellees, Poland's western border, and the whole subject of the Recovered Territories, became in the language of the nomenklatura, one of 'German militarism, revisionism and revenge'. From the time of the foundation of the two German states in 1949 the differences between the two were underlined. Ten years after the Treaty of Görlitz of 6 July 1950 in which the German Democratic Republic (GDR) recognised Poland's western border, Gomulka said:

> Until the Potsdam decisions are executed in all Germany, as they were in GDR, militarism and the spirit of revisionism will live in the other German state . . . the Polish nation must be vigilant and Europe will not be certain of lasting peace.
>
> (Gomulka 1968: 118)

Throughout the entire period of 'really existing socialism', the Polish population was reminded of this apparent German threat. The BdV and its associated *Landsmannschaften* were presented as fascist associations, who were waiting to seize the Recovered Territories. However, from the middle of the 1960s, this negative portrayal of Germany and the Germans began to change. Although the general public still possessed a negative attitude towards Germans in general, and the expellees in particular, the cultural, social and political elite was beginning to enter into a tentative dialogue with sections of German society. Although communist propaganda continued to portray Germans in lurid terms, independent Polish writers and journalists began to seek common ground with their German counterparts. In 1965, such steps were famously supplemented by the Catholic and Evangelical churches. The well-known letter of the Polish bishops to their German counterparts of that year is considered as marking the real start of Polish–German reconciliation. For the first time, the Polish episcopate spoke about the expulsions, a series of events which, in Poland, had simply been glossed over for the past twenty years. The bishops' request for forgiveness was a brave attempt to promote reconciliation with Germany. This gesture was roundly condemned by the communist authorities, and wider public opinion in Poland was similarly hostile. It seems that majority of society considered the tough reaction of the government toward the episcopate to be justified. Given that a large majority of society supported the church in every other regard, the reaction of the general public shows how deep was the antagonism of Poles towards all things German. Antipathy toward the expellees was so great, that most people lost sight of the fact that the bishops explicitly rejected any thought of re-positioning Poland's western border and defended post-war Polish *raison d'état*. During the commemorations of the twentieth anniversary of the defeat of Germany, the Polish primate, Cardinal Wyszynski, said: 'We were here and again we are here! . . . This is not German property, this is our Polish soul'. The standpoint of the church on that issue simply reflected the standpoint of the communist party and of the society as a whole.

In the 1970s, after the signing on 7 December 1970 of the Treaty on the Mutual Renunciation of Force with the Federal Republic, relations between Poland and the Federal Republic thawed a little. The new government of Edward Gierek softened the tone of anti-German propaganda. In addition, expellees were allowed to visit Poland, and in exchange for trade credits and loans, for the first time since the late 1950s, Polish citizens of German descent were allowed to migrate to the Federal Republic in number. However, the issue of the expellees continued to be used by the authorities as a bogey with which to scare the remainder of society. It was only in the 1980s, with the growth of the Solidarity movement, that a real impulse toward dialogue became apparent. This was important, because, at last, Polish perceptions of the expellees began to change in some meaningful way. More and more (prominent) Poles began to call for an improvement in

German–Polish relations. The wartime generation of Stanislaw Stomma, Tadeusz Mazowiecki, Jan Jozef Lipski, Andrzej Szczypiorski, Wladyslaw Bartoszewski and Mieczyslaw Rakowski had their counterparts among those born after the war. The period of activity of such as Aleksander Kwasniewski, Janusz Reiter and Wlodzimierz Borodziej overlapped with the collapse of the post-war order. Their re-evaluation of Polish perspectives of what occurred between 1945 and 1949 in turn formed the basis of the sea change in Polish–German relations which occurred in the 1990s.

## Toward dialogue and debate 1989–91

Signs of real progress between the two sides first became evident in the period 1989–91. The traditional, monochrome image of the expellees inculcated into Polish society started to fade. Some BdV activists, such as Hartmut Koschyk and Herbert Hupka, commenced a direct dialogue with the Poles. Although there was as yet no consensus there was at least communication. The two sides started to discuss the past and with that the fear of direct contact decreased. As this debate became more widespread, it influenced the discussion of stereotypes and taboos. Of course, tensions and problems remained, but both sides began to put personal prejudices and hurt to one side, and began to listen to one another. This was especially hard for many Poles, who for years had thought of the expellees purely as culprits and never as (fellow) victims, and general public opinion still lagged some way behind that of elite groups.

The introduction into the Polish political and social language of the term 'expulsion' (*Vertreibung*), to describe what had happened, was a symptom of the attempt to overcome stereotypes of the expelled. The term was used for the first time in an official state document in preamble to the Polish–German border treaty of 14 November 1990. For decades in Poland, use of this term was perceived almost as treason of the national interest. This particular taboo had prevented Poles from perceiving the tragedy and misfortune of millions of German who had been deprived of everything they had possessed. Use of the word expulsion slowly ceased to be inconvenient. Until 1989, Poles were simply used to hearing the apologies of Germans for crimes committed during the war. They avoided facing the problem of their own actions in the context of the expulsions. However, for people who perceived themselves as having been the victims of aggression and not the perpetrators of wholesale revenge, it was difficult to take a step forward and admit to responsibility for these actions. Since 1989, the issue of the expulsions has been debated regularly in the mass media, has been the subject of research, and has appeared in the social conscious more and more often. Gradually, the tragedy of what had happened to the expellees reached the consciousness of most Poles. They started to talk about the crimes committed against Germans after the war in concentration camps such as those in Lambinowice, Potlice, Milecin and Jaworzyna. By the second half of the 1990s, sections of the Polish public were demanding that those perpetrators of such crimes be brought to justice. The destruction of the Cold War European order and the construction of a new order of relations with Germany forced Poles to re-evaluate the past. Such developments showed that Polish society was slowly coming to terms with the fact that the process of expulsion had been tainted with evil. A little more than a decade after Jan Jozef Lipski in 1981 had drawn attention to the moral aspects of that evil in his essay 'Two Homelands-Two Patriotisms' (Lipski 1981), real progress was being made. This is despite the fact that many of the expellees also found it difficult to perceive Poles in terms of anything other than negative stereotypes.

During the period 1989–90, the expellees aimed to keep the border and property ownership questions open. They based their arguments on domestic German law, the decisions of the Potsdam conference, and a completely unrealistic assessment of both domestic and wider European political realities (*Pressemitteilung der BdV*, 25 January 1990). Such arcane and archaic arguments simply served to have a negative effect on Polish public opinion. Symptomatic of the attitude of the BdV was their initiative of the expelled 'Peace through a free vote' (*Frieden durch freie Abstimmung*), a scheme which caused widespread revulsion in Poland. The idea was to collect signatures in Germany in support of a plebiscite on the future of the Recovered Territories. Prominent individuals within the BdV, such as general secretary Hartmut Koschyk and its long-standing president, Herbert Czaja, labelled the initiative as 'the biggest political offensive by the expellees since the controversy over the eastern treaty in 1970' (Pressemiteilung der BdV, 5 April 1990). Their aim was to collect a million signatures in favour of such a plebiscite and to use such a petition as a means of influencing the 2+4 negotiations in their favour. In Poland, such fantastic schemes were taken as evidence that the BdV was simply pursuing a more subtle form of revanchism.

As a 'concession', it was proposed that those Poles born within the boundaries of pre-war Germany also be allowed to vote in the envisaged plebiscite. The voter was to choose one from three alternatives. The first was to 'confirm' that the territory continued to be part of Germany. The second was to opt for the 'Europeanisation' of the territory under the auspices of the EU and a joint Polish–German commission. The third option was to 'cede' the territory to Poland. The BdV actually favoured the second option, which one might just about construe as progress of a sort. It felt that such a solution would satisfy both sides, facilitate the settlement of property ownership and restitution questions, and guarantee the future of Poland's remaining German minority.

Unfortunately, Polish public opinion was not appraised of political realities in Germany, and was unaware of the fact that the BdV simply lacked the support needed to have this idea taken seriously. Thus the actions of the BdV caused an increase of anti-German sentiment in Poland. Different polls in 1990 showed that as many as 79 per cent of the population held that Germans had no rights to the Recovered Territories. At the as much as 89 per cent supported the Polish government's standpoint in the 2+4 negotiations. Luckily, the idea of a plebiscite proved to be a fiasco. Instead of the expected one million signatures, the BdV could manage only 208,989. Conversely, the failure of the BdV showed the Poles that the real strength of the BdV was much less than as presented in communist propaganda.

After the collapse of the plebiscite idea contacts between the BdV and with representatives of the newly legalised Federation of German societies in Poland (*Verband der deutschen Gesellschaften*, VdG) came to play an ever more important role in the wider public arena. The VdG had begun to establish itself from the late 1980s and was particularly strong in parts of Upper Silesia. The BdV had, in fact, been instrumental in the establishment of the VdG and its affiliate organisations, and the latter organisation quickly assumed the role of political spokesman for the remaining Germans in Poland. That it could do so was partly through the failure of rivals to institutionalise themselves, and partly due to inaction by the Polish government to foster alternatives. This in turn was caused by the failure of virtually the whole of Polish society to recognise that several hundred thousand of their co-citizens actually thought of themselves as Germans.

Co-operation between the BdV and the German minority was particularly visible in the context of negotiations on the German–Polish Treaty on Good Neighbourly and Friendly Co-operation of 17 June 1991. On 26 October 1990, the BdV and the governing council of the VdG produced a memorandum of sixteen items addressed to the governments of Germany and Poland. Once again both the demands of The BdV and the language employed caused consternation in Poland. It was also suspected, and not without justification, that the prime objective of the memorandum was to secure a special autonomy statute for those areas in which, according to the BdV and VdG, significant numbers of Germans still lived. The contents of the memorandum and the general tenor of the BdV and its supporters did little to undo the damage caused by the aborted plan for a plebiscite. Aspects of the memorandum, which once again appeared to call into question Poland's territorial integrity and which demanded positive discrimination for Germans, were particularly unwelcome (Berlinska 1991: 40). Both the Polish government and the majority of Polish society possessed a shared conviction that the issue of the rights of Poland's (newly visible) German minority were a purely internal affair. They rejected the idea that the BdV should act as some kind of mediator, and also rejected the erection of bilingual signs in areas of German settlement. Neither were they keen on allowing members of the German minority to (re-)apply for German passports, although this point was eventually conceded. Similarly, the wholesale right of return and restitution of property was deemed by the

Polish side to be beyond the pale. Either way, the majority of the ideas put forward by the BdV and the VdG did not find their way into the final text of the treaty, although many of the points raised in the memorandum were left open. Once again, the results of opinion polls show that the demands of the BdV had a negative opinion upon the Poles themselves. About 50 per cent of respondents demanded that the rights of the German minority be in some way constrained, and that only 29 per cent agreed that the German minority should be allowed to manifest and demonstrate its culture. As many as 32 per cent actually thought that remaining Germans should be encouraged to emigrate (*Polityka*, 14 April 1990).

On the other hand, the treaty of 1991 did provide a new basis for broad discussion on a whole range of issues. Having said that, it did not go down well with elements of the BdV, who perceived the treaty as some kind of sell out. The most spectacular manifestation of internal tension within the BdV was the resignation, as general secretary of Hartmut Koschyk on 26 June 1991. Koschyk evaluated both the treaty and the changing attitude of the Polish government in a positive manner. He believed that future Polish membership of the Council of Europe and the European Union (EU) would provide a forum for overcoming the 'weak points' of the treaty (*Pressemitteilung der BdV*, 9 June 1991). Koschyk recognised that the signing of the treaty marked the beginning of new phase of relations with Poland. He was of opinion that the expellees and German minority in Poland should co-operate with both governments in order to reach a comprehensive mutually beneficial agreement. He also called on the expellees to visit their places of birth and to become involved in the development of bilateral relations and to focus upon the here and now and the future and not solely upon the past. He advocated cross-border regional co-operation, youth exchange programmes, and the involvement of all sections of society in this programme of rapprochement. In short, he was advocating that Poland and Germany repeat in the 1990s, the experience of France and Germany in the 1950s. Interestingly, prior to the spring of 1991, Koschyk's standpoint had been barely indistinguishable from that of his more orthodox colleagues. His conversion to a more moderate programme was symptomatic of a deeper cleft between the generations within the BdV.

For several reasons during the middle of the 1990s, Polish fears of Germany and the Germans continued to decline. The fact that Poles could now witness through free contact with Germany the patent marginalisation of the BdV played an important role here. In addition, many BdV activists became involved in direct dialogue with Poles, and thereby made their own contribution to a lessening of tensions. Since 1990, Hupka and Koschyk have simply been the most prominent of the hundreds and thousands of expellees who have visited Poland, and form the vanguard of those who have taken part in public discussions and academic conferences. They have appeared in the mass media and have organised bilateral symposiums together with Polish partners. The extent to which the expellees have embraced the idea of dialogue with Poland at the beginning of the new millennium has led to a situation in which the BdV receives greater media attention in Poland than in Germany. In addition, a huge swathe of publications on the expulsions and their aftermath has appeared in Poland. There has also been an upsurge in former German territory in the true history of these areas, as opposed to the bowdlerised and, on occasion, falsified histories as presented by the communists. Small museums and memorials dedicated to outstanding German figures have come into being in some towns and cities. In effect, Poles have begun to demonstrate a sense of inner security by accepting the achievements of those who lived in the area before them. Stereotypes of 'a thousand years of hostility' between Poles and Germans have been revised. The Polish political elite has played its part by repeatedly condemning the process of expulsion. Former Prime Minister Wladyslaw Bartoszewski's speech to the German Bundestag in 1995 was the most spectacular example of this phenomenon. Undoubtedly, all those factors influenced a change in Polish perceptions of the expellees and the process of expulsions. According to opinion polls, sympathy for the German position has increased since 1991 by a few percentage points. In 1995, as much as 65 per cent of all Poles considered the expulsions as necessary in order to promote internal stability and consolidate post-war Poland. Yet only 50 per cent approved of the means used. By 1997, results showed that as much as 47 per cent of the population recognised that harm had been done to innocent civilians, with only13 per cent were refusing to admit that any harm had been done at all (Borodziej and Hajnicz 1996: 49–50). The data demonstrate that there has, in recent years, been a change in Polish perceptions. This has come about as a result of an open airing of the reality of what occurred between 1945 and 1949, and the resultant German–Polish dialogue on that issue and the dialogue with the expellees. Large numbers of Poles have gradually freed themselves from previous complexes, as have most Germans. As we shall now discover, after negotiations with the EU over Poland's envisaged membership of that organisation commenced, the debate continued and intensified.

## The expellees, Poland and the EU

Formal negotiations on Polish accession to the EU began in March 1998. In September 1998, Helmut Kohl lost power in Germany. This was a double-edged sword for the Poles. The new Social Democratic/Green coalition in Berlin has little time for the BdV. By the same token, neither do they accord Poland the same degree of importance as do the Union parties. With the commencement of serious negotiations, platitudes had to be replaced with serious discussion of those issues where common ground may be difficult to achieve. This new situation has forced the Polish public to pay closer attention to the issues of common concern to Poland and Germany, which have been left open by the treaties of 1990 and 1991. The Polish public began to perceive these issues, such as the possibility of allowing foreigners to live and work in Poland, especially Germans in general and expellees in particular, the issue of bilingual signage, and the rights of foreigners to own real estate, within the context of the membership negotiations, but with half an eye upon the BdV. As the negotiations have progressed, the issue of real estate has become highly contentious and has served to revive prejudices toward the expellees. The myth that the Germans would simply buy Poland as opposed to invading it, has been revived by the Peasant's Party (PSL), and various national Catholic organisations. In 1996, the 1920 law on real-estate ownership was amended, with the result that fears of an imminent 'German capital offensive' were revived. According to the amended law, foreigners have to acquire special permission from the Ministry of the Interior in order to buy land or property. Foreigners who have lived in Poland for at least five years and persons in law which have their head offices in Poland were exempted. Since 1996, foreigners can buy a plot of non-agricultural land of not more than 0.4 of a hectare. Although the amounts of land involved are not great, the amendment was not without significance in former German areas. Above all, it was feared that Germans with their superior purchasing power would start making offers for (their former) homes that a large majority of Poles simply could not compete with. There was also a fear that Germans had been abusing the previous law by buying land through the use of 'straw men' in essentially bogus joint venture companies. The theory postulated that having completed such deals, the German partner would then simply buy out the Polish partner, and 'return' such property to German ownership. The extent to which this has happened is unknown. Either way, two things have to be made clear at this point. The first is that the amendment is not retroactive, and that such deals that may have been concluded are legally valid. The second point is this: the fact that this became an issue in the absence of any proof that it was a widespread phenomenon, demonstrates the extent of Polish sensitivities on the problem. German companies have sought to buy land in former German areas. However, whether or not this has been done on political as opposed to economic criteria is a moot point. In addition, Germans who have openly admitted to putting in a bid to buy back their former homes have overwhelmingly met with an outright refusal to sell. What this admittedly rather lengthy discourse shows is this: that of the thirty-one items of negotiation between Poland and the EU, the question of the right to buy real estate is the most contentious. Such contention is, in turn, the consequence of Polish–German history. In an effort to mollify passions in Poland, the Polish government recently proposed that it be granted a five-year transitional period for the purchase of non-agricultural land, and eighteen years for the purchase of agricultural land by foreigners.

The BdV can rightly be accused of having deliberately and provocatively drawn attention to this issue. In 1997, they encouraged expellees to bombard both Polish officialdom and individual Poles with letters pointing out that Polish ownership of former German territory was open to contestation in EU and international law. The campaign was also in part designed to put pressure on the Polish government to adopt a less rigid stance on the issue of property restitution to former German owners. It was pointed out that Hungary and Estonia have passed laws providing for compensation and the restitution of citizenship, and that Romania has allowed German expellees the right of return. In addition, the letter writers argued that a return of Germans and German capital could aid in the regeneration of economically depressed areas.

It goes without saying that such ideas are completely unacceptable to an overwhelming majority of Poles. The protestations of BdV activists that they are no longer demanding restitution on a one-to-one basis are also treated with disdain. Unfortunately, the BdV seems to have created the impression among many Poles that large numbers of Germans spend their spare time searching for title deeds to property that lies beyond today's border. Those Poles taken in by this unlikely alliance of Polish nationalists and German fantasists believe that: 'Germany supports the accession of Poland to the EU because it will allow them to win a war without a shot. They will come back for their property, and they will enclose the Poles in reservations' (*Polityka*, 13 June 1998). The despatch of these letters did nothing more than damage the progress made in recent years. As we have already noted, Polish Germanophobia weakened in the early and mid-1990s. However, it never completely disappeared, and the realisation that Polish real estate laws are incompatible with superior EU legislation, coupled with the ruthless exploitation of that fact by the BdV, has done undoubted damage to both Poland's relationship with Germany, as well as to Poland's prospects of early accession. The BdV has long been of the opinion that the German government forms an explicit link between Polish accession to the EU and the right to restitution, compensation and return. We have already seen how the treaty of 1991 left the question open. From the Polish point of view the restitution of property in east Germany to former owners is seen as evidence of what could happen to Poland, despite the difference between the two cases.

There seems to be particular concern in Poland over the attitude of east Germans. This may have arisen as a result of the partial failure of unification and the comparatively higher incidence of attacks on foreigners in east Germany. Some estimates assess the percentage of east Germans who were either born in former German territory now in Poland or in pre-war Poland, and their descendants as being as high as 25 per cent of the entire population. Unlike their co-nationals in the Federal Republic, expellees who became citizens of the GDR received no special financial assistance from the government. Although they have been eligible for such assistance since unification there is a feeling in some Polish quarters that many east Germans have an unfulfilled land hunger, and that they might compensate for an inferiority complex vis-à-vis west Germans with aggression towards Poles. Once again, such fears say more about Polish than they do about German society. Whereas it is true to say that the German communists did as little to break down German–Polish stereotypes as did their Polish counterparts, the large majority of east Germans have preoccupations completely unrelated to the events of 1945–49.

Although the Polish Ministry of Foreign Affairs has replied firmly that in principle, the issue of property restitution is closed, many Poles do not believe such assurances, and have doubts as to whether the matter of property has disappeared in the context of international law, following the conclusion of the treaties of 1990 and 1991. As evidence they cite the unclear position of international law on the matter, and the fact that the government itself says exceptions may be made in the cases of Jews and members of Poland's pre-war German minority (*Wprost*, 7 June 1998). The assurances of the Ministry of Foreign Affairs that EU legislation is invalid when it comes to former German territory are treated with similar scepticism, as are the assurances of the German government that they have no interest in the matter.

Polish anxieties are further increased by the fact that most are still rentiers as opposed to proprietors. On 8 March 1946, the incoming Polish authorities confiscated all property from ethnic Germans. Real estate was then distributed on a series of 99-year leases. In September 1997, in an attempt to solve this problem, the law was amended to grant leasehold in perpetuity. Once again the fear is that Polish law may conflict with international law, and that any claim brought by an expellee may be found to be valid. These fears are exacerbated by statements by the Polish Ministry of Foreign Affairs that the expellees do have a moral if not a legal point and that Poland will not avoid the painful questions of who was harmed by the war and history. The fact that according to the Treaty of Rome the contestation of property ownership must be decided by the courts of the country in which the property lies, does little to allay Polish fears. This particular set of fears is justified by the commonly held fear that the Polish legal system is in part incompetent and corrupt.

Despite the fact that the German government has repeatedly declared that as far as it is concerned this issue is closed, there is of course a rump of politicians within the Union parties connected to the BdV for whom it is very much open, as was evidenced by a declaration of the Bundestag on 29 May 1998. This resolution which has absolutely no legal weight in Germany stated that the 'The expellees and the German minority [in Poland] are the bridge between Germany and its eastern neighbour'. The resolution itself was more than anything else aimed at securing the expellee vote for the Union parties in the upcoming general election. The resolution also affirmed that in the view of its supporters the process of EU enlargement should facilitate the preservation of the German cultural heritage in East-Central Europe, and expressed the hope that the federal government will continue to support German minorities in the countries of Central and Eastern Europe. Inevitably, what raised Polish hackles was the repetition of the view of the resolution's supporters, that the expulsion of ethnic Germans from Poland and elsewhere and the related seizure of German real estate was contrary to international law.

Inevitably the resolution provoked a Polish counter-reaction. The Euro-sceptic and sometimes Germanophobe PSL sponsored a counter-resolution in the Polish Sejm. The deepening crisis of Polish agriculture and the escalation of radical protest associations of farmers, fuels the scepticism of the PSL. We must not forget that up to 30 per cent of Polish society can be counted as (part-time) farmers and peasants. They are wary of the EU, Germany's motives for supporting Polish entry, and are especially wary of the expellees. The text of the resolution ignored changes in German–Polish inter-state and interpersonal relations after 1989, and despite the fact the government withheld its support, the resolution was still passed (*Polityka*, 11 July 1998). The inner contradictions of the resolution, which included a number of ill-worded phrases, shows that even among the political elite there are still unconscious fears of Germany. The resolution states that the Polish membership of the EU cannot in anyway effect either Poland's borders or Polish title deeds. This is despite the fact that neither EU law nor the Bundestag's resolution call either into question. That both parliaments still contain members who have seemingly not been able to break with the past indicates that at both elite and mass level much work still needs to be done (*Polityka*, 5 September 1998).

The fact that such a resolution, grounded as it was on misunderstanding and misconstruction of the facts was passed, shows that wide sections of Polish society still has not engaged seriously with the reality of the debate on European enlargement. It cannot be denied that in the minds on many Poles the BdV is much stronger than it is in reality. Similarly, there is widespread ignorance of what Polish membership of the EU will actually mean in terms of costs and benefits. It is pointless either to shirk this fact, or to pretend that these problems do not exist (*Tygodnik Powszechny*, 12 July 1998). Many Poles living in former German areas simply cannot comprehend a situation in which foreigners, including expellees, could be allowed to reside in Poland, as long as they fulfil criteria agreed in Brussels by the EU member-states. Neither do many Poles understand that in EU and international law, expellees might just have a case against the Polish government with regard to the expulsions of 1945–9, and the subsequent refusal, a tiny fraction of cases to one side, to pay any form of compensation.

## A balance sheet

With regard to the wider issues of the German–Polish relationship, much depends on how Germany treats Poland in the immediate future. Comparison is often made with France. Whereas this comparison is valid in the sense that Franco-German reconciliation forms a worthy model for Germany and Poland to follow, in other ways it is not apt. The Franco-German axis within the EU was formed for a specific political purpose. Although Germany is Poland's largest trading partner, and indeed largest creditor, Poland does not possess the same political weight as France, and the circumstances of the 2000s are not the same as those of the 1950s. Besides which, Franco-German relations are not burdened by a continual debate over the 'events' of 1939–49 and their legacy. What is more, as the prospect of integration looms ever larger, the German public, more concerned with the here and now, as opposed to history, is growing ever more wary of the potential 'flood' of cheap Polish labour into an already saturated labour market. They are also aware of the fact that whereas Germany is and will continue to be for some years, the main contributor to the EU budget, Poland will be a net beneficiary.

However, none of these issues means that Polish–German relations are about to regress to the pre-1989 depths. Closer relations have become possible thanks to an increase in cross-border trade, the huge increase in tourism, direct human contacts, political dialogue, the open presentation of Polish–German history in the Polish media and a recognition that murder and expulsion was a fate shared by Poles and Germans. All these factors, coupled with the general increase in economic co-operation between the two states, has led to an increase in mutual trust. Public opinion polls show that positive evaluations of Poles toward Germans have gradually increased each year since 1989. On the other hand, they also indicate that a certain ambiguity still exists. Ancient fears and prejudices still lurk in the background, and in some ways effect the interactions of elite groups who themselves are largely free of such concerns.

There is little doubt that at the beginning of the twenty-first century a lot of the enthusiasm of the early 1990s has faded. Having said that, economic, political and military relations remain excellent, and Germany still performs its role as de facto Polish ambassador to Brussels, although dangers remain. A majority of Germans may now oppose Polish entry of the EU on the grounds earlier stated. The BdV could also try to influence matters here. Paradoxically, however, given the total disinterest that most Germans have in the fate of the expellees, the BdV is likely to have a greater impact in Poland than in Germany. Here its shrill and incessant demands can be blown out of all proportion by the Catholic right, the PSL and their allies, and be used as a device to keep Poland out of the EU. A lack of knowledge of domestic German politics and uncertainty concerning rights within and the structures of the EU may lead to an increasing sense of doubt in Poland. A substantial number of Poles and the expelled very often behave as autistic people who live in their imaginary worlds, without ever communicating with external reality. It is to be hoped that this intellectual autism is not allowed to blight an otherwise promising landscape. In order to do that, however, Polish society needs to come to terms with the reality of the expulsions and the consequences, and rid itself of the idea that the BdV is a major political actor in Germany. Once a sense of proportion has been achieved, it may at last be possible to bid farewell to the ghosts of history.

## Bibilography


Bachmann, K. and Krenz, J. 'Przeprosic za wypedzenie ?': Warszawa: Znak, 1997

Berlinska, D. *Procesy demokratyzacyjne w Polsce a mniejszosc niemiecka na Slasku Opolskim*, Poznan: Przeglad Zachodni, Bd 2, 1991.

Borodziej, W. and Hajnicz, A. *Kompleks wypedzenia-raport koncowy*, Warszawa: Fundacja Schumana, 1996.

Kersten, K. *Repatriacja ludnosci polskiej po II wojnie swiatowej*, Wroclaw: Ossolineum, 1994.

Lipski, J. 'Dwie ojczyzny–dwa patriotyzmy', *Kultura* 10, 3–29, 1981.

*Narodowy Spis Powszechny z dnia 3 Lipca 1950*, Warszawa: GUS 1955,

Gomulka, W. *o problemie niemieckim*, Warszawa: Czytelnik, 1968.

*Polityka*, various issues April 1990–September 1998.

*Pressemitteilung der BdV*, 25 January 1990.

*Pressemitteilung der BdV*, 5 April 1990.

*Pressemitteilung der BdV*, 9 June 1991.

*Tygodnik Powszechny*, 12 July 1998.

*Wprost*, 7 July 1998.

Ziolkowski, J. 'Przeobrazenia demograficzne i spoleczne na Ziemiach Zachodnich', *Kultura i spoleczenstwo* 3, 1, 129–48, 1959.

# 11 The European Union and Ukrainian–Polish relations

*Andrzej Dybczynski*

This chapter has a dual purpose. The first is to reveal the connection between Poland's aspiration to become a member of the European Union (EU), and Poland's policy towards its Ukrainian minority. The second is to assess Polish–Ukrainian inter-state relations and the potential ramifications of halting the process of European integration at the Polish–Ukrainian border. In order to achieve these objectives, it will be necessary to outline a number of themes. First we will consider some of the general issues surrounding the rights of ethnic minorities in Poland, and how they relate to the question of Polish accession to the EU. Second, within that same framework we will analyse bilateral Polish–Ukrainian relations. Finally, we will consider the sometimes bitter history of Poland's Ukrainian minority between the years 1918 and 1999.

## The Polish state and its national minorities

Since the beginning of the 1990s Poland has set its sights on membership of the EU. In order to achieve this objective, Poland is undergoing a vigorous programme of internal transformation. This transformation has not only affected the political system, but also touches the very fabric of Polish society. Hence, in the literature dedicated to processes of transformation in Poland, scholars mainly refer to the overall transformation of society and its institutions, and the deep changes of mentality that are taking place.

Contemporary Polish governmental policy towards its indigenous national or ethnic minorities is to a large extent determined by its aspiration to join West European supranational organisations, most particularly the EU. As a result, in recent years successive Polish governments have sought to adapt Polish law and practices to those normally found in the EU. This applies to its national minorities just as much as it does to any other aspect of the civil code. From the beginning of the 1990s Poland began to take steps which would achieve precisely this objective.

At one level, these and other changes which the governments of the time initiated could be classified as 'examinations in democracy'. In other words, successive governments drafted laws and parliament passed legislation with half an eye to the West. Having said that, it has come as something of a surprise to many sections of Polish society that people in the 'West' think far less about Poland than they initially believed. For many observers of the Polish scene, governmental policy toward national minorities is the litmus paper of the young Polish democracy. Similarly, given the ferocity of past inter-ethnic conflicts in this part of Europe, the Polish political elite realised that in order to demonstrate its commitment to pluralism there would have to be a transparent break with past practices.

Apart from anything else, a country prone to internal instability is hardly likely to be allowed to join the EU. It was therefore in Poland's national interest to alter its policies towards indigenous ethnic minorities, lest it become prey to accusations similar to those regularly posited toward the Turkish government with regard to its Kurdish minority. This is not to say that the situation in Poland is any way comparable to that of contemporary Turkey. However, Polish policy-makers were aware of two things. First, that Turkey's treatment of its Kurdish minority is one reason why Turkey's application to join the EU remains in limbo. The other is that, since 1918, relationships between the majority Polish community and indigenous minorities have been complex and sometimes tragic. Before moving directly into the case study itself, we should pause to consider which factors, other than the desire to join the EU, help to determine both mass and elite attitudes towards indigenous minorities in today's Poland.

For the large majority of society the issue of national minorities is not crucial because at around 2.5 per cent of the total population, they are not very numerous. Following the huge demographic changes that took place between 1939 and 1945, and the passage of time, many of the old conflicts have quite simply faded. In today's Poland, society's view of a particular minority is very often governed by its view of that minority's 'parent state'. Thus, attitudes towards Germany determine Polish attitudes toward the German minority in Poland. Similarly, attitudes toward Ukraine determine societal attitudes toward the Ukrainian minority resident in Poland. This tendency is re-enforced by the fact that a majority of Poles rarely if ever come into regular contact with members of the country's minority groups, and as a consequence have little first-hand experience of them.

History still does, of course, play a part in shaping contemporary perceptions, as does the current value system. The practical consequence of all these factors is that, as we have already seen, far from there being a uniform attitude toward Poland's minorities, each minority is viewed differently. As a consequence, given that the 'East' is now viewed with distrust in Poland, so many Poles view their own Belorussian and Ukrainian minorities with distrust. In other words, a negative stereotype continues to prevail. On the other hand, the generally positive attitude which exists toward both Germany and the Czech Republic has resulted in a more positive assessment of those Czechs and Germans native to Poland. This does not, of course, mean that even in the latter cases there are no problems. Rather, it is to say that any conflicts which arise tend to be local in character and of a non-fundamental nature. As a consequence there is little exposure in the national media of any issues concerning such minorities.

## Ukrainian–Polish relations: past and present

Having so completed our overview, let us move directly into the case study. The case of the Ukrainian minority and Ukrainian–Polish relations is instructive for two reasons. The first is the complicated nature of Ukrainian-Polish relations especially during the twentieth century. The second is the character of the Polish–Ukrainian border, which according to some authors separates two cultures, and possibly two different worlds (Huntington 1996). Hence observation of the mutual relationship of those two distinct, but very closely connected worlds is extremely interesting. According to this perspective, German–Polish relations are conducted between peoples of a common civilizational core. Polish–Ukrainian relations, however, are not only relations between two nations, they also represent the contact of two different cultures, the opposition of individualism to collectivism, and of Catholicism and Orthodoxy.

Polish policy towards the successor states of the former Soviet Union is by no means uniform. Above anything else it is determined by geopolitical factors. Although Polish–Ukrainian relations go back to medieval times, the factors which shape their contemporary form are relatively recent. In the case of Ukraine, contemporary relations are hampered by the complicated pattern of Ukrainian–Polish relations since 1918. Yet, the Polish government is supportive of Ukrainian independence. It has sought to bolster the Ukrainian economy, and act as Kiev's ambassador in Brussels. However, for obvious reasons Poland is constrained in terms of what it can do. Let us now assess contemporary Polish–Ukrainian inter-state relations.

In the 1990s Polish-Ukrainian relations displayed a twofold character. At the level of high politics, in December 1991 Poland was the first country to recognise the independence of Ukraine. This act was complemented in May 1992 by the conclusion of a treaty on Good Neighbourly Relations and Friendly Co-operation. In 1994 the Polish and Ukrainian ministers of foreign affairs issued a joint declaration establishing the basis of future co-operation between the two states. The culmination of this process came in 1997, when President Kwasniewski of Poland and President Kuczma of Ukraine signed a joint declaration of reconciliation.

The new Polish political elite quickly realised how important an independent Ukraine was to the security of Poland. This importance stems from the very difficult and unpredictable situation in Russia, which still has aspirations of returning to superpower status. Some elements of the Russian political class have hinted that if the opportunity arose they would attempt to reconstruct the former zone of influences. The means that

Russia might use were outlined in a document produced in 1994, and military methods were not excluded (*Zalozenia polityki zagranicznej Federacji Rosyjskiej' 1994*). From the Polish standpoint, as long as Ukraine remains an independent, democratic state, the attempt of Russia to become a superpower in the old style will be impossible to execute. In effect, Poland has begun to create a 'strategic partnership' with Ukraine. This aspiration dovetails perfectly with Ukrainian objectives which are to strengthen ties with the western part of the continent. In such a situation, Poland has become a natural partner in Ukrainian *Westpolitik*. So Poland plays for Ukraine a role analogous to that which Germany plays for Poland. Poland acts as an advanced and more experienced advocate for Ukraine in its attempt to engage with the EU and other supranational European organisations.

As a result there is close co-operation between Warsaw and Kiev. However, in terms of policy outputs, there is much that is left to be desired. In spite of all the previously referred to initiatives and agreements, ancillary co-operation has been slow to develop (Gill and Gill 1997). The reasons for this failure are to be found in the continued economic weakness of both countries, especially Ukraine. Despite its success in restructuring the economy, Poland is still in no position to offer substantial amounts of aid to its eastern neighbour.

Unfortunately, everyday interpersonal relations do not seem to have developed as well as those at official level. The negative image of Ukrainians held by many Poles has not been overcome, and in fact seems to be growing. In a 1998 survey, only 13 per cent of respondents claimed to have a positive image of Ukrainians. At the same time, 59 per cent of those questioned described their attitude towards Ukrainian as 'negative' (CBOS 1998). Only Romanians and Roma (Gypsies) received lower rankings. Poles still tend to stereotype Ukrainians as chauvinists.

This negative image of Ukrainians has been strengthened by phenomena typical of the market economy that came into being in both countries. After the opening of the borders, thousands of Ukrainians started to trade in Poland. In the first half of the 1990s, visitors from the East selling cheap low-quality products became very common in Polish markets, bazaars, streets and railway stations. Together with their appearance there came an upsurge in crime, for which the media tended to blame Ukrainians. At the same time, many Poles looked down upon the visibly poorer Ukrainians, forgetting that with regard to Western Europe it was the Poles who were often treated warily for precisely those reasons that they in turn used to justify negatively stereotyping Ukrainians.

This 'Polish inferiority complex' had a crucial role in fortifying the negative image of Ukrainians in Poland. A majority of the Polish population is keenly aware of the difference in the standard of living between Poland and most of Western Europe. This can be evidenced with reference to Polish attitudes toward Germans, who are admired and respected by most Poles, but are not necessarily liked. The easiest way to compensate for such feelings of low self-esteem is to find identify someone who is palpably worse off and transmit feelings of inadequacy toward them. For many Poles, Ukrainians play precisely that role.

This negative image of Ukraine has been increased by conflicts concerning remaining traces of Polish life in west Ukraine. The example of the Polish cemetery in Lwow is significant. Many Polish soldiers who died fighting Ukrainian nationalist forces in 1919 are buried there. Attempts at renovation of these graves are a sensitive matter for the young Ukrainian state, and especially for the right-wing Ukrainians. Every few months Polish graves are desecrated. As a result there is a constant stream of complaints from Poland that the Ukrainian government is doing nothing to stop such attacks. On top of that, the approach of some sections of the Polish media to this whole issue does little to ease tensions over the matter.

## Ukrainians in the first Polish Republic

After the partitions of Poland at the end of the eighteenth century, most Ukrainians found themselves living under Russian rule, and were subject to a policy of Russification. However, the Ukrainians of eastern Galicia found themselves under the rule of Vienna, and it was in those areas which found themselves under the more relaxed rule of the Habsburgs that the Ukrainian national movement came into being (Chalupczak and Browarek 1998: 55). At the end of the First World War, Ukrainian nationalists attempted to establish an independent state. A four-cornered war broke out between Ukrainian nationalists, the Poles, the Red Army and White Russian forces, and by 1920 the independent Ukrainian People's Republic had ceased to exist. Following the end of the subsequent Russo-Polish war in 1921, Ukraine was divided between Poland and Bolshevik Russia. As a consequence, around five million Ukrainians found themselves to be citizens of the new Poland. Accounting for between 14 and 16 per cent of the population they constituted the most numerous national minority. In fact, in the four south-eastern *voivodships* (provinces) in which they were largely concentrated, Ukrainians constituted between 34 and 72 per cent of the total population. It is also calculated that Ukrainians accounted for as much as 60 per cent of the entire population in the territory seized by Poland to the east of the Curzon line (Chalupczak and Browarek 1998). To put it another way, due to the prevalence of Ukrainians and other non-ethnically Polish groups, ethnic Poles were in a distinct minority in the recently conquered area. Ukrainian society was overwhelmingly peasant in character (80 per cent), with urban dwellers constituting a mere 4 per cent of the total. In terms of religious affiliation, around 60 per cent were Uniates, with the remainder being Russian Orthodox.

During the inter-war period national minorities throughout East-Central Europe were ostensibly protected in both national and international law.

However, in Poland, as elsewhere, the reality of the situation was somewhat different. A treaty of 1919 guaranteed the protection of political and civil rights, allowed for the creation of minority schools, and provided for other linguistic rights. However, Polish public opinion regarded the treaty as a diktat and a violation of Polish sovereignty. In 1934 the Polish government suspended the treaty, and replaced it with new provisions in the constitution of 1935.

Ethnic Ukrainian parties of various stripes also established themselves during this time. There was also a Ukrainian language press which faced a constant battle with the censor. In 1922 the parliament voted to introduce autonomy in eastern Galicia, to create a Ukrainian university, and to make Ukrainian the official administrative language of the region. The legislation was however never implemented. Inter-communal relations were unsurprisingly tense. Ukrainians tended to boycott parliamentary elections and acts of terrorism were not uncommon. The Polish authorities acted with measures of mass repression. By 1930 some predominantly Ukrainian areas were effectively beyond the reach of the local administration, and a decision to 'pacify' them was made. The pacification measures consisted of the closure of Ukrainian schools, house to house searches, the destruction of property, mass arrests and acts of random and organised violence against suspected Ukrainian nationalists. The results of these actions were predictable. The population at large was radicalised, and many Ukrainians who previously had been loyal to Poland switched allegiance. In 1935, the government began to moderate its stance, and some improvement in the lot of the Ukrainian minority occurred. Nevertheless, the government continued to exploit issues of ethnicity in areas of Ukrainian residence, and the Uniate Church in particular faced a hostile state.

Yet, in September 1939, following the German invasion, most Ukrainian organisations declared their support of Poland, although in the Volhynia region attacks on Polish state property as well as individual Poles took place. When on 17 September the Soviet Union invaded eastern Poland and re-took the territory lost to Poland in 1921, the Ukrainian population was split in terms of its attitudes. Some supported the new Soviet power. Others rejected it or attempted to remain neutral.

The Ukrainian population now found itself partitioned between the Germans and the Russians. Although for the most part the Germans banned all Ukrainian political activity, the Organisation of the Ukrainian Nationalists (OUN) was tolerated. Indeed, the Germans returned churches to the Uniate Church, helped to establish a Ukrainian schools system, and granted Ukrainians special economic privileges. In the areas under Soviet control, those non-communist activists who did not flee were arrested. The communist party took control, and proceeded upon the Ukrainisation and Bolshevisation of the whole of society.

Despite the hopes of many Ukrainian nationalists, the Germans did not create an independent Ukraine following their assault of June 1941 upon the Soviet Union. Some of these disappointed nationalists continued to lobby the German authorities for independence, whilst at the same time working on plans to create the Ukrainian Insurgent Army (UPA). Plans to formulate a common Polish–Ukrainian resistance to both the Germans and the Soviets came to nothing (Chalupczak and Browarek 1998: 87). By the beginning of 1943 the UPA, with the acquiescence of the Germans, commenced attacks on the Polish civilian population. The objective was to create mono-ethnic communities in areas which had previously been multi-ethnic in character. Inevitably, Polish resistance fighters became involved in this struggle, and between February 1943 and July 1944 it is estimated that between 70–100,000 Poles and 20–30,000 Ukrainians were killed. Unsurprisingly, to this day this episode is still a matter of controversy between Poles and Ukrainians.

## The post-war aftermath

Following the defeat of Germany, the number of Ukrainians living in Poland was dramatically reduced. Poland's new eastern border ran along the Curzon line with small deviations in favour of Poland. As a result of the shift in borders, Poland's Ukrainian minority declined to a total of around 700,000. At one level, the Soviet authorities and their Polish allies were trying to create an artificial ethnic border between Poland and the Soviet Union. A honeymoon period between the Polish communists and ethnic Ukrainians had ended as early as September 1944 when the Lublin government struck a deal with its counterpart in Kiev concerning a forcible exchange of populations. As for the Ukrainians who were due to 'transferred', they resisted by all the means at their disposal. A bitter and complicated struggle broke out involving on one side the UPA, and on the other, Polish communist security forces, backed by where necessary the Red Army. At the same time non-communist Polish resistance forces were fighting the Red Army and their Polish allies, which led them on occasion to enter into tactical alliances with the UPA. By 15 August 1945 a total of 'only' 222,509 Ukrainians had been deported (Drozd 1998). If anything, by this time the UPA had actually gained the upper hand, forcing the Polish government to send massive re-enforcements to south-east Poland in September 1945. The programme of mass deportations was carried out with renewed ferocity, and by the end of 1946, around 480,000 Ukrainians had been expelled from post-war Polish territory. According to a subsequent census of that year, approximately 162,000 Ukrainians remained in Poland, although in reality the figure may have been as high as 200,000. Despite the fact that the Polish government wanted to deport the remainder, for reasons of their own, the Soviet authorities refused to sanction any further deportations (Drozd 1998).

Thus thwarted, the Polish authorities decided to displace and disperse the remainder of the Ukrainian population to the formerly German

'Recovered Territories' in the north and west of the country. In so doing it was hoped that in the short term the UPA would once and for all be crushed, and that it the long term, remaining Ukrainians would be assimilated into Polish society. This policy of forced deportation to other parts of Poland was labelled *Akcja Wisla* (Action Vistula) and commenced in April 1947. Inevitably, *Akcja Wisla* proceeded in a brutal manner. Rape, robbery and sundry acts of violence were the order of the day. UPA suspects were sent to the former German concentration camp in Jaworzno, along with members of the clergy and intelligentsia, to join the German and Polish inmates already held there. At least 3,873 people, including 700 women and children passed through the camp, and 161 persons are known to have died there (Misilo 1993).

*Akcja Wisla* lasted until 15 August 1947, although individual deportations continued up until 1952. Eventually, a total of over 150,000 persons were deported. These events caused a further economic collapse in south-east Poland. Dozens of churches, farms, villages and small towns lay in ruins. As for those who survived in the Recovered Territories, they found themselves under the surveillance of the security services and subject to a variety of restrictions concerning the areas in which they could live and in what number.

A wave of anti-Ukrainian propaganda had accompanied *Akcja Wisla,* which of course served to increase anti-Ukrainian sentiment among ordinary Poles, and sparked attacks upon the deportees (Drozd 1998). Quite understandably, anti-Polish sentiment hardened among the Ukrainians, and rather like the Germans of Upper Silesia they reacted by turning inward and by cutting themselves off as far as possible from the wider world. Paradoxically, this self-isolation led to a superficial integration within Polish society, especially as there was no possibility for autonomous political organisation. Such trends were noted with satisfaction by the government in Warsaw. In order to further the cause of polonisation and prevent the re-emergence of Ukrainian nationalism, programmes of economic assistance were gradually initiated. A decisive change came in 1956, when as part and parcel of the overall policy of relaxation, the Ukrainian minority was allowed to form its own cultural society, the Ukrainian Social-Cultural Society (UTSK), and a small Ukrainian language press came into existence. Promises by the authorities of support for Ukrainian educational and cultural activities proved to be largely empty. Besides which, the fact that the Ukrainians were so scattered made it difficult to establish such institutions. For their part, Ukrainian spokesmen cautiously requested the right to return to their original homes, financial compensation, the compulsory teaching of the Ukrainian language in those schools which had Ukrainian pupils, Ukrainian language radio broadcasts, and increased contacts with Ukrainians living in the Soviet Union (Zabrowarny 1989).

In turn, the authorities reacted with similar caution. Between April 1957 and July 1958, around 20,000 people were allowed to return to south-eastern Poland (Zabrowarny 1989). The government was afraid that if a greater number were allowed to return, such returnees would re-settle in close-knit communities, thus making the objective of polonisation more difficult. Although Ukrainian language provision did increase, it covered no more than 1,500 individuals (Drozd 1998). In short, Ukrainian cultural and religious activity developed very slowly and met with obstacles and hostility from both the government and indeed ordinary Poles.

This period of liberalisation was extremely brief, and in the late 1950s and early 1960s, the authorities restricted the independence of the UTSK, turning it into yet another transmission belt. Its role was now to pass on the directives of the party to the Ukrainian community, which in fact led the organisation to all but wither and die. Also at this time Ukrainian national sentiment underwent a change of orientation, and became focused on the right to return and attempts to foster tradition. It also began to lose its anti-Polish character. However, these changes went unregarded by the authorities which continued to use anti-Ukrainian, German and Jewish sentiment as a means of bolstering their domestic legitimacy. The obvious contradiction of attempting to assimilate a group of people who were simultaneously targeted as internal enemies, seems to have been lost upon the communists.

In 1968, conditions for the Ukrainian minority took a decisive turn for the worse. The anti-Zionist, i.e. anti-Semitic, campaign of that year fuelled distrust toward Ukrainians, by means which included negative stereotyping of them in the schools system. The authorities redoubled their attempts at polonisation, and attempted to increase their stranglehold upon the UTSK, which in turn provoked a counter-reaction from some Ukrainian activists. The very existence of the UTSK called the alleged mono-ethnic character of Polish society into question. That is why national minorities policy was in fact geared toward their liquidation. Thus, for example, in 1977 about 120 Ukrainian place-names were polonised, although the increasingly weak authorities were forced to re-instate the Ukrainian originals in 1981.

In this field, as with so much else in Poland, the breakthrough came in the early 1980s. A resolution calling for freedom of expression for national minorities was accepted by Solidarity at its inaugural convention. Having said that, in later years it became clear that many Solidarity activists were not well informed of the real situation and numbers of such minorities, and were in fact in some cases in favour of continued polonisation (Drozd 1998). In turn, Ukrainians perceived the political changes as a chance for the reconstruction of their political and cultural life. The UTSK fractured between those who wished to push for change, and those who sought to preserve the status quo. Attempts at independent action on the part of the UTSK met with severe counter-measures on the part of the authorities. However, as the decade progressed, so resistance increased. During the 1980s Ukrainian students began to become active, and some gains, such as the return of Uniate churches, by order of the pope, were achieved.

## The Ukrainian minority in Poland after 1989

It is very difficult to estimate the number of Ukrainians living in Poland today. The common assumption, in the absence of any census data, is that the community numbers some 300,000. Some estimates place the number as low as 200,000, with others placing the number as high as 500,000. In fact the community can be divided into two distinct groups – those who live in the south-east of the country, and those who live in and around formerly German cities such as Wroclaw, Legnica, Szczecin, Koszalin, Slupsk and Olsztyn.

A further division can be made in terms of levels of national consciousness. The first and smallest group, is composed of Ukrainians of high national consciousness who know the Ukrainian language and culture, and who cherish Ukrainian traditions. The second group consists of persons who are less conscious of their identity, who rarely use the language, but who take part in religious festivities and cultural activities. The third and largest group consists of persons who are conscious of their Ukrainian origin but who consider themselves as much Polish as they do Ukrainian (Drozd 1998).

With regard to the minority, one of the biggest problems is how to overcome the negative stereotyping of Ukrainians which exists among ordinary Poles. This objective is extremely hard to achieve for at least two reasons. First of all, by their very nature, stereotypes tend to be long-lasting. Additionally, the position of the Ukrainian minority is quite simply not relevant to most Poles. As a result, the majority of Poles do not see the need to change their attitude toward Ukrainians. This is despite the fact that as many as 69 per cent of the Polish population believes that the continued existence of an independent Ukraine is vital to Poland's national interests. At the same time, most Poles acknowledge that reconciliation with Ukrainians is necessary, but the chances of achieving it are regarded more sceptically than are the chances of achieving reconciliation with Germany. A CBOS poll of 1999 indicated that whereas 57 per cent of Poles believed reconciliation between Poles and Ukrainians to be possible, 40 per cent of respondents did not (CBOS 1999).

During the campaign for the semi-free election of 1989, Ukrainian activists aligned themselves with Solidarity. A representative of the Ukrainian minority, Wlodzimierz Mokry, obtained a seat in parliament. The new political climate heralded many positive changes in the situation of the Ukrainian minority. In the 1990s, censorship of Ukrainian publications was abandoned and the status of the Uniate Church was regulated. Responsibility for the protection of ethnic minorities has shifted from the Home Office to the Ministry of Culture and Art, and Ukrainians possess the possibility to articulate their desires in a much more conducive atmosphere. In 1990 the old UTSK was wound-up, and in its place the Association of Ukrainians in Poland (ZUwP) was created. The main objectives of the ZUwP include: the defence of the civil rights of Poland's Ukrainian minority; to lobby the Polish state on behalf of that minority, and to develop Ukrainian culture and identity in Poland. At present the ZUwP is estimated to have a membership of around 7,500, a figure which indicates that for one reason or another it is finding it difficult to mobilise Ukrainians around the badge of ethnicity. On the other hand, a clearly negative phenomenon since 1989 has been the re-appearance of overt anti-Ukrainian sentiment on the part of elements of the Polish population, who accuse Ukrainian activists of having adopted an 'anti-Polish' attitude. For example, in 1995, a number of organisations from the city of Przemysl in south-eastern Poland in which a fairly substantial Ukrainian population resides, demanded that the ZUwP be banned.

In the 1990s, Ukrainian activists vociferously demanded the annulment of the decree of 1949 under which Ukrainian-owned property was confiscated. Although in 1990 the Senate condemned *Akcja Wisla,* to this day the 1949 decree remains in force. Moreover, much to the dismay of Ukrainian activists, the more powerful Sejm has passed no analogous resolution. The post-communist Democratic Left Alliance (SLD) is particularly wary of any formal revocation lest the question of the role of its communist predecessor be brought up. Other opponents claim that repeal of the law would open the way for a flood of demands for the return of property. One proposed solution has been to deal with the issue within a general law on the reprivatisation of property, but as of the autumn of 1999, such an eventuality still had not come to pass.

On the occasion of its fiftieth anniversary in 1997, leading Polish politicians and intellectuals condemned of *Akcja Wisla* and expressed solidarity with the victims. Yet, from time to time, local conflicts appear which make the task of reconciliation difficult. Most of these conflicts are connected with monuments erected by members of the Ukrainian minority on the graves of UPA soldiers. Such activities have objections from Polish civilians and army veterans. Another problem is allegations that festivals of Ukrainian culture in Przemysl are a front for Ukrainian nationalist propaganda. In truth, it has to be said that those who complain loudest about these 'provocations' are usually pursuing a nationalist agenda of their own (*Polityka*, 31 May 1997).

## Minority rights and the Ukrainian community in Poland today

The Polish state is signatory to a series of international agreements aimed at securing the rights of national minorities. Although these acts often have a moral as opposed to a legal and political significance, the necessity to abide by them is widely recognised by the Polish political elite. With regard to domestic law there is variety of legislation which in one way or another deals with the rights of national minorities. The most important is the constitution of 1997. Others include the School Systems Law, the Law on Radio and Television, and the Law on Association.

In addition, members of ethnic minorities have equality before the courts, freedom to identify themselves as members of a particular minority, language and cultural rights, the right to be educated in their mother tongue, the right for unconstrained formation of association and expression of opinions, and the right to maintain international contacts. Acts of incitement against members of Poland's national minorities are punishable in criminal law.

The government has also established an Office for Ethnic Minorities situated within the Ministry of Culture and Art. This office supports cultural events organised by ethnic minorities and financially supports minority language publications. Almost inevitably, the Ukrainians like all the other minority groups in Poland regard levels of support as being insufficient. Whereas this may be true, in all likelihood such deficiencies arise as a consequence of general budgetary constraints, rather than any desire to choke off the supply of funds to the minorities.

Turning to political representation, we find that at national elections Polish electoral law states that ethnic minorities are exempt to the thresholds which apply to all other parties. Due to their dispersal around the country, and inertia on the part of many who live in the south-east, there is no Ukrainian parliamentary caucus. Instead, Miroslaw Czech of the Freedom Union (UW) informally represents Ukrainian interests. Although representatives of the Ukrainian minority have gained seats at sub-national elections, representation is once again limited for the reasons previously stated.

Perhaps the biggest issue facing the minority today is that of language rights. Because Ukrainians are to be found throughout the country, it is hard to execute some of the rules adopted by the EU in the 1987 Resolution on the Languages and Cultures of Regional and Ethnic Minorities in the European Community. The ethnic minorities' school system is organised in three ways. First, there are schools where the mother tongue forms the language of instruction. Second, there are schools which provide supplementary lessons for those who wish to learn their mother tongue. Finally, there are schools which offer the aforementioned classes for groups of children who otherwise attend different schools. The problems of dispersal and apathy have resulted in a situation where, as of the mid-1990s, only about 2,800 children attended Ukrainian schools. Ukrainian as the language of instruction functioned in forty-two primary schools and in three secondary schools (Mikolajczyk 1996).

At the time of writing, the National Minorities Bill, although prepared, has not yet been passed. In part this is because there is a feeling that existing legislation is sufficient, so there is no immediate need for further regulation of these issues. Second, it is argued that parliament has such a heavy legislative programme that it simply does not have time to deal with the issue. The draft bill defines an ethnic minority as: 'those groups of people who are in a minority in relation to the remainder of the community, and are particularly characterised by the aspiration to preserve their own culture, tradition, language, and national or ethnic consciousness' (Lodzinski and Bajda 1995). The bill also includes a catalogue of ethnic minorities and the rights of such minorities. They include the right of free association, the right to use non-Polish personal names, and the right to religious freedom. The bill, if passed, would also outlaw forcible assimilation, and bilingual place-names would be permitted. It is also envisaged that a Plenipotentiary for Ethnic Minorities would be appointed, along with a Council of Ethnic Minorities. The envisaged council would consist of two representatives each from the German, Ukrainian and Belorussian minorities, plus one representative from each of the further ten scheduled ethnic minorities indigenous to Poland. The council would have opinion-making and representative competencies, and would be able to initiate legal action in the Constitutional Court.

What in light of the above, can we say about the relationship between the Ukrainian minority in Poland and the Polish government's application to join the EU? The answer is in fact quite controversial. The overwhelming majority of Polish society is completely unaware of any such relationship. Interestingly enough, support for Polish accession to the EU has dropped from 77 per cent in 1994 to 64 per cent as of December 1998. At the same time the number firmly opposed to membership has increased from 6 per cent to 19 per cent. This change has little if anything to do with any of the national minorities in Poland, including the Ukrainian minority. It does, however, tell us something about changing Polish perceptions of the EU.

A large majority of Polish society regards European integration in symbolic and ideological as opposed to pragmatic categories. Integration with the EU is seen as a route to prosperity. Most Poles do not in fact realise what this project is about, and that there will be both positive and negative side effects upon Poland once membership is achieved. It may be added that this mentality is by no means absent among considerable sections of the political elite. Opinion poll results confirm these findings, as does the lack of serious debate about the issue in the Polish media (Mach *et al.* 1998).

Second, a sizeable section of Polish society appears to accept the need for membership precisely because others also accept it. In other words, membership is not conceived in terms of costs and benefits. In fact the only group in Polish society which seems to consider accession in those terms is the peasantry, which for the most part is actually in favour of staying out. Similarly, despite the fact that Poland must achieve a certain standard of protection toward its ethnic minorities as a condition of entry, most people simply are unaware of the existence of any such connection. Poland is, in effect, for the most part an ethnically homogeneous state. The large majority of the population has no direct contact with members of the minority groups, and is ill-informed of the nature of communist discrimination against them (Chalupczak and Browarek 1998). There are, however, three groups we can identify who recognise the connection between EU accession and domestic policies toward indigenous ethnic minorities. Although they comprise an extremely low percentage of society, the third group is of decisive importance to the future of the country

The first and least important group in terms of their impact upon wider society, consists of those academics who research into the affairs of ethnic minorities in Poland, and who in their enthusiasm for their subject matter sometimes lose sight of the overall picture. The second, and more important group, consists of minority activists. Because of their high level of national consciousness and commitment to their cause they are naturally sensitive to processes which can influence the situation of ethnic minorities. In other words, they see accession as a means of redressing imbalances, correcting historical injustices, and ensuring that Poland will not be able to act against its minorities in a unilateral and arbitrary manner (Drozd 1998).

The third group, and by far the most important group, is Poland's political elite. Among them, a large majority is convinced that Poland should become a member of the EU. Despite their often primarily symbolic perception of European integration these people know that Poland must meet certain requirements on its way to EU membership. One of such criteria is the regulation of ethnic minority issues. Therefore, since the beginning of the 1990s, the Polish political elite has undertaken a series of activities aimed at ensuring that Polish law and practice is comparable to EU norms and standards. The problem is that whereas the general public is by and large unaware of this relationship, and therefore may be manipulated into a nationalist counter-reaction, the minorities themselves often claim the government has not gone far enough.

It is to be hoped that following Polish accession and as Polish society in general becomes richer, the situation of the Ukriainian minority will improve. No doubt Ukrainian activists hope they will be the recipients of extra funding to preserve their language and culture and that south-eastern Poland will receive large amounts of development aid. Another more controversial consequence is likely to be that more stringent visa requirements will be placed upon Ukrainians wishing to enter Poland. This process has in fact already begun, and has been the cause of some friction between Warsaw and Kiev. The problem is that such requirements may be perceived as a means of isolating Ukrainians living in Poland from their compatriots on the other side of the border. In other words, although the EU will place no restrictions upon any of its citizens from entering Ukraine, the reverse will not necessarily apply.

## Bilateral perspectives

In this final section the ramifications of halting the eastward expansion of the EU on the Polish–Ukrainian border are assessed. The first point to note is that there are no concrete proposals for the admission of Ukraine into the EU. First of all, the EU has more than enough on its plate in attempting to integrate the current round of applicants. Second, the parlous state of the Ukrainian economy, general social problems, and latent tensions between Ukrainians and non-Ukrainians, coupled with uncertainties over which direction Ukraine will actually take, combine to push any serious application for membership many years hence. As for the Ukrainian minority in Poland, their situation is very different.

In theory, at least, the creation of a 'fortress Europe' which excluded Ukraine could precipitate retaliation from Kiev. However, given the imbalance in resources between the two, and the current spirit of co-operation, this is extremely unlikely. Nevertheless, the point remains that a tightening up of visa procedures could contain unforeseen dangers. Most importantly, if the EU is perceived as discriminating against Ukrainians and Ukraine as a state, such perceptions could adversely affect the fragile democracy of that country. This is an important point. One of the reasons that liberal democracy has taken root so quickly in Poland is the fact that after 1989, Poles were easily able to visit liberal democratic countries. Their own first-hand experiences of such societies created a positive impression, and encouraged them in the attempt to emulate what had in effect become a role model. Since the collapse of the Soviet Union in 1991, Poland has played an analogous role with regard to Ukraine, and Brussels should carefully evaluate the potential consequences of policies which might inadvertently disturb this relationship (*Magazyn Kresowy*, 2 June 1993). Poland is, and hopefully will continue to be, a bridge for Ukraine to the West. If this bridge is closed, Ukrainians will not be able to become the members of the Western community, any more than they will even will be able to observe it at first hand.

A second dimension to this web of relationships is of a political economic nature. Lack of contact between Ukraine and the EU can serve only to deepen the gulf which already exists between the two. It would lead to the creation of a zone of poverty and instability along the eastern border of the EU. The tensions and dangers arising from such a situation are as legion as they are dangerous. In the event of such a scenario coming to pass, at best the Polish–Ukrainian border would come to resemble the US–Mexican border with hundreds of thousands of migrants attempting to reach some kind of promised land. At worst, Ukraine could collapse as a state. Approximately 28 per cent of the population of the country is not in fact ethnically Ukrainian. Russians form the largest minority group, to which must be added the fact that many Ukrainians are russophones and don't actually speak Ukrainian at all. As such, their level of Ukrainian national consciousness is often low. In such a situation, Russia could conceivably be tempted to annex either part of or even the whole country (*Zalozenia polityki zagranicznej Federacji Rosyjskiej* 1994). The potential dangers for the EU of such a situation are self-evident.

It is clear that in the foreseeable future Ukraine will not become a member of the EU. The question is one of how to prevent any of the aforementioned gloomy scenarios from coming to pass. The answer is that the EU must abandon short-termism and embark upon a programme of long-term aid aimed at restructuring the economy and strengthening liberal democracy. Poland cannot deliver substantial amounts of aid on its own. Poland's role should be, above all, to promote Ukrainian interests in the international arena. One practical example has been Polish support of Ukrainian applications for assistance from the International Monetary Fund (IMF). The Ukrainian minority in Poland can also play a part in the construction of such a policy. It can act as a bridge between the countries, and become an example to other Ukrainians of what can be achieved. Let us not forget that in the estimations of some, Ukraine is one of the most important states in Europe (Brzezinski 1998). In the long run, the EU cannot afford to treat it as a pariah.

## Bibliography

Brzezinski, Z. *Wielka szachownica. Glowne cele polityki amerykanskiej*, Warszawa: Swiat Ksiazki, 1998.

CBOS, Swiat wokol nas, July 1997.

—— Aktualne problemy i wydarzenia, November 1998.

—— Polacy o mozliwosci pojednania z Niemcami I Ukraina, September 1999.

Chalupczak, H. and Browarek, T. *Mniejszosci narodowe w Polsce 1918–1995*, Lublin: Wydawnictwo Uniwersytetu Marii Curie-Sklodowskiej, 1998.

Czarnocki, A. (ed.) *Samoidentyfikacja mniejszosci narodowych i religijnych w Europie Srodkowo-Wschodniej. Problematyka politologiczna*, Lublin: Instytut Europy Srodkowo-Wschodniej, 1998.

Drozd, R. 'Ukraincy w Polsce w okresie przelomow politycznych 1944–1981', in P. Madajczyk (ed.) *Mniejszosci narodowe w Polsce. Panstwo i spoleczenstwo polskie a mniejszosci narodowe w okresach przelomow politycznych (1944–1989)*, Warszawa: Instytut Studiow Politycznych PAN, 180–244, 1998.

Gill, W. and Gill, N. *Stosunki Polski z Ukraina w latach 1989–1993*, Torun: Adam Marszalek, 1997.

Hrycak, J. 'Jeszcze raz o stosunku Ukraincow do Polakow (z Rosja w tle)', *Wiez* 3, 15–32, 1998.

Huntington, S. *The Clash of Civilizations and the remaking of World Order*, New York: Simon & Schuster, 1996.

Lodzinski, S. and Bajda, P. (eds) *Ochrona praw osob nalezacych do mniejszosci narodowych*, Warszawa: Helsinska Fundacja Praw Czlowieka, 1995.

Mach, B. *et al. Polacy wobec integracji z Unia Europejska. Trwalosc zmian i postaw spolecznych wobec integracji Polski z Unia Europejska*, Warszawa: Fundacja im. Friedricha Eberta, 1998.

*Magazyn Kresowy*, 2 June, 1993.

Mikolajczyk, B. *Mniejszosci w prawie miedzynarodowym*, Katowice: Wydawnictwo Uniwersytetu Slaskiego, 1996.

Misilo, E. (ed.) (1993) *Akcja Wisla. Dokumenty*, Warszawa: Panstwowe Wydawnictwo Naukowe, 1993.

Motyka, G. 'Ukrainska orientacja', *Karta*, 23, 18–53, 1997.
*Polityka*, 3 May 1997.
——, 21 June 1997.
Zabrowarny, S. 'Geneza I poczatki dzialalnosci Ukrainskiego Towarzystwa Spoleczno-Kultralnego', *Zeszyty Naukowe* INP: 16, 133–56, 1989.
Zalozenia polityki zagranicznej Federacji Rosjskiej, *Eurazja*, 5–6, (aneks) 1994.

# 12 Conclusion

*Karl Cordell*

All that remains for us now is to consider two basic issues. The first is now, in the light of our survey, to assess the prospects for Poland's admission into the European Union (EU). The second is to assess the effectiveness of the process of internal reform, and to highlight the impact such reforms have had upon Polish politics and society.

At one level, we can answer the first question in a concise and straightforward manner. Poland will become a full member of the EU sometime between the years 2003 and 2006. This is not to deny that problems remain, rather what is being stated is that despite outstanding problems and issues, failure to achieve compromise on those issues which still remain to be resolved is unthinkable. In other words, it is now too late for either party to withdraw from the negotiations. Once negotiated, the final terms of membership will eventually be put to the Polish population by means of a referendum, and we can be sure that there will be a vociferous campaign for a 'No' vote. We can be equally sure that this campaign will be led by the Polish Peasant's Party (PSL), together with elements of the Movement for the Restoration of Poland (ROP), and Solidarity Electoral Action (AWS). We can be sure that radicals of both the left and right will also campaign for a 'No' vote. Yet, the fact of the matter is that at the time of writing (October 1999), there is no evidence to suggest that such a coalition commands anything like the majority necessary to thwart the accession process. Having said that, Brussels should note the fact that organisations such as Polish Agreement are seeking to turn frustration over delays in completing the negotiations into hostility toward the EU.

Those problems which remain are, however, genuine. To repeat, they concern issues such as the future of agriculture, the fate of heavy industry, and environmental regeneration. To a lesser extent they also include issues concerning property ownership rights, the right of foreigners to live and work in Poland, and the ability of Poles to work in other member-states. There is also the possibility that German expellees from post-war Poland may obtain the right to some form of compensation for the material and other losses suffered in the aftermath of World War Two. Nevertheless, there is once again no reason to assume that any of these issues are of such fundamental importance to either side, and that workable compromises cannot be reached.

The fact that such issues are capable of fairly straightforward processes of resolution in part helps to answer the second question posed at the beginning of this piece. Contemporary Poland is in fact a remarkably normal society possessed of a political system and culture that has more in common with Western Europe than it does with a majority of former communist states. We have noted how it pursues foreign policy goals that are not marked by either extreme demands or unrealistic expectations. We have also noted that the majority of Polish society supports the primary objective of the government's foreign policy, namely accession to the EU. Similarly, although some political parties, politicians, members of the clergy and the agricultural lobby remain deeply wary of the whole process, as stated neither they nor their supporters have any real chance of bringing it to a halt.

In terms of its political development, Polish political behaviour continues to pursue a path of correlation with the western part of the continent. This is not to say that Poland is becoming some kind of clone of, for instance, Sweden, the United Kingdom or Germany. Poland has its own history and its own traditions. This history and such traditions are in part unique to Poland, but in many cases form part and parcel of a shared Central European heritage. It would be both unreasonable and churlish to expect Poland simply to attempt to mimic any of the countries of Western Europe. Yet, as we have noted, correlation and convergence is taking place. Political campaigns in Poland now lean heavily on North American and West European experiences. The ideological bases of the party system are now becoming clearer. The contours of the party system are less blurred than they were in the early 1990s, and there is widespread agreement among supporters of three main electoral actors that Poland should, and indeed must, join the European venture.

With regard to reform of the processes of government and the overhaul of the machinery of state, once again, it cannot be denied that progress has been made. However, as we have seen, problems still remain. The process of reform is not complete, and there are complaints that the reforms have in part been poorly constructed. There is also the issue of the remnants of the nomenklatura. Whilst it would be unrealistic to claim that remaining elements of the nomenklatura wish to disrupt the process of reform, or are capable of so doing, they are quite capable of indulging in bureaucratic inertia. Given that such individuals do actually possess administrative expertise, and in part have to be relied on in order to ensure that policy design and implementation is effective, reformers have little choice but to proceed with caution. The resolution of this problem cannot be achieved simply by administrative fiat. It is also a question of changing the mindset, and of rooting out individuals who are unwilling or unable to adapt to the requirements of a competitive society. This problem is apparent at both the national and sub-national levels of government. In the case of sub-national government, the new structures can attain legitimacy only if they are seen to function effectively. This in turn means that they must be adequately financed, and staffed by competent professionals who are appointed and promoted on the basis of merit.

Turning to external matters, Poland's diplomatic and economic relationship with Germany continues to prosper. However, rising concerns among Germans that they could be 'flooded' by an unwanted wave of cheap labour upon Polish entry into the EU continue to grow. Similarly, issues surrounding the expellees could conceivably become a complicating factor as negotiations reach their final stages. These remarks are not intended to belittle the very real achievements of the past ten years. Rather, the point is that in both countries stereotypical perceptions of the 'Other', although on the decline, are still by no means uncommon. That this is the case should come as no surprise to anyone who has even a passing interest in German–Polish affairs.

What is true of Polish–German relations is also largely true of Polish–Ukrainian relations. We have already noted that with regard to the EU, Poland is doing as best it can in attempting to do for Ukraine what Germany has done for Poland. There are, however, crucial differences between the two cases. First, unless accession criteria are radically changed, there is no possibility of Ukraine joining the EU in the foreseeable future. Ukraine is quite simply economically and politically too weak. Second, the task of breaking down negative Polish–Ukrainian stereotypes is not as advanced as is the endeavour to break down their German–Polish counterparts. Nevertheless, as is shown earlier in the volume, progress has been, and continues to be made.

On balance, the prognosis for Polish membership of the EU is good. We should not allow ourselves to become despondent as a result some of the observations made earlier. Poland has made remarkable progress since 1989, and there is little sign that the gains of the past few years are about to be lost. Perhaps the real question which confronts Poland today is not one of in which year will accession take place. Rather it is one of when and if Poland will meet the criteria for economic and monetary union, and if that day comes, will Poland wish to cede further sovereignty to the EU? As the British example shows, for some, such objectives go straight to the heart of notions of national identity and sovereignty. Given the vigour with which Poles approach politics, there is no reason to assume that a proposal issued by the government in Warsaw would not stir the most vigorous of debates.

# Index

90 0449958 2

WITHDRAWN
FROM
UNIVERSITY OF PLYMOUTH
LIBRARY SERVICES

SEVEN DAY LOAN
This book is to be returned on
or before the date stamped below

| | |
|---|---|
| 18 FEB 2002 | 18 FEB 2003 |
| - 1 MAR 2002 | - 4 MAR 2003 |
| - 1 MAY 2002 | 29 APR 2003 |
| - 8 MAY 2002 | 22 OCT 2003 |
| 16 MAY 2002 | - 6 NOV 2003 |
| 24 MAY 2002 | - 2 MAR 2004 |
| - 5 JUN 2002 | 30 SEP 2004 |
| 14 JAN 2003 | |

UNIVERSITY OF PLYMOUTH

PLYMOUTH LIBRARY
Tel: (01752) 232323
This book is subject to recall if required by another reader
Books may be renewed by phone
CHARGES WILL BE MADE FOR OVERDUE BOOKS

3,4,5